WAR DIARY OF A COMBAT ARTIST

Captain Harry Everett Townsend. *Courtesy of the New Britain Museum of American Art, New Britain, Connecticut.*

WAR DIARY OF A COMBAT ARTIST

※

Captain Harry Everett Townsend

Edited by
Alfred E. Cornebise

UNIVERSITY PRESS OF COLORADO

Copyright © 1991 by the University Press of Colorado
P.O. Box 849
Niwot, Colorado 80544

The University Press of Colorado is a cooperative publishing enterprise supported,
in part, by Adams State College, Colorado State University, Fort Lewis College,
Mesa State College, Metropolitan State College of Denver, University of Colorado,
University of Northern Colorado, University of Southern Colorado,
and Western State College.

Library of Congress Cataloging-in-Publication Data

Townsend, Harry Everett.
  War diary of a combat artist / Harry Everett Townsend; edited by Alfred E.
Cornebise.
     p. cm.
  Includes bibliographical references and index.
  ISBN 0-87081-231-9
  1. Townsend, Harry Everett — Diaries. 2. Artists — United States — Diaries.
3. World War, 1914–1918 — Art and the war. 4. World War, 1914–1918 —
Personal narratives, American. I. Cornebise, Alfred E. II. Title.
N6537.T66A2 1991
740'.92 — dc20
[B]   91-12287
                                                                              CIP

The paper used in this publication meets the minimum requirements of the American
National Standard for Information Sciences—Permanence of Paper for Printed Library
Materials. ANSI Z39.48–1984

∞

10 9 8 7 6 5 4 3 2 1

Design by Carol Humphrey.

CONTENTS

MAPS

❧

All maps are from American Battle Monuments Commission, *American
Armies and Battlefields in Europe: A History, Guide and Reference Book*
(Washington, D.C.: U.S. Government Printing Office, 1938).

ILLUSTRATIONS

ILLUSTRATIONS

EDITOR'S PREFACE

This diary was written by Harry Everett Townsend, an artist who was commissioned a captain in the U.S. Army Corps of Engineers and sent to France in 1918 to record on canvas the events of the U.S. involvement in the Great War.

While I was engaged in research into a history of the eight official combat artists of the American Expeditionary Forces in Europe in World War I, I discovered this unpublished diary at the New Britain Art Museum in New Britain, Connecticut. A quick perusal of its pages revealed that it was an unusually interesting document bearing on the U.S. experience during the war, and arrangements were promptly made to publish it separately.

Townsend's account is not merely the usual diary; it is also an apology and an explanation of sorts. It is clear that the artistic work produced by the eight official U.S. artists did not altogether live up to expectations. The British created splendid war art of the period, but U.S. artists, largely due to circumstances beyond their control, failed to emulate them. Among other things, the U.S. involvement in the war was too brief; the artists only learned their way around just as the armistice came. There was confusion, too, as to what sort of art they were to produce: propaganda for immediate use or art of a permanent historical nature. Then again, their art was frequently and unaccountably detained in Europe and did not arrive promptly in Washington, where it might have been put to some immediate use. Those pieces that did arrive, especially in the early weeks, seemed hurriedly done and of inferior quality. Nor were the artists given the time they needed to produce permanent art after the conflict. Though Townsend, among others, worked in Europe for a few months following the end of hostilities, attitudes toward the war changed rapidly, as did the conditions on the battlefields, and the moment to produce the kind of work that they desired passed, never to return. And though Townsend attended the Paris Peace Conference early in 1919, he did not produce any significant art from that experience.

In the event, the artists were soon discharged, their work relegated to the Smithsonian Institution, where most of it remains. It has been used to some extent to illustrate studies and accounts of the Great War, and the artists themselves published examples of their creations. But their accomplishments remain little known. Townsend's diary helps redress the balance, both as to the experiences of one keenly observant U.S. officer, who was unusually well placed and trained to record events of the war and its aftermath, and as a record of an arm of the AEF about which little is known: its official combat artists.

Townsend's diary, over 200 wartime sketches and paintings, letters, and other papers pertaining to his service in the American Expeditionary Forces in World War I were sold to the New Britain Art Museum by his widow, Cory Townsend, in 1970. These are now part of the museum's Sanford Low Memorial Collection of American Illustration and are catalogued as: "Portfolio of World War Sketches," Sanford Low Fund, 70.57.1-214 LIC; and "World War I Sketches," Sanford Low Fund, 70.58.1-3 LIC. The museum also possesses a charcoal picture by Townsend, entitled "Lincoln With Harriet Beecher Stowe" and filed as Sanford Low Fund, 66.45 LIC, and an oil, "Portrait of the Artist's Wife," listed as 75.93 LIC.

I have drawn upon other sources to enhance and help explain Townsend's account, notably from Record Group 120: "Records of the American Expeditionary Forces (World War I), 1917–23"; subseries, "Censorship and Press Division (G-2-D)"; Entry 224, "Artists with the AEF," Case 70, Drawer 3, Folders 2–10. These are in the National Archives, in Washington, D.C. Other works that have been useful in preparing this edition of the diary are listed in the bibliography.

The first several pages of Townsend's diary were written in a scrawled longhand, after which he, fortunately, turned to the typewriter. However, if his artwork bore the marks of a careful workman, the diary was typed by an amateur, which posed some problems for me. In addition, though Townsend clearly possessed some knowledge of the French language, his spelling of French words exhibited great variation. I have corrected these and have also taken the liberty of correcting mistakes in grammar and spelling. For example, Townsend always spelled "Boche" as "Bosche"; I have substituted "Boche." However, I have retained his spelling of "thro" for "through," "tho" for "though," and "strait" for "straight." I have used lowercase in many instances when he used upper. I have, however, not been consistent with abbreviations, often leaving them as he wrote them. I have usually linked together the numerous incomplete sentences in the diary forming completed ones. In addition, I have introduced paragraphing where needed. Finally, I have excluded many allusions to people, places, and other material that now seem inconsequential or obscure, using ellipses to indicate the omissions.

ALFRED E. CORNEBISE

ACKNOWLEDGMENTS

I would like to acknowledge the assistance of Daniel DuBois, director of the New Britain Museum of American Art, New Britain, Connecticut, and Lois L. Blomstrann, administrative manager, and Jane Darnell, researcher, of the same institution, for their considerable assistance in completing this project, especially providing a duplicated copy of the diary. In addition, the New Britain Museum of American Art's Sanford B.D. Low Fund has granted permission to publish the diary and the use of the portrait of Captain Townsend as the frontispiece. Other illustrations have been provided, as indicated, by the Smithsonian Institution and the National Archives.

The Faculty Senate Research and Publication Committee of the University of Northern Colorado, Greeley, also provided funds for the purchase of necessary materials. The editor wishes to acknowledge this timely help.

WAR DIARY OF A COMBAT ARTIST

INTRODUCTION

When the United States entered the Great War on April 6, 1917, even artists were mobilized for action, to serve in many ways. President Woodrow Wilson, recognizing the value of propaganda in modern war, created the Committee on Public Information by executive order eight days later, placing the energetic journalist George Creel in charge.[1] One of the units created by Creel was the Division of Pictorial Publicity. He soon enrolled such artists and illustrators as Charles Dana Gibson, Charles Falls, Wallace Morgan, Jack Sheridan, Cass Gilbert, Herbert Adams, Frederick McMonnies, Joseph Pennell, and Harry Townsend, the author of this diary, in his propaganda operations.

While engaged in drawing posters, Townsend received a letter from Major General William M. Black, chief of engineers, U.S. Army, at the War Department in Washington, D.C., that revealed another way in which the artists were to be employed. Dated February 15, 1918, this letter informed him that he had been recommended for a commission as a captain in the Engineer Reserve Corps, with a view to his assignment to the American Expeditionary Forces in France. His specific — and only — duties would be to prepare "oil paintings, portraits, sketches, etchings, etc., within the war zone for historical purposes."[2] Townsend responded promptly, and, after meeting the physical and mental requirements, he was commissioned on March 21. He soon set sail for Europe, departing from New York in a snowstorm. After a few days in Great Britain, he crossed the English Channel to France and reported for duty on May 1, 1918. In this swift fashion, Captain Harry Everett Townsend went to war.[3]

He joined seven other U.S. artists and illustrators who had been similarly recruited: William James Aylward, Walter Jack Duncan, Harvey Thomas Dunn, George M. Harding, Wallace Morgan, Ernest Clifford Peixotto, and Jay André Smith. The men had been appointed in response to the belief of many artists and officials in the United States that photographs and movies, which the U.S. Army Signal Corps was making in great numbers, could not adequately convey the essence of combat and its effects — that only the artist could truly see beneath the surface of things and produce work of lasting artistic value or for immediate propaganda use. In this, the United States emulated the Allies, who had long since fielded numbers of artists with good results, using this art for the practical purposes of assisting in recruitment, bond drives, and the like and as a means to provide a permanent pictorial record of the conflict.

Following several aborted attempts to launch the U.S. program, General John J. Pershing, the commander in chief of the AEF, agreed to the appointment of the eight artists, who arrived shortly thereafter in France. Though in the Engineers, they were attached to the Press and Censorship Division (G-2-D) of the Intelligence Branch (G-2) of the General Staff, located at Chaumont, France, in AEF Headquarters. Their operational base was at the press headquarters in Neufchâteau, northeast of Chaumont.[4] There, they were not too far from the battlelines where U.S. forces were becoming a significant presence on the western front. The men were usually assigned billets with French families, and Townsend resided with the Bathos family at No. 41, Jules Ferry Street in Neufchâteau. This became his home and studio until January 1919, when he relocated in Paris, establishing his quarters and studio at No. 4, rue Belloni.[5]

The men were given permanent passes signed by both high U.S. and French military officers that, together with their rank, gave them access to many areas of operations. Though they were forbidden to engage in actual combat operations, they found themselves under fire on occasion and were certainly close enough to the action to observe its immediate effects. They were eventually assigned two National automobiles, and, though these were not adequate to meet the men's transportation needs, other means were often found to maintain their considerable mobility.

Freed from normal military duties and given carte blanche and unstinting support by Headquarters to determine their own agenda and activities, the artists found themselves in an enviable position. They took full advantage of their opportunities and were soon energetically engaged in seeking appropriate artistic subjects. Though there was some misunderstanding about the sort of work they were to create — whether it was to be primarily propaganda material or permanent historical art — the men eventually produced several hundred interesting war scenes. They hoped that their art would have a lasting historical value and resisted attempts by several people in Washington to use it primarily for momentary propaganda purposes. They also blocked attempts by the Pictorial Section of the Historical Branch, the War Plans Division, at the War Department in Washington, to dictate how they were to operate.[6] They were able to assert themselves in the matter of control, recognizing direction only from Chaumont, but they did have to acquiesce when their work was sent to Washington for use and display in ways that they sometimes objected to.

They also did not get their way, for the most part, regarding the establishment of a permanent exhibition of their art after the war. They had hoped to stay in the army, perhaps for several years following the end of hostilities, gaining time to turn their sketches, field notes, and impressions of battle and its consequences into permanent form. But they found themselves caught up in the rush to get the men home and discharged as quickly as possible after the war, and by the summer of 1919, all eight of the artists were out of the service as quickly as they had entered it, civilians again. Their plans seemed in ruins; their task, as they saw it, lay incomplete. Their art was soon transferred to the Smithsonian Institution for short-term display and eventual storage, where most of it remains today. Peixotto, Harding, and Smith published accounts of their activities in France, but only Townsend produced a full-scale diary.[7]

The future diarist and painter was born to William Jarman and Jane Elizabeth (Houghtaling) Townsend in Wyoming, Illinois, on March 10, 1879.[8] His father was a prosperous farmer and merchant. He also operated a peddling wagon that Harry, as a youth, used to deliver supplies to farms throughout the countryside. However, young Townsend soon developed an interest in art and began to make money by painting signs for local businessmen. Resolving not to join his father's business, he made plans to become an artist; after his graduation from Wyoming High School, he took his savings and traveled via bicycle to Chicago to enroll in that city's well-known art institute. There, he studied with painters Frederick Freer and Frank Duveneck and with sculptor Lorado Taft. He worked his way through school by setting up and servicing farm implements for the McCormick Harvester Company on farms in Illinois and Iowa during the summers. He also interested the Rock Island and Santa Fe railroads in his drawings and made several trips to the U.S. Southwest, painting and sketching native Americans and scenic attractions to be used in advertising.[9]

Following the completion of his studies at the Chicago Art Institute in 1900, Townsend continued his training for the next three years under the famed illustrator Howard Pyle, who maintained a school and studio in Wilmington, Delaware, and at Chadds Ford, Pennsylvania. Subsequently, he studied for a time in Europe, especially in Paris (at the Academie Moderne, the Academie Julien, and Colarossi's studio); he also worked in London. Townsend then returned to Chicago to teach in the Academy of Fine Arts. Shortly thereafter, on July 20, 1904, he married Cory Schiedewend, of Chicago, who had been a fellow student at the Chicago Art Institute.

The Townsends soon left Chicago for the New York art scene, establishing a home and studio nearby in Leonia, New Jersey. Harry rapidly rose to the front ranks among U.S. illustrators, with his work appearing frequently in books and in such major magazines as *Harper's, Century, Everybody's, Scribner's* and *McClure's*. In addition, he exhibited regularly in the leading art shows in the area. He still found time to study sculpture with Herman MacNeil and developed his skills in etching, woodcutting and lithography. Eventually, he acquired an expertise in all forms of pictorial art, from magazine illustration to mural decoration.[10]

In 1912, the Townsends, who now had a daughter named Barbara, went to Europe, where Harry worked for London magazines. They resided in Montreuil-sur-Mer in northern France, giving them easy access to both the London and Paris art markets. They were in France when the war broke out in 1914 and immediately returned to New York, establishing themselves in Greenwich Village. Townsend again worked for the magazines and book publishers.

Following the U.S. entry into the war in 1917, Townsend found himself in the army and on his way overseas. Almost immediately after his arrival in France, he began keeping a diary. Fortunately for those with an interest in the World War I era, he faithfully kept a detailed account of his activities and those of some of his colleagues during his service abroad.

The diary is informative in many respects. The unlimited pass that Townsend and his fellow artists possessed proved of inestimable value. They became far-ranging observers of many aspects of the war and recorders of its myriad scenes. Some of the men, including Townsend, were in Paris to see the Bastille Day celebrations on July 14, 1918, which took on a decidedly martial character in the midst of war. The effects of the shelling of Paris by "Big Bertha" or the "Paris Gun" at this time were also recorded, as were the results of the frequent air raids on the city.[11] But, as the diary reveals, even at the height of war there was time for sumptuous eating and theatrical entertainment; Paris remained, after all, the City of Light, if made a bit drab by the events of those days.

At the front, Townsend gave a graphic and amusing account of his first shelling, and his observations of French refugees and the war-torn countryside are of interest. His artist's eye could not fail to see haunting, if tragic, beauty in war scenes.

Townsend also recognized aspects of this war that set it apart from preceding struggles. He was aware that the lavish use of modern artillery, as well as tanks and aircraft, defined a new sort of war. He saw the artistic possibilities of the new hardware of battle and could be lyrical in his descriptions of it, especially regarding aircraft. He was already emotionally conditioned to see airplanes in a special light due to the untimely death of his brother Henri, only three weeks after arriving at the front with a Royal Air Force bomber squadron, a victim of German fire. Henri had left his job as a toiletries representative to enlist in the Royal Flying Corps in Canada. Trained as a pilot, he was commissioned and sent to England for advanced training, reaching France just prior to Harry's arrival. The brothers were no doubt planning a joyous reunion there, but it was not to be.[12] One of the legacies of this personal tragedy was Harry's preoccupation with aircraft art: He soon became the specialist among the eight artists for the Air Service, as well as tanks and artillery. These interests dictated where Townsend would spend some of his time, notably with the squadrons making up the famed 1st Pursuit Group of the U.S. Air Service. Townsend's accounts of visits to these outfits are therefore noteworthy. His first flight, which he took following the end of the war, was graphically described in his diary.

The artists found that they were so rushed and their activity was so intense that it was difficult to produce finished work. But they persevered and were able to mount a monthly show at Chaumont for the benefit of AEF Headquarters. There, the pictures met with considerable acclaim. But getting the art to the United States proved difficult at times and for various reasons, and shipments lagged, much to Washington's annoyance. These developments also frustrated the artists and caused some controversy, mainly with officials in the United States.

Meanwhile, the artists were free to follow closely behind the U.S. troops as they launched their successive campaigns, especially those in the St. Mihiel salient and in the Meuse-Argonne. Townsend made detailed observations regarding these operations.

As the war ended with a rush, Townsend's diary conveyed a sense of the expectations preceding the final armistice with Germany, which came on November 11, 1918. The cease-fire with the smaller Central Powers had already been concluded, raising hopes for an end to war at last. Townsend's pages enable us to relive these hopeful days.

Beyond this, Towsend's decision to journey to Metz, in the Lorraine, as early as possible after the armistice was an inspired one. There, he and some of his colleagues observed the end of Germany's domination of the area. It had been in German hands since 1871 and the end of the Franco-Prussian War, when the French had to surrender the territory and many French citizens to Germany. It is interesting to note, as Townsend described it, how the Lorrainers nonetheless managed to regain an upper hand, which the Germans, in their turn, then had to endure while contemplating their uncertain futures. Many no doubt planned to return to Germany, having no intention of living under French control. But not all Germans in Lorraine seemed concerned. The *patron* of the Hotel de l'Europe in Metz was clearly an exception, and Townsend's account of the ease of the man's transition from one set of circumstances to another are entertaining and enlightening: His rooms were filled as before, and his tables had a steady stream of customers, even if the uniforms were different — all without missing a day's business!

Other notable observations concerned the health of the population. Townsend made it clear that none of the people in Lorraine — whether French or German — seemed pinched for life's necessities. The well-to-do French Lorrainers had learned over the years to sail before the prevailing wind and were clearly able to do more than merely survive under German domination. Townsend was even able to find cameras and film on sale in a store in Metz — a rarity, indeed, even in Paris and London during the war years.

Journeying to Luxembourg, Townsend faithfully recorded the attitudes and actions of another people emerging from a four-year occupation. That beautiful country had its usual enchanting effect on the first-time visitor, and Townsend the artist was duly impressed. His graphic observations on the lilliputian duchy are amusing as well as informative, and his views on the relations between the citizenry and the recently arrived U.S. forces are of interest.

Perhaps no better example of how wise the high command was in giving the artists complete mobility can be found than in the fact that they were permitted to accompany the U.S. forces into Germany. According to the armistice terms, the Germans were to withdraw behind a line thirty miles east of the Rhine. The Allied forces were to follow closely behind and then establish themselves in zones of occupation; the Belgians in the north, the British around the Rhine city of Cologne, the Americans pushing down the Moselle to Coblenz on the Rhine, and the French into Mainz. All eyes were focused on Germany and the sights anticipated there. Fortunately for readers of his diary, Townsend and the other AEF artists were among the first to arrive in Coblenz. His initial impressions focused on the great contrasts between devastated France and Belgium and Germany's tranquil, untouched countryside. Though the German people had had to tighten their belts and the poorer ones had suffered some privation (largely because of the years-long British blockade), Townsend had the distinct impression that tales of their suffering were exaggerated. Again, he had no difficulty in finding good food and lodging. The relative willingness of the Germans to accommodate their conquerors was also apparent, though the attempts to divide the Allies were abundantly clear, especially their efforts to detach the U.S. troops from the British and French. They had some success at it, too, for many of these men manifested considerable anti-French sentiment, for various reasons; even Townsend himself was not immune. The fact that many of the U.S. troops were descendants of German immigrants and still spoke German contributed to the situation. And never was this more apparent than at Christmastime, as many of the U.S. servicemen recalled a common heritage. Germany was also a clean and tidy place, which could not fail to make a good impression upon these troops, who had been living in the omnipresent filth, dirt, dust, and debris of war in the shattered areas of France. Townsend's graphic descriptions of the German Rhineland at this time are especially useful to the student of this era, in particular regarding U.S., French, and German attitudes. The art produced by the AEF artists in Germany is also among the most interesting and useful that they created.

Subsequently, the official artists split up, some returning almost at once to the United States. Townsend, though, was one of those who remained. He was the only artist of the eight to make sketches of persons and scenes surrounding the peace talks that began in Paris in January of 1919, though no use was made of them. His descriptions of the great personalities of the day — including President Wilson; Georges Clemenceau, the French premier; and Lloyd George, the British prime minister — are compelling, as are those he made of many of the less important personalities present. His comments on the issues of the time reflected a sense of how some of the doughboys were still caught up in a crusading spirit. To many men in the AEF, Wilson had emerged as the leader of a righteous cause — though some were certainly disillusioned — and when he ran into European intrigue and opposition, he was seen as the just man set upon by the forces of an age-old evil. Townsend was among those appalled by the opposition that developed in the United States against Wilson and his policies; had it been left to them, no doubt the country would have speedily ratified the Treaty of Versailles and subsequently participated in the League of Nations.

Townsend's determination to produce permanent art of historical value was apparent, and the pages of his diary detailed his attempts to get back to the old battlefields to recapture the scenes of war. He was thwarted in these ends by the cold and rainy weather of the spring of 1919 and by the fact, immediately obvious to him, that the battlefields had already lost much of the character that they bore in the midst of war. These considerations, coupled with the concerns of his wife as to why he tarried abroad, convinced Townsend to return home. He departed Europe on May 24, 1919, and was discharged from the army a few days following his arrival in the States, on June 3.[13]

Thereafter, Townsend had little time to worry about combat art and what he might have been able to create given the time and opportunity. He was soon engaged in his own pursuit of "normalcy." After briefly reestablishing himself in New York, he and his family departed in 1921 for Connecticut, a state that had become a center of artistic and cultural activity. The Townsends chose Norwalk as their home, where they bought an old red barn at West Avenue and Stevens Street, and transformed it into a lovely house and studio.[14]

Townsend became a familiar figure on the Connecticut artistic scene. He was a charter member of the influential Silvermine Guild of Artists, founded in 1922 in New Canaan, and served on its board for the remainder of his life, with a term as president from 1926–1927. He was active in the Westport Artists' Market and exhibited in numerous shows of the era. He also continued to teach art, particularly for the Silvermine Guild, and conducted painting classes at his studio in Norwalk.[15]

The many murals that he executed in the 1930s are of special interest. When the Public Works Administration's art programs were created in the New Deal years, Townsend, perhaps in need of funds, made many pictorial records of life and activities in the Civilian Conservation Corps (CCC) camps and parks, notably in the Finger Lake district of upstate New York.[16] He later painted murals for the city hall of South Norwalk and historic scenes for the auditorium of that town's Benjamin Franklin Junior High School.[17] Not long thereafter, however, Townsend died at his home, on July 25, 1941.[18] He was survived by his widow and fellow artist, Cory, and his daughter, Barbara, who became a writer on art and a watercolorist in her own right; for a time, she was on the staff of the Museum of Modern Art in New York City.[19]

As an artist, Townsend was skilled in various media. And as a draftsman, he was widely recognized, conveying in his art not only "a decorative appeal" but also "a wistful quality which carries one into the realm of the imaginary," as one commentator expressed it.[20] He thus sought to go beyond mere draftsmanship, though he believed that this had to be done meticulously in order to affect the emotions and to bring out the spiritual side of a subject. He once advised his brother Lee, who studied at the Chicago Art Institute in 1915–1916, on the subject. He urged him to seek that fundamental quality of a subject that he defined as "that inherent moving power of a particular form or relation of forms, of a line or relation of lines, or of both masses and lines which gives through the eye that aesthetic thrill — peculiar, mysterious, haunting, personal and intangible, without which no graphic or plastic expression can truly be called a 'work of art.' "[21] The emphasis, he never tired of explaining, should be on creativity — on expressing oneself as an artist and at the same time, pursuing simplicity and sincerity. He was the first to admit that this was a large order, and the artist's greatest challenge. A study of Townsend's war art reveals that he took his own instructions seriously, all of which adds to its interest.

Over 200 of Townsend's wartime sketches and paintings, many of them uncompleted, are at the New Britain Art Museum in New Britain, Connecticut; these were not turned in to the army as part of his official work. On January 28, 1920, the Historical Branch of the General Staff of the War Department transferred 503 pieces of combat art from all eight of the official artists to the United States national museum, the Smithsonian Institution, in Washington, D.C. Later, three additional works were added to the collection. Of this total, Townsend created forty-seven. These remain at the Smithsonian as his contribution to the U.S. effort in the Great War.[22]

Although he was certainly a better artist than writer, Townsend's labors in his diary nonetheless provide much of interest for the student of the World War I years. To be sure, he enjoyed an unusually privileged position. Commissioned a captain without any previous military experience, he remained a "summer soldier" — one who had the privileges of an officer with few of the responsibilities. And the mobility enjoyed by the official artists must have been a sore spot to those less able to move about at will: Enlisted men must have wondered about these unusual officers. Then, too, the "rah-rah, college-boys-on-a-lark," lightheartedness that Townsend's diary sometimes reveals conveys a somewhat distorted picture of the war, which was hardly a vacation for most men of the AEF. Townsend, though he observed the harshness of the combat military environment, did not have to endure its hardships for an extended period. And he could find relief in more pleasant surroundings; he could go to Paris to attend the theater or eat a tasty meal almost at will. These amenities enabled him to avoid the bleaker aspects of service familiar to many other U.S. troops caught up in the struggle.

Nevertheless, Townsend was in a unique position to observe the grand events of the war. An educated, thoughtful, and well-placed observer, his writing transcended the more familiar diaries of trench-bound soldiers, and his fresh insights are unfailingly stimulating.

CHAPTER I

ARRIVAL

When the United States declared war on April 6, 1917, the U.S. Army consisted of 127,588 Regular Army officers and men and a National Guard of 80,446 members — a total of only 208,034 troops.[23] Clearly, a greatly expanded force was required. High officials soon decided that a draft was needed to obtain the necessary numbers, and on May 18, a draft bill was passed. By the end of hostilities, over 4 million U.S. men were under arms, about one-half of those serving in Europe.

Also in May, Secretary of War Newton T. Baker appointed General John Pershing to command the American Expeditionary Forces.[24] He and his staff, numbering 191 officers and men, sailed from New York on May 28, 1917. Arriving at Liverpool, England, on June 8, Pershing's group conferred in London with British high officials before sailing five days later to Boulogne-sur-Mer, France. They traveled to Paris, where they turned to establishing the AEF, amidst much hope on the part of the Allies that a huge U.S. army would arrive shortly. They would initially be disappointed, for U.S. troops would only trickle in over the next months. It was not until 1918 that large numbers would begin to arrive.

Meanwhile, from his Paris offices in the rue de Constantine, Pershing began the massive task of organizing the AEF. On June 26, the first elements of the U.S. 1st Division, consisting of about 14,000 men, arrived at St. Nazaire. The soldiers, most of whom were raw recruits, were billeted in many small villages near Gondrecourt, in north central France, and began their training. As other branches arrived, schools were set up to accommodate them: the artillery center at La Valdahon in the Vosges Mountains of Eastern France; general staff offices at Langres; aviation training fields at Issoudun; and numerous other bases covering all phases of military operations.[25]

After some time in Paris, Pershing moved away from the capital and its numerous distractions on September 6, 1917, establishing his headquarters

at Chaumont, a provincial city on the Marne River that lay approximately 150 miles southeast of Paris. This location placed General Headquarters (GHQ) in close proximity to the main sector of the western front where U.S. soldiers would serve — in Lorraine. Pershing's staff included five major sections: administration, intelligence, operations, coordination, and training, under a chief of staff of the AEF. A technical and administrative staff was also created, composed of the chiefs of fifteen separate departments, corps, and services, such as the Medical Corps and the Air Service. The massive supply apparatus consisted of the Line of Communications, divided into Base, Intermediate, and

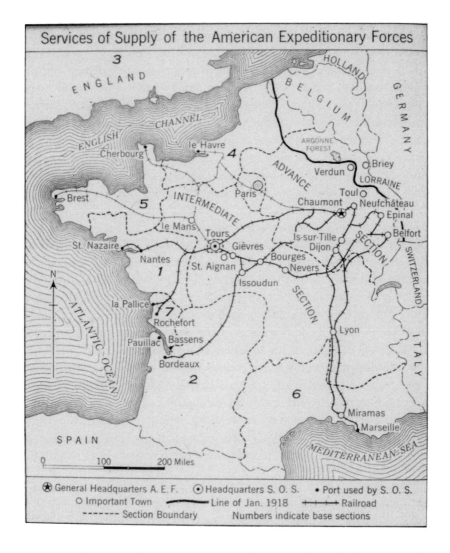

Services of Supply of the American Expeditionary Forces

Advance Sections. There were eventually nine Base Sections, one in London, one in Belgium, another in Italy, and others at several French ports. At Nevers, Bourges, Gièvres, St. Aignan, Le Mans, and elsewhere, other major bases and supply depots were also established. To facilitate the purchase of the vast quantities of matériel needed, the General Purchasing Board was created in August of 1917, headed by Lieutenant Colonel Charles G. Dawes.

The AEF also created a distinctive organization for its infantry divisions. These included two infantry brigades, of about 8,500 men each, and a field artillery brigade, together with a machine gun battalion, a signal battalion, and other units. With some 28,000 officers and men, seventy-two guns, 260 machine guns, and 17,666 rifles, a typical division was commanded by a major general. These large divisions were two to three times the size of their counterparts in the armies then engaged in the conflict. In action, they were later to be combined into corps, consisting of two or more divisions under a major general, and armies, each of two or more corps, commanded by a lieutenant general. An army group was to be made up of two or more armies, led by a general. In actual fact, the AEF would only create two armies during hostilities. Pershing was initially in charge of the 1st Army, and in October of 1918, Major General Robert Lee Bullard and Major General Hunter Liggett were assigned to command the two new armies, receiving their appointments as lieutenant generals on November 1. Pershing also briefly commanded the AEF's sole army group. After the armistice in November 1918, the 3d Army was formed to occupy the U.S. zone in the Rhineland of defeated Germany.

When the Chaumont headquarters also became congested, eleven of the technical and supply bureaus were transferred to Tours, in central France, on February 16, 1918, where they were placed under the Line of Communications, by then called the Service of the Rear. Somewhat later, this was redesignated the Services of Supply. Known widely and derisively as the SOS, duty in this vast organization was usually hated and shunned by those soldiers who hoped to serve where the action was. At Chaumont, the General Staff's five sections were redesignated as G-1, administration; G-2, intelligence; G-3, operations; G-4, coordination; and G-5, training. Most important to the official artists would be G-2, the Intelligence Section, for they were placed under G-2-D, the Press and Censorship Division of G-2, and assigned to Press Field Headquarters at Neufchâteau, northeast of Chaumont and closer to the site of U.S. operations.

After three months in France, where they were tutored by French instructors, the 1st Division troops were ready to be sent into a quiet part of the front, the trenches in the Toul sector. This occurred on October 21, 1917, and from that date until the armistice, U.S. troops were always somewhere in the lines. The first artillery shots were fired at the Germans

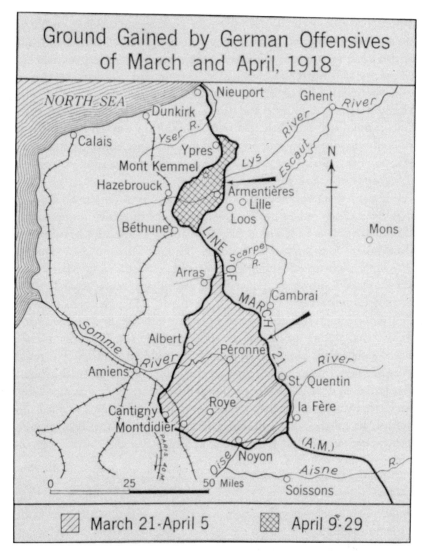

Ground Gained by German Offensives of March and April, 1918

March 21-April 5   April 9-29

two days later. By March 1918, there were about 350,000 U.S. troops in France, with daily arrivals swelling those numbers.

Meanwhile, the Germans began planning massive drives along the western front, hoping to break through before the U.S. troops arrived in sufficient numbers to make winning the war an impossibility for Germany. On March 21, therefore, they began the first of a series of five drives. The initial effort, after the heaviest German artillery bombardment of the war, was aimed at splitting the French and British forces. The British bore the brunt of this assault when seventy-one German divisions hit twenty-six British ones; suddenly, the front had a forty-mile gap in it. In a seventeen-day fight, the Germans advanced to the villages of Montdidier and Cantigny and threatened to break out toward Paris, though the Allied lines held. Among the results of the German initiative were the appointment by the Allies of a supreme Allied commander, Marshal Ferdinand Foch, and General Pershing's decision to commit U.S. troops to large-scale action.

But the first sharply fought U.S. battle was waged on a small scale. In early April, Foch pulled the 1st Division out of the quiet Toul sector in Lorraine to prepare for action farther to the west around Cantigny and Montdidier. The 1st was replaced by the 26th Division (or "Yankee" Division), made up of New Englanders and commanded by Major General Clarence R. Edwards. The division was in position by April 3, 1918, in the trenches around the town of Seicheprey. The Germans held the high ground opposite, dominated by a hill near the town of Montsec. Hoping to capture prisoners for interrogation, the Germans massed special storm troops to attack the newly arrived U.S. soldiers. The result was a series of inconclusive trench raids. The Germans then launched a large strike on April 20, with over 3,000 men involved. At first successful, the Germans were ultimately forced to withdraw, having sustained numerous casualties while inflicting heavy losses on the U.S. troops. Seicheprey was the first engagement in which the U.S. forces were involved in some strength, providing a foretaste of much action to come.

The second major German attack along the western front began on April 9, in the British sector at the northern extremity of the front. This resulted in a seventeen-mile advance in the Lys Valley by the end of the battle on April 29.

The third German assault commenced on May 27, resulting in the capture of Soissons. Four days later, the Germans reached the Marne River Valley, scene of major battles in 1914, where the French had checked the German invasion and saved Paris, forcing the Germans to withdraw and thereby creating the stalemated western front. From May 27 to June 5, 1918, the U.S. 2d and 3d Divisions were thrown into the lines and, by blocking the German advance at Château-Thierry, helped

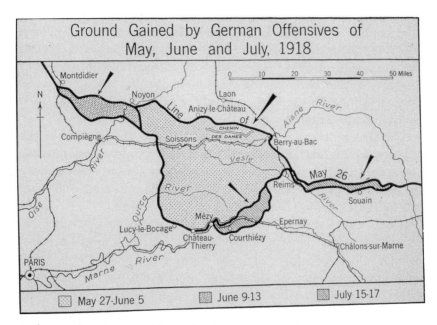

Ground Gained by German Offensives of May, June and July, 1918

May 27-June 5 | June 9-13 | July 15-17

to thwart the German drive. The 2d Division subsequently recaptured Bouresches, Belleau Wood, and Vaux.

Meanwhile, having created two salients in the western front, the Germans mounted their fourth attack on June 9, which lasted until June 15, but the French held, supported by the U.S. 1st Division, which even before the drive began (on May 28) had captured the town of Cantigny, one of the first significant U.S. offensive operations on the front.

Harry Townsend reported for duty in France on May 1, 1918, in the midst of these developments. He was stationed at Neufchâteau and from there proceeded to tour U.S. areas of operations. His first visit was to the Toul sector and included sites in and around Ménil-la-Tour, Domèvre, Martincourt, Pont-à-Mousson, and Seicheprey, the scene of the recent battle. He made later excursions to Baccarat, Lunéville, and Dombasle to the east of the Toul sector. In Toul, he visited with the 94th and 95th Squadrons of the U.S. Air Service, part of the 1st Pursuit Group.

In early June, Townsend and other artists journeyed to the Château-Thierry area, where several U.S. divisions, especially the 2d, were in action. This division was made up of army regulars and marines. The marines were engaged in bloody operations in Belleau Wood; in the twenty-day battle, the brigade sustained over 5,000 casualties. However, because of several censorship slips, the marines received much publicity, while the army components of the 2d Division, as well as the 3d Division that was also involved in the area, were left in obscurity. When the army brigade of the 2d Division captured Vaux in a skillful attack, it received little attention. The omission rankled for a long time to come, facts which Townsend discussed in his diary.

The German advance in these weeks had produced waves of French refugees, which Townsend reflected upon while making notes, sketches, and photographs for future work. He normally worked in this way, using the materials that he gathered during his excursions to produce finished canvases in his studio at Neufchâteau.

Townsend's account of his stay in hotels and his sumptuous meals contrasted his situation with that of the French refugees, as well as the lot of the U.S. troops engaged in action. However, in the Château-Thierry area, Townsend came under artillery fire for the first time, perhaps earning his privileges at last.

May 22, 1918

With Louis Raemaekers, Heath Robinson, Peixotto and Lieutenant Parks, we set out for Ménil-la-Tour.[26] A delightful sunny day. Country was truly beautiful. After looking around a bit — are watching the troops with their heavy packs of variegated makeup as they come into barracks, and the many strange trucks — mule and motor — that rumbled by, Peixotto and I went over to YMCA huts to inquire about dinner. I went to tell Raemaekers to meet us there. Soon he came, and a Captain Maris recognized him, as he came over, from press portraits of him — so he came and introduced himself, saying he wanted to meet Raemaekers. Captain Maris is a Philadelphian — a descendent of Benjamin West — also related to the Dutch painters the Marises.[27] Also he knows practically all the younger artists of Phila. and knew all the old Howard Pyle crowd at Wilmington.[28]

Had a fine lunch, then Captain Maris, knowing we were bent on seeing artillery — and being Captain of a heavy battery — ten-inch marine guns — suggested that we go out afterwards to his batteries, which were supposed to be models of excellence. He took us over first to his park where his trucks, etc., were — to show us the motor mounts for transporting them. Tremendous trucks — seventeen tons each. Saw also their anti-aircraft defense. School for truck drivers also, where they must drive around in small circles of iron stakes — just far enough apart to clear wheels by careful driving. Then went with two autos to his battery — passing Andilly and skirting around Royaumeix — the old church which is visible from everywhere. It quite commands the eyes of all — for it seems always in sight first. Stopped at Domèvre — battery headquarters — where we met Major Miles in command of batteries. Fine, clean type of man.

Then on thro Manonville where there is a fine old 12th-century château — now occupied by the military. It has been under shellfire. Then on out past our balloon and off to Martincourt — where there is another old château very much shattered by shells. Right near here, wonderfully tucked away under a high roadbank and quite out of sight of Boche balloons, was Maris's battery. How wonderful they looked, and how wicked — yet human — they seemed. They seemed alive but oh so patient and ready to be up and "at them." The guns themselves are in sunken pits — are nicely camouflaged — and have over the top of each pit a screen — tubes and branches on wire netting — so that it will roll back and let the muzzle of the gun be raised sufficiently — thirty degrees about. How handily they can be elevated and lowered. Went down also in their bomb-and-gas-proof shelter — about thirty feet underground — a trifle less — but with a thick layer of rock and soil above them, they feel comparatively safe.

The old château nearby is a fine, old tumbled-down establishment; it has been struck by shells several times. From this old château at Martincourt, which sits on the edge of the plateau, one looks away across the valley to hills guarded by Germans, their balloons on the lookout above. Off to the left is Pont-à-Mousson — not visible, however. In the valley just below the château, is a lovely winding stream and a tiny village, 500 feet below perhaps.

We went thro the château — admiring the wonderful old timbering — intricate and heavy. Then up a tiny stairway from the court to a path around the embattlements — getting wonderful glimpses from the portholes, that once held cannon, perhaps, and crossbowmen guarded the place in all directions. From these points too, we could look down, to the ground floors, into the great wells of shattered beams and walls made by the Boche shells. Yet it is by no means a ruined building, and is occupied by French troops now. The court is filled with trucks, and also farm implements, and in the center is a corral with eighty-four asses, many of which are arriving as we were there, carrying slung packs of bailed hay — twice as large as they.

"Firing a Big Gun." *Courtesy of the Smithsonian Institution, NMAH, Division Armed Forces History. 46436.*

Then back to the guns, the men having elevated one a bit for us — I made a slight sketch. What a thrill goes thro one at the sight of these monsters — conscious of their own power — lying there, serenely waiting — waiting for what, tho? Will it be first a German bomb — or will they manage to keep their position secret until after they have gotten in their own deadly work and have served most of their usefulness? Captain Maris tells me that in ten days about, they are to move them by night to a position being prepared for them, fifteen kilos away — I think, put them in place — and from this new position, fire heavily one night only, then back to their home at Martincourt. It seems there's a big move or surprise about to be sprung in that section by the French — and we are to help of course — a counteroffensive to the expected and certain Boche offensive in the north. He has thrilled me with expectation and has asked me to come over when they move the guns. It's a very, very fascinating spot to me — the positions here. How cunningly they are concealed from the enemy planes, and the great shells standing ready under the ledge along the road on either side of the placements, covered with their camouflage nets — and the tiny railroad and tiny trucks to carry them down on their way to the Boche — covered, too, with painted cloth. What a pride Maris must take in these big children of his. It's called officially Battery Maris. May they keep their secret there — until they've done their work.

"The Hurry Call, Night of May 20, 1918." *Courtesy of the Smithsonian Institution, NMAH, Division Armed Forces History. 46453.*

On our way back, we stopped in places along the military road under observation by Boche balloons, to search out with our glasses various well-known spots on the front — Seicheprey (where so many of our boys in an uneven fight went gallantly, tho perhaps foolishly, to their death — held under long gas concentration), Flirey, Beaumont, and Foret-du-Bois-le-Prétre. As we stood there in the strong sun, and as our auto sailed along leaving its trail of white dust behind, we could not resist the thought of how the Boche would have liked to know that Raemaekers was there — what a time they would have given us — and how likely that they could have gotten us — having the range of that road as they do, and so many guns to trail us with. Raemaekers was greatly amused, too, at the thought. What a fine simple soul he is.

Stopped at Manonville — went thro the fine 11th-century château there — up into its towers with their glorious views of the entire valley. Looked out thro a hole in the roof at the mark of a fragment of a shell that grazed the tower. Great brick houses are built in the walls of the towers; what a den one of these tower rooms would be. The owner, haute bourgeoisie — name I didn't get — has gone to safer climes, but has left his things behind. One of the salons has a large collection of stuffed birds of

Lorraine — truly thousands of them, all different — unbelievable almost. The keeper assured us that a certain one — flamingo we were sure, was a swan!

Then across the street to an ambulance, first U.S. in France, and still working with the French. Gordon Stevenson in command. They saved our lives with a large bach pitcher of Pinard lemonade, wonder-of-wonders with ice in it.

Took pictures of the château, then back to Ménil-la-Tour thro hordes of Annamites, not unlike Chinese coolies only dark-skinned, almost, as Africans.[29] All sorts of weird costumes and kits. Many carried very long balances of swinging dishes and gas masks . . . swinging from them. And all were chattering like so many birds.

Stopped at Andilly. To come back tomorrow. Met Tom Ball's son at Ménil-la-Tour — he's guarding camouflage material.[30] Very interesting boy, making himself known in the U.S. before the war with his costume and stage design. Quite a change. Another sort of a show.

We were loath to leave. In fact, we paused a long time before reaching home. Three blowouts halfway between Toul and Colombey-les-Belles — no telephone near — held us up till 10:30. Lieutenant Parks and I walk across fields to a little, sleepy village to find phone out of order. Peixotto goes into Colombey on a truck and phones HQ [headquarters] to send relief. Meanwhile, we all go back again to our village to hunt supper. Raemaekers proves himself by inducing the innkeeper's wife at 9:00 to prepare us an omelette. So with beer also, and cheese and salad — and after words and a search by Mme. — some bread, we dined very well indeed. Took hard-boiled eggs and beer back to our driver who stayed with the car.

Then we waited. And as we waited we could see — and hear — for hours, it seemed, the RFC [Royal Flying Corps] bombing planes rising from their camp over to our left — take the air, flash a few signals and roar away on their deadly work.[31] Somehow it makes one feel that after all — the Allies, inactive as they may seem, waiting, waiting so anxiously for the impending blow of the Boche to be delivered soon — are far from inactive, and are using their air forces to the limit. And day after day we do get the reports of Huns down, and eleven or twenty-two tons, as the case may be, of bombs dropped on enemy works. . . . Even Cologne has been bombarded. So away into the night they kept going — and returning — and I imagine going back again. And from over the front we got the report of guns which — while we knew better — did sound as tho it might be their loads of bombs — effective somewhere there — and then the flash of rockets as of distress, going up along the line — and flares that stayed a moment — and flicker of bursting shrapnel from archies here and there.[32] Of course all of this — save the archies — had no connection with the raiders; yet the illusion was there. It was weird and exciting, watching it all. How it brought dear old Henri back to me tho — for it was to me as tho the throb of his motor mingled with the rest. Then I'd try to realize the facts as I knew them, but no picture would come, and oh it seems he must still be here — doing his work that he knew and loved so well.[33]

Finally our relief came. Then home.

May 23, 1918
❧

*B*ack to Ménil-la-Tour and Andilly today. Had lunch with Captains Maris and Holmes. Sketched around Andilly all afternoon — talked with the boys just returning from the front — Seicheprey and around there— 102d and 103rd Infantry was coming in for rest — to be sent on — they didn't know where.[34] Told me of a recent phosgene gas attack they had to suffer. Lost in Co. C, 103d Inf., twenty men dead—130 severely gassed — this a surprise. They seem to dread the English type of mask — swore by the French one — and say they have found it to be comfortable and effective for five hours and that they prefer two of them to the discomfiture of the other type — all pay glowing tribute to the quality and quantity of food given them in front lines. No complaints in general.

There was very great activity in Andilly all day. Great camions driving in — American and French.[35] Machine gun companies. Field kitchens. Signal Corps line carts, all sorts, and what a mixture of people. French, American, Italian and the ubiquitous coolie or Annamite — garrulous and lively, and every one washing either their clothes or their persons. And in the midst of it all, dozens of Frenchmen with more dozens of horses — or it may be Americans with horses, come thundering down and splashing into the little stream for water, riding up it to another street and then exit. How they seem to enjoy it all. Upstream are a couple of poor, sick horses tied to a footbridge in the stream. How utterly dejected they seem. Nothing matters to them it seems — too much trouble even to shake an ear infested with flies — or else flies seem as nothing to what they may have been thro, which is more likely.

How open to the world is the barrack or homelife to these soldiers here. And how interesting, and apparently not too uncomfortable either.

"Infantryman." *Courtesy of the National Archives. 111-SC-57036.*

We learn that Elsie Janis is to give an entertainment, so decide to stay for it.[36] Up near the barracks is a boxing ring — elevated. The 101st Regimental band is there and fifty nurses seated in front.[37] Soldiers, countless soldiers are packed around. Seats have been saved for us. Soon Elsie appeared, dressed for an indoor performance, and as it is cold, she objects to taking off her wraps. Her mother, who is with her also, appears

"Our Cavalry." *Courtesy of the National Archives. 111-SC-57031.*

to be upset because they hadn't been told. However, she begins with stories, then a song. Then the band plays an air which starts her feet, and in a moment of forgetfulness, she throws off her coat and is Elsie Janis — in thin black dress — and she does her very best. An enthusiastic crowd. Soon she is whisked away to a performance at an aviation camp, making the third performance for the evening. So she keeps it up, day after day. The officers were having a dance afterwards, hence the fifty nurses. We would have stayed, but Robinson insisted on returning as he was to take an early train in the morning. Hard luck!

May 24, 1918

*T*ook trip to Baccarat today for the first time. It's a fine ride — via Nancy, St. Nicholas, Lunéville — passing Dombasle of salt and chemical fame, where the girls work the factories entirely in knickerbockers and tight blouses. Many we saw actually wore silk stockings and shapely shoes, as tho they had tried to make themselves as attractive as possible. Why not? They certainly were plentiful — it was noontime when we passed.

On to Baccarat. Dined at Cafe de la Gare. Five francs. Good. Then to HQ. 166th at Reherrey, which was very, very quiet in spite of its being at the front.[38] Went over to a nearby village to meet Colonel Hough in command who was playing in a ball game there. Brought back Lincoln Eyre and Captain Harrington, engineering officer of Dijon.[39] Took dinner with them at club.

May 25, 1918

Went to Toul and to 94th and 95th squadrons — *chasse* — there, where we talked with some of the pilots.[40] Discussed death of Lufbery, and the talk of the Boche plane involved being armored, for it seems the French, who engaged it first, emptied all their bullets into it without effect — also one American before "Luf" went up, determined to shoot at the pilot himself, so there seems no doubt of it.[41] No news there.

Home — to supper — and then to bed early.

May 26, 1918

Saw long procession of girls — in white dresses and veils — being led by gorgeous priest and boys in scarlet with embroidery and banners — and followed by priest in wonderful golden gown or surplice — and followed by more boys in scarlet — on their way to first communion. Didn't go on trip today. Am expecting arrival of equipment from Paris. Glorious weather!

June 5–8, 1918

In company with Captain Wallace Morgan and Captain Adams (F.P.A.), I left Neufchâteau for Château-Thierry to get as close as possible to the big fight then going on between the Boche and our boys, supported by French artillery.[42] The drive up took us thro Gondrecourt, Ligny-en-Barrois, Ancerville, St. Dizier, Vitry-le-François, Sommesous, Sézanne, Montmirail and Viels-Maisons — all of them interesting old towns and most of them scenes of the first Marne battles.[43] In fact, on much of the way up we passed over the old battlefields — marked here and there with reminiscent crosses, faded and dust-covered now — the once brilliant French *cocarde* on each washed with the rains and almost obliterated with the sun — and on top of all the dust. In places the very thickness of the tiny graves tells a mute story of the fierceness of the old battle. Dust! Dust are they indeed now. In a world of dust! As tho in proof of the old saying — the battlefields of the Marne, with their countless French and German dead (for there are many faded black crosses mixed with them all) are truly in a world of dust. It's as tho the power on high was determined to obliterate every trace of the old struggle, save only the glorious memory. But he has to do it . . . by the fierceness of the new struggle — the struggle of today with its very threat at times of overrunning the fields. For the steady, the fierce incessant streams of camions loaded with every sort of munition of death — tearing frantically over these strait, heartless roads — as well as their same kind, empty, hurrying breathlessly back — have beaten and churned their surface until the whole countryside is a veritable inferno of noise and a wilderness of dust, white and cutting as the alkali of the plains. Forgetting almost the lovely country thro which one is passing, one can with difficulty see the traffic that is tearing back on its eternal quest for supplies, and one is in constant danger from the sudden stopping of the line in front. What a sight and an experience it all is. Dust, dust, dust! Till the human element in the great struggle forward and back, white with it all, seems to peer out at one with great cavernous eyes like ghouls, and the sudden opening of mouth creates at once a strange elemental mask, almost terrifying in its mystery.

The June sunshine pours down with almost the vehemence of a summer sun at home. In front and behind us the road is a long white ribbon in the sun, strait and inexorable as Fate. When there is the slightest break in the backward convoys, we swerve out and past the ones going forward, and often, in turn, are we passed by some swift staff car. In spite of the long procession of heavy guns and troops and munitions and of the nameless supplies that pass over the roads day after day, and in spite of the ceaseless dust whipped up from their surface, the roads continue wonderfully smooth. Till one feels that, after all, they were built for this very possibility, this sudden need against the Hun.

Here and there we pass a prison camp, from which the Boches stare out with vacant gaze. Then there is an aviation field, perhaps, the machines drawn up as on parade ready for the sudden alert or for patrol. In a corner of one field and near the road is a pile of wrecked machines, their wings scorched or torn, their engines with cylinders exposed, holding out, as it were, maimed stumps of arms for sympathy. Here and there we pass gangs of roadmenders, Italian, Chinese or Russsians, who straiten bent backs to look at us.

As we stare into the fields searching thro the dust we see sometimes a farmer with his oxen at his work, tho generally the farmer is the woman of the family. Or the girl, even, of tender age, who struggles at a man's tasks from early morning till late into the dusk. Everywhere there are the wonderfully beautiful scarlet poppies that struggle thro the dust for light and breath. How beautiful they are here in the fields of France away from this dust, how pathetic they are here in the midst of it, how like to the women folk of France who suffer, too, in this war zone. Overhead an aeroplane goes humming on its way free from it all.

At last we near the front, or the immediate zone back of it, passing long trains of refugees for many miles, grey in the dust, patient-faced, leaving their homes for the second time to who knows what fate, and going back into the more-or-less unknown rear to await the final day. Many of them were smiling as they waved their hands at us as we messed, and always were the children gay. Little did they seem to comprehend the meaning of it all. Lucky they!

Two of these groups of evacuees I shall never forget. One was led by the father, a more-or-less ordinary looking man, kind-faced, not over-strong, who struggled up the slight hill pushing a barrow loaded to the skies with things that he had felt he must not leave behind. Behind him was a lovely girl of eleven or twelve years with big, wide-brimmed, beribboned straw hat and in white dress who was carrying, with great difficulty, a roll of rugs on her shoulder. And behind her was her mother, a wonderfully refined and handsome woman, bareheaded, who pushed a baby carriage loaded to overflowing with bundles and clothes and parcels hanging from the handles, and down in the midst of the carriage was a wee, smiling baby. I couldn't help wondering about this family or where they were from — what kind of a home — or where did they think to go? How full of this sort of sad flight, tho, France has been.

Later, we met or passed, as she rested by the roadside and gazed at us with strange, distant look, a tall, rather gaunt, woman, alone with all the belongings she was apparently able to bring with her. She stood at the head of a large, black horse hitched to a cart loaded with furniture and bedding and hay, and with a coop on top filled to overflowing, almost, with

"Refugees From Château-Thierry Section." *Courtesy of the Smithsonian Institution, NMAH, Division Armed Forces History. 46435.*

chickens and ducks. She was hatless and shaded her eyes with her left hand from the glaring sun. With the other hand she held the leash on three fine cows who struggled and tugged to reach the grass at the roadside. Beneath the cart a faithful dog panted in the heat. She seemed alone in the world. Her *marié* at the front, living or dead, and she left behind to manage their apparently prosperous little farm. This great threat had again come to them and she had had to pack and flee, as she had once before done, till the menace was passed. Alone but not alone, for "*enceinte*" as she was, she carried with her that great hope, to give joy soon to that soldier husband of hers when he heard the news that he was father to a son, another soldier someday for his beloved France. And failing his return, or even her return ever to their old home, she stood there looking, as it were, into a future that bore for her a son, consecrated to her and to that other mother, France. One glance at her and one sensed all this.

Further on we pass a small boy in an old dilapidated "peram" who, hitched on behind a large cart, was having the time of his young life, innocent of the crisis at hand. When one thinks of the countless children that have been born and raised their few young years within sound of the

"Viels-Maisons, Near Château-Thierry." *Courtesy of the Smithsonian Institution, NMAH, Division Armed Forces History. 46448.*

guns, and even under or within gun fire, and know nothing of a world beautiful and at peace!

Instead of taking the road that leads from Montmirail up to Château-Thierry, we decided to go on to Viels-Maisons and report to Division Headquarters there to prevent any difficulties further on.[44] We were glad that we did, for we found it a delightful old town, and we saw passing thro there a regiment of French Chasseurs, fine, tall, aquiline-looking men different from any other class of men we had seen in the French service. How beautifully they were mounted too, and how well they sat their mounts. Their long, thin lances, sharp and shining in the sun, their gaze neither to left or right, but strait ahead as tho intent only on the business in hand, which was death and destruction to whatever foe they met, they seemed like the crusaders of old. And with cartridge belts slung on their horses' necks, as the English do, with their carbines on their back, their gas masks and their other accoutrements built up about them, they carried a very business-like air. I took some snaps here — tried to make a few sketches of them, and made a slight sketch of a very interesting old house at the end or turn of the old main street which I thought would be useful in any picture I might make of incident here. Then shortly after, we ran back to have supper and spend the night at Montmirail, having taken about seven hours to make the run up from Neufchâteau to Viels-Maisons.

Thank goodness we were directed by an MP [Military Police] to the Hotel Verte Galante. For aside from the excellent accommodations that we found, we found also Le Maître Gaston Mirabelle, and we wouldn't have missed him for the world. After a more-or-less anxious query to the nominal proprietor at the desk, and after a more or less satisfactory reply, in answer to a vigorous appeal, Gaston appears. And with his appearance, it is as tho one were suddenly confronted with the opening act in some quaint French farce or Opera Comique. A thin, pale man with a sparse, black, waxed mustache and a sparse beard appears on the scene. He is wonderful to look upon with the white suit of the chef and the tall, white cap with the roof on top. He comes toward us, dry cleaning his hands, a smile in his otherwise frightened-looking eyes; a smile on his thin, pale lips. He bows nervously, twitches his shoulders, wrings his hands again and assures us that he has room for us, and will we have the kindness, etc., and we are shown to nice, clean, little rooms at three francs the night, and yes he has one for our driver, Anderson, too. So we are fixed for the night. Now our car must be fixed for the night as well, and Gaston, in his white suit and white cap, leads it into the court and locates it to the inch as he would have it put. It is plain to us at once that he is the real master of the Verte Galante.

At the very good dinner with very good wine, which in time is served us by Mirabelle himself as tho he feared for some reason to trust his good wife, who has waited on most of the others there, we discover that he is also a wit and keen with his bit of by-play too. Adams decides at once that he is a find of a lifetime, a real individual, and he certainly was a bright spot in what was a trifle depressing, tho interesting, day.

As we drove up to the hotel we found that Hubbell and Hatrik and Sergeant Duff, still and movie men for the Signal Corps who had been up in the Château-Thierry fight for several days, were spending the night there and were going back to what was also our objective in the morning. They told us something of what they had found there when they came up — for they had a tip that things were to happen there, and had hurried up in a Cadillac, and were there waiting when our boys had arrived to relieve the French who were being driven back with heavy loss. And of how, when the train pulled in with our troops, they had to get out and move the wounded French, and I believe they said also the British, who were lying in stretchers on the tracks. And they told us of, and pointed out to us, an American nurse, Miss . . . who alone practically had been caring for these poor wounded men for a couple of days and had stayed with them after the French doctors had flown in the face of the Boche advance. And our men had arrived in the nick of time, hurried there, as we know, by every means possible to stem the tide, as they had done, too, so heroically, and the stand they made and their resistance . . . and their sturdy fight and advance against the Hun in that first Château-Thierry fight, will go down in our military history, and in the records of the Marines.

In the morning, Morgan and I, in a little walk, discover near us, in a little "place," a machine gun outfit that is just pulling out to go up to the relief of their men in the fight. We have a very interesting talk with a lieutenant who has had charge of the supplies for them up there all thro the fight, and it was thrilling. Also he had told us of how, when they had pulled into the little park there the day before, they had found it full of French cavalry that had been all cut to pieces by the Boche artillery fire and how pitiful it was to see the poor horses so.

When we get back to the hotel, we find that the cameramen have gone. In a few minutes we are off. They had given us instructions as to how far it was safe to take the car, and just how to manage to walk most safely on to get a good view of the continued shelling of the town.

Approaching Château-Thierry at last, and what a glamour of conflict had been cast around its very name! We find the road up there full of feverish activity and soon we are passing the heavier artillery that now and again bursts into a desultory action. Soon we arrive at the clump of trees near some French ambulances where we are to park our car, and go on afoot. . . . Walking up the road, which is under observation from two Boche balloons, we are soon opposite some 75s that are in positions in an open field hidden only by the brow of a little hill.[45] These are firing regularly, and over our heads there goes the intermittent whistle and scream of the heavies that we have passed as they go on their errand over into the Boche lines. It all is quite thrilling to me, for it's the first time I have been so near to actual conflict.

We are plodding on up the road, separated by considerable distance and hugging the trees as much as possible to lessen the chances of arousing the Hun observers' suspicions, when there appears over the hill and bearing down upon us with all the speed at its command, what turns out to be the boys' car, and the fellows in it are frightened to the limit, as well they might be. We had heard the bursting of German shells not far away and they had been firing at them. I shall never forget the looks on their faces as they came rushing down the road and pulled up in front of us and told breathlessly of it — of how taking their car up farther than they should have perhaps, and then scattering and going on afoot, they had been spotted by the balloons, and a little further on had been shelled vigorously. They had beat it back to their car and had been followed up the road. One can well imagine the state of fright they were in to have the bursts around them. A second or two before they reached us one had fallen right by their side, had come tearing and screaming at them, capping their fright, only to land, a "dud." But it had done the work, for they were in quite a state when they reached us. They piled out of the car for a minute to tell us of it; Hubbell had his trousers ripped pretty badly, and Hatrik his hand cut, from throwing themselves into the ditch to protect themselves. We were pretty nervous over it all; I know I was, for it was all new to me. Then there came a parting shell from the Hun which fell over in the field not far away, and they were thro.

Soon the fellows drove on back to Montmirail, leaving us to whatever fate we found. We talked for a time to some French ambulance men waiting there for any call that might come. The heavies in our rear had begun to throw shells over pretty constantly now and, thro lack of experience, we were not always able to know them as ours, tho it should have been easy. The Frenchmen were a bit amused, I am sure. Morgan decided he was going to try to go on up the road and if possible get a glimpse of the town from the top of the hill, and if possible a slight sketch, even. Adams was for going, and I was too, tho I somehow didn't like the look of it with those two balloons watching the road now even as they had when the others had been caught. But we split up, Morgan to go first, Adams next and then I. We were to keep at the side and under the thin trees which were on either side of the road. I watched their getaway. Before I could make up my mind to start, there were several shells that seemed to pass pretty close, judging from the terrific screech they made, and Morgan and Adams must have mistaken them even as I, for I could see them suddenly throw themselves to the ground. I went into the bushes several times, then decided to start. But a half mile, perhaps less, up that road picking my way from tree to tree, and incidentally out of the ditch from time-to-time, and finally with a sprained wrist, I hesitated. My poor heart was trying to beat its way out of its weakening cage. Go on I could not, however much I knew I ought. Here to do the war and showing yellow, it seemed! But then it seemed a physical impossibility. I tried a few rods farther and had to give up. My misery then at finding that I couldn't make myself go, willing as my spirit seemed to be, under pressure perhaps, this, along with the physical agitation I was undergoing, was considerable.

I managed to get back to the Frenchmen, who, strangely enough, seemed to understand and be a bit sympathetic. This was like a tonic to me. I felt better at once and had a slight desire to try it again when I had

"Sketch, French Soldier." *Courtesy of the Smithsonian Institution, NMAH, Division Armed Forces History. 46450.*

"A Roadside Repair Station, Northwest of Château-Thierry, 2d Division." *Courtesy of the Smithsonian Institution, NMAH, Division Armed Forces History. 46432.*

learned from them that none of the shells they had watched me duck were Hun but instead were bound Hunward. But then I discovered Adams on his way back, ducking and diving as on the way up, and soon came Morgan head down plodding along back. He apparently was "on" by now for he was quite himself, it seemed. But Morgan had been under shellfire several times before, and whatever nervousness he may have shown at the start was caused by the unfortunate experience of Hubbell's crowd.

I was ready to leave. So were the others, so we decided to go around over to the other side of the river and the town where the Marines were operating with the 2d Division. This led us back thro Viels-Maisons where we had a nice dinner at the officers' mess. . . .

La Ferté we found a very beautiful old town with many marks of the Hun still on it from the first battle of the Marne. The ruined bridge, perhaps wisely, has never been rebuilt, a temporary one-way or single crossing span having been thrown across. This we found very congested owing to the traffic in both directions, which meant long waiting. The Marne here is beautiful, and the ride out on the far side of town, looking down over the Marne Valley as one approached Montreuil-aux-Lions, was

"Northwest of Château-Thierry." *Courtesy of the Smithsonian Institution, NMAH, Division Armed Forces History. 46443.*

truly wonderful. We are only a few kilometres here from the action that is taking place on the road that leads out past the Ferme de Paris to Château-Thierry. The division headquarters are at Montreuil-aux-Lions where we are going to report.[46] The roads here are alive with all sorts of activity. The country on either side of the roads is filled with French reserve troops, infantry and cavalry. Ammunition trucks come and go, and one hears at all times the roar of the artillery on ahead.

We soon come to the evacuation hospital which is unloading ambulances as fast as they arrive. We meet them coming. There is a large, well-guarded ammunition dump farther on. Trucks here are busy loading . . . and officers and clerks are busy pegging typewriters here and there.

As we arrive at HQ, a lone German prisoner is being brought in looking as tho he really believed he was to be killed soon, as they are taught by their officers. This one was quite a young boy, and seemed so scared. We were told that many had been brought in earlier in the morning.

We reported, and were soon on our way up the road to where the batteries were. We drove up thro a very inferno of fire from heavy guns hidden in the woods on either side. Strange to say, I seemed a different person now. For some strange reason, I was thoroughly happy, gay in fact, and I seemed to get into the spirit of the Hell that we were then giving

"Salvage. Clearing Up the Fields." *Courtesy of the Smithsonian Institution, NMAH, Division Armed Forces History. 46452.*

them. We left our car soon and went on foot, making a few sketches on the way. There seemed to be little or no reply to the American guns; here and there a shell would break, but it seems that the Huns had been prevented in the recent forced retreat from getting any of the big guns in position, for the Marines had been pushing them back a little each day. Reserve batteries of 75s were hidden here and there in the woods waiting an order to position farther front, and some of them rushed out as we were passing. It all spelled business of a lively sort.

The guard posted at Regimental HQ, a Marine, in conversation asked us where we were from. New York? Why then maybe we used to follow the races and remembered Johnny Baker who used to ride many of the winners at Belmont Park? We assured him that his name was familiar. He was one of those thin, rat-like creatures that the war has changed so many of our boys here into. One sees so many of them that have been thro much of the hardest of it. Thin faces, with staring eyes that look at you but thro and beyond; strange, patient, long-suffering eyes. Thin bodies trimmed down, as it were, to meet necessity. Thin legs that in their wrapped puttees give little mark for flying fragment or machine gun bullets. Fate seems to

"Field Sketch, Roadside YMCA Canteen, Northwest of Château-Thierry." *Courtesy of the Smithsonian Institution, NMAH, Division Armed Forces History. 46449.*

be trying to protect them as well as she can, till the thing is settled and they mean to see it thro.

We went forward to the advanced 75s which were keeping up a steady fire. Shrapnel was bursting down in the fields in front of them but they didn't have the range. Our boys were down in the wheatfields over a little range of hills but we were as far forward as we dared to go. Off to the left I saw an officer on horse galloping down into it, apparently directly under the shrapnel. The air was full of balloons, ours and the enemy. When I say ours, I mean of course French, for as yet we have only one I believe that is really ours. There are many aeroplanes overhead, busy with their work. All is activity.

On our way back, we hear that twelve horses had just been killed by a shell that fell in their midst a couple of hundred yards to our right. They are then dragging a horse that had been killed by a piece of shrapnel in another spot. One pities the poor horses in this war and hopes that it will be possible to completely motorize it soon. Why not?

We go back to the ammunition train to make some drawings and meet Major Fairfax, and Captain Cox, an old League student, and at their

"Officers' Mess, Ammunition Train." *Courtesy of the Smithsonian Institution, NMAH, Division Armed Forces History. 46447.*

solicitation, have supper and spend the night there with their outfit.[47] It gives promise of interest so we stay. Fine supper. Champagne, song and stories after. Major Fairfax and F.P.A. vie with each other far into the night with all the old popular songs, and it was amazing and interesting to hear and to suddenly awake to the fact that many of them were pretty good old songs, too. While we listened to the songs, we watched an air raid on Meaux, then the archies after them. It was very exciting. Over on the front, too, there were many star shells, and the flare of the guns which kept up a steady fire.

We found a good bed for Anderson on the seat of one of the trucks. Adams was given an extra cot by one of the officers, and Morgan and I curled up in our blankets in our National. Night went pretty well, save that along about three o'clock, I think, there came a hurry call for a number of trucks up at the front to bring back the wounded, for the boys had gone over the top for a big gain but with terribly heavy losses, so much so that the ambulances were unable to care for them. All morning they were hurrying by to the evacuation hospital which was only a couple of hundred yards down the road. After breakfast, we went down to see the boys there. They certainly were a brave bunch, and how the slightly wounded ones cursed to think that they were put out of the fight, and how eager they were to get back into it. That hospital was a pretty trying place, for they were coming in in terrible shape, some of them.

We left in time to get our dinner on the way back at Montmirail with Gaston Mirabelle and, on the way there, saw right near us two Hun planes slip up on a balloon, set it on fire, saw the observer jump with his parachute which opened successfully, saw the sausage flame then explode and fall, and saw the Huns hurry away, pursued by a long trail of shrapnel bursts. It was very dramatic and we couldn't have had a better view of it. At once another balloon was sent up in its place.

A good dinner, and a dull trip home, or most of the way, for we realized that, after all, we hadn't slept, "*sur les belles étoiles*," as well as we thought, and we dozed most of the way home. When we reached Joinville, we thought we discovered a shortcut home, and found a really beautiful route thro a country that I am sure had seen no American officers that way before. Lovely little towns filled with children and cattle and sheep. It was night now and they were bringing them in from the grazing.

In the morning, before we started back, we heard that while we had been having our supper the night before down the road, Floyd Gibbons had gone out with Major Berry to inspect some machine gun nests or positions of ours. In order to reach them, they had to cross a wheatfield under fire from Boche machine guns. The Major was hit and fell. Gibbons, a distance away, went to his rescue crawling towards him. He, too, was hit, one bullet going thro his helmet and thro the frontal bone taking his eye out completely.[48] Two bullets went thro his left shoulder coming out down the arm, fracturing the bone. He has been sent in to the hospital at Neuilly. It looks bad, and is the more regrettable in that he went out into unnecessary danger, altho he was game all thro, they say, and insisted that wounded soldiers in great need of surgical attention be cared for first. When he was found, he had been lying there an hour and a half with his eye on his cheek and had been conscious all the time. It must have been a strange and hopeless situation for a man to be in, fearing to try to crawl back to his own relief and not knowing when other relief would come. His wife at Dijon was sent for, and she is nursing him at the hospital, I hear.

Morgan, Harding and I take a trip over to Baccarat and out to Reherrey to see if we can find Aitken who is in a machine gun company — Captain — in the 77th Division which we had heard was just in there, having relieved the 42d. We find, tho, that the exchange is still taking place, and that the machine guns were not yet arrived. It was a very cloudy day, tho it had been a beautiful trip over. But now that we were there, it

"A Quiet Sector in Lorraine Opposite Domèvre." *Courtesy of the Smithsonian Institution, NMAH, Division Armed Forces History. 46427.*

began to rain hard. We looked around Reherrey, then walked out beyond the town toward the front line as far as the 75s, or really beyond them, looking out over the landscape which was certainly peaceful enough to look at.

Then on the way back, we hunted up the gun positions back thro an orchard. Here we found the 42d's batteries still in position and a very engaging lieutenant in charge who insisted in taking us around to all his batteries, showing us with satisfaction the high polish on all their polished gun parts, then pointing with a shrug at the (by comparison) unpolished French ones that were in a position nearby. He told us that the Germans had their batteries all registered and he showed us with great pride one of his guns that has had direct hits made on her three times and all that remains of her, as she came out there, is the axle. All the other parts have been replacements. He has great respect for the German artillery. In talking about the situation there and about the front line, he suggested that we might like to see the Germans over the other side of No-Man's-Land at Domèvre. This sounded good to us, especially as he explained that since it was too stormy for them to put up their balloons, they would be unable to make any observations. [A portion of Townsend's diary is missing at this point.]

CHAPTER 2

JULY 1918: BASTILLE DAY AND THE LAST GERMAN OFFENSIVE

The French went all out in celebrating their national holiday on July 14, 1918. Townsend was among the U.S. troops who attended, yet another example of his exceptional mobility. His observations on the rather mediocre showing of the U.S. contingent on the occasion echoed those made by others on the scene. To be sure, soldiers who are good on parade are not necessarily good fighters, but at a time when the Allies were seeking encouragement, appearances perhaps weighed unduly heavily. Of course, as Townsend observed, the men of the 1st Division were bloodied veterans of the Montdidier and Cantigny battles; they may well have regarded the parade through Paris as a nuisance and were apparently tired from the long march into the city.

Townsend's visit to Paris coincided with other events as the German cannon, "Big Bertha," began again to shell Paris. If not creating panic, it caused considerable official concern. The gun originally began shelling Paris on March 23, 1918, continuing intermittently until May 1, when it suspended operations. It resumed attack in mid-July, as Townsend recounted.

Also while Townsend was in Paris, the Germans launched their fifth and last major attack, after a month of comparative quiet. Beginning on July 15, it came on both sides of Rheims. But to the east of the city and to the west, where the Marne River was crossed, only a few gains were made. In this battle, 85,000 U.S. troops were engaged, mainly those of the 42d, the 3d, and 28th Divisons. Three days later, the Allies seized the initiative and launched a counteroffensive to the west of Rheims. The U.S. 1st, 2d, 3d, 4th, 26th, 28th, 32d, and 42d Divisions, as well as large contingents of French troops, were employed. When the operation was completed on August 6, the German salient was pushed back and the

Allied line then ran from Soissons to Rheims along the Vesle River. The turning point of the war had arrived. The initiative had passed irrevocably to the Allies.

Townsend's continuing interest in aviation is apparent in his entries during these weeks. The 1st Pursuit Group, one of his favorite organizations, was the U.S. Air Service's most famous unit. It was created in February of 1918, when the 95th Pursuit Squadron arrived in the Toul sector, to be joined by the 94th — the "Hat-in-the-Ring" — Squadron in March. One month later, the two squadrons formed the 1st Pursuit Group. Meanwhile, three U.S. observation squadrons were formed into the I Corps Observation Group, under French tactical control. About the same time, captive observation balloons began operating with the U.S. divisions near Toul. The first U.S. day bombardment squadron to go into service, the 96th, initiated operations in June.

By the time of the armistice, the United States had about 740 aircraft at the front in France, constituting some 10 percent of the Allied air strength. The Air Service carried out 150 bombing attacks, while U.S. air crews destroyed 781 enemy planes and seventy-three balloons, losing 289 planes and forty-eight balloons to enemy action. These figures included fifty-seven planes flown by U.S. pilots operating with the British, French, and Italians. Some seventy-one U.S. fliers became aces — by shooting down five or more enemy aircraft each.

The 1st Pursuit Group was in the forefront of U.S. aerial activity and included the most famous of the nation's World War I fliers. One of these was the highest scoring airman in the United States — Captain Edward V. Rickenbacker, commander of the 94th Squadron, who shot down twenty-six enemy aircraft. Another was Lieutenant Frank Luke, Jr., of the 27th Squadron, famous for his exploits against German observation balloons, though he shot down a total of eighteen German airplanes as well. From August 21, 1918, the group was commanded by Canadian Major Harold E. Hartney, a combat veteran who had earlier flown with the Royal Flying Corps. It eventually consisted of the 94th, 95th, 27th, and 147th Pursuit Squadrons, as well as the 4th Repair Park and the 185th Night Pursuit squadron. Also on August 21, the group became part of the U. S. 1st Army and was placed under the command of Brigadier General Billy Mitchell. Shortly thereafter, the group was based at Rembercourt, arriving there from Saints near Touquin where it had been stationed since July and where Townsend visited it following his trip to Paris.

July 13–15, 1918
᠅

Captain Morgan and I decide to go up to spend the "Quatorze" in Paris and see the celebration there. From there I am to go on out to Meaux where press HQ is, counting on getting transport from there to the 1st Aero Pursuit Group.[49] We are taken up from Chaumont in a car with Colonel E.R.W. McCabe.[50] A delightful man and it made a delightful and easy trip. The route from Chaumont to Paris was new to me and we went thro very lovely country and some fine old towns, including Provins, which is French Army GHQ.

He took us to the Regina where we found two connecting rooms with bath at seventeen francs each per day, *"bains et petit déjeuner compris."* Too much, but as it's only for the night or possibly two, we take it without murmur. This is the hotel where our dear friends the Thomases of Chicago used to stay and where we have visited them so I knew its accommodations were good. We found them so now.

Colonel McCabe, on leaving us, had said that if we reported in the morning at Hotel St. Anne, he might be able to arrange to take one or both of us on up to British HQ with him. But this wasn't arranged, so we forgot our disappointment in our enjoyment of the celebration. We had tried to get numerous taxies to take us up to the Bois to witness the ceremony and review of the troops there by the President at 9 o'clock sharp. This struck us as an unusual hour for an affair but it seems to be custom here now. But it was just as well, for it took us some time to find a suitable place from which to get a decent view for any sketches we should want to make and we are bent on this. Finally, at the last it occurs to me that if we went to the Red Cross HQ, corner Rue Royal and Place de la Concorde, which is the place where it is to end, dispersing in the Place there, we might, by inquiring for Thomas B. Wells, Editor of *Harper's,* now in the American Red Cross, get a place on one of their balconies. It did look like a long chance, for they were besieged with a great crowd bent on the same quest as we were. But our rank got us attention at once and a RC [Red Cross] officer, whose name I don't recall now, tho I should out of gratitude, took us at once to a large balcony that was reserved for a few of their leaders, and we had a wonderful opportunity to see it from there.

We spent our time till it should appear making sketches of the setting for what was really a wonderful and truly inspiring parade, or procession of troops of all the Allies. None were left out I think. Tcheke-Slovaks [*sic*] we saw for the first time as a group. Also it was my first sight of the Portuguese to know them as such. How wonderful the Highlanders were with their plaid skirts covered with the brown trench skirt or apron. On their heads were shining black helmets, and with that great strong stride of theirs, with their bare legs and vigorous swinging arm, they were a remarkable sight. It was thrilling and very touching, this long line of fighting men, all of whom, save the Slavs, had been but recently in the midst of this terrific war. Perhaps I do the Slavs an injustice, for the group here may have been picked men from the front, too.

Soon came our boys, a little disappointing as to their marching, for they seemed to lack a spirit that was characteristic of the others. They looked tired, and they were tired, for they were men from the 1st Division who had been thro the Montdidier and Cantigny scraps and not only was there that, but they had been marched, we heard, some sixteen miles the night before to get in for the show, and they knew there was to be no leave for them in which to see Paris, for they were to be taken right out after the parade. So it all reflected in their spirit. But, at that, they were a mighty business-like looking lot. For the others all were on parade and dressed for it too. Ours looked as if they were in the midst of a war. Whereas all the others carried flowers — had been literally loaded with them all along the line — ours had evidently refused them all, for at the end where we viewed them, they bore none, in contrast to the others. And there was great enthusiasm for our boys, too, so that one was proud of them, and I know I was moved as only on one other occasion, the memorial service at Ménil-la-Tour.

Great amusement was furnished everyone by a number of French girls who, after their flowers had all been given to the passing soldiers, began to kiss all comers. They found they were being hampered by their hats, so off come the hats, and they go at it with new vim. As each soldier passed, there was a girl to grab him around the neck and plant a kiss on his cheek. This made a great hit with everyone, even with the soldiers. There was one Frenchman, much older than the others, who for some reason or other had gotten out of his formation, had lagged behind, and was now following along trying to catch them, stroking his beard as he went, and gazing ahead with far-seeing eyes. He was just strange enough looking and droll to make one smile at his nonchalance. He has just passed the girls, unsuspecting their dangers, oblivious to everything, in fact, when one of them starts after him, grabs him from behind, as it were, a surprise attack, wheels him around, almost taking him off his feet, throws her arms about his neck and kisses him, then lets him go. It is all over in a second, the attack was so swift. He is too dazed by it all to know what has happened. He looks around, startled, blinks . . . unconsciously wipes his mouth with one sweeping movement of his blue sleeve and goes on, eyes strait ahead, but with him one got the impression that he a bit resented it. But it was great sport; there was something fine, too, about the spirit of it, and one was surprised and greatly impressed with the character, apparently, of the girls who bestowed their kisses so abundantly. Not that one necessarily has any preconceived notions about the type that might do such a thing, tho there is undoubtedly a convention, but here were girls who impressed you as a different, more innocent, sort.

The last troops passed, the girls put on their hats and, the gendarmes giving way, the crowd closed in behind and became a mob. In all, it was a memorable occasion and we were glad to have been part of it too.

We look up Cameron Mackenzie, now correspondent for the *London Chronicle*, in the afternoon, and while later Morgan calls on Miss Barclay, I go back to the Red Cross balcony and make some detail sketches of points I want from there. In the evening we dine at Voisins with Mackenzie. This is a fine old place, wonderful food. . . . Colonel William Mitchell, Chief of our air forces in the field, came in . . . and I had him come over to eat at my table and had a good long talk with him about a number of things about aviation.[51] He knew I was going to handle the aviation end as official artist, so he talked freely, and seemed glad that I was on my way out to see the 1st Pursuit Group then. He promised also to be of all the help he could at any time and said that he would arrange to give me the necessary flying to be able to attack the work properly.

There was no air raid. But on awaking in the morning found that the German offensive had begun in the night. The guns had been heard very distinctly as they began. . . . A sudden note added by the Boche to the festivities of the celebration.

July 15, 1918
❧

. . . At the Press Section — Hotel St. Anne — I arrived to find great excitement. Captain Stone from the Bourse came with the morning communiqué saying that the Boche was driving thro Château-Thierry. That they had shelled the large towns back of the lines and bombed them from the air — Meaux, La Ferté, Montmirail and Châlons. This didn't sound so good. I was bound for Meaux.

Then at 2 P.M., out of a breathless silence, tho there were holiday crowds, for Monday had been declared a Fête also, there boomed a shell burst. Big Bertha had commenced again after a long silence. Paris laughed, tho coming as it did with the heavy offensive, I'm sure there was just a bit of apprehension in their minds. People waited the old accustomed fifteen-to-twenty-minute interval for the next visit. But it is 5 before she speaks again. Then 5:20, then 6. These all sound as tho they might be over across the river, too, for we hear that the first one fell near the old ferris wheel, over in our old section of the city. Or near. At 8, as we are dining at the Cafe de la Paix, another, and much closer one, fell. It was very striking the way this one affected the diners and the passersby, for there were laughs and smiles and shrugged shoulders as tho it were all a joke, the Boche thinking he could in any way disturb the morale or the tranquility of Paris. Nor did he seem to do so.

When the 5 o'clock shell fell, I was again on the Red Cross balcony completing a drawing there. Bennett Schneider, of the Red Cross transportation office, an old Château friend of ours, was with me. He had been telling me how he had seen the first one strike or burst in a building across the block from the rear of his apartment as he was eating his dinner. How great the concussion seemed to be, and that there were several people killed there, including the inmates of a taxi that was on the street in front of the demolished apartment house. Then as we sat there, the 5 o'clock one fell, and we could see the cloud of smoke and dust that arose from the wreck it made over in back of the Luxembourg, as it seemed to us.

After dinner, Wallace Morgan and I take a walk up the Champs Élysées and finally sit and watch the couples pass, the eternal lovemaking of Paris, the everlasting quest, the course of the hunter and the hunted . . . How amused we were, too, at the sight . . . of the Highlanders, with their bare legs and their short skirts, as they sauntered by with their arm about some painted smiling fancy they had found. How the streets teemed with life and muffled laughter. Cafes closed their doors and took in their tables and chairs at 9:30, and now people sat or walked on, waiting for a raid they sensed was due. But no raid came. We laughed again over an old-fashioned Frenchman we had seen that afternoon on the Rue du Rivoli, who sat astride an old highwheel bicyclette and, stiff and conscious as a judge, pedalled it down the street to the gaze of what must have seemed to him a million people. How old-fashioned it was. And then I thought of the first bicycle I ever rode, one of the same sort. Then to the Hotel and to bed. . . .

July 16, 1918
*

*D*id some necessary shopping in midst of which, at 10:30, the *gross* cannon spoke again. What a strange feeling to have things like that dropping out of a quiet sky, onto one never knew just where next, with its death and destruction and that awful mess of ruined building and scattered plaster, and jumbled rubbish slid into exposed cellars. . . . And it is true that a palace looks as mean and sordid and worthless as a peasant's hut after a shell or a bomb. They all have the same sad, indefinable damp smell, and the same coating of dust. And here I was, not only going out this morning to Meaux, a town that was both being shelled and bombed, but I was to take the train from Gare de l'Est, in the very part of town that was bearing the brunt of Big Bertha's malice.

Wallace Morgan went back to Neufchâteau to get his things in shape, get the car, hurry back up to Meaux and out to the aviation field for me, when we would cover the front together. I dug up a gas mask and a helmet in Paris, for they were necessary in Meaux, no doubt, and out I went with a bit of trepidation, for no one knew in Paris just what was in store for one's arrival there. So little news gets into the city, and so much speculation and rumor is always in the air there. But I had the facts from the Press Bureau, and I had reason for taking precautions. I shall never forget my feelings as we approached the danger zone. . . .

Things at the Press HQ I found at 6s and 7s. Transportation was far from satisfactory and there seemed little chance for me to get anywhere to do anything, so inasmuch as Wallace Morgan was coming up at once and would get me at the aviation field, I decided to go there the first chance that I had. This, too, looked difficult, for now that the big fight had developed into an offensive on our part, and they were keen to follow it up, the correspondents had lost interest in the work of the aviators, and there seemed no cars going there. So I waited.

Looked around the town a bit, found it a beautiful old city, with a cathedral that seemed justly famous for its beauty as well as its history. The old mills that span the river on two fine old arched bridges, for all the world like the prints one has seen of the old London Bridge, are very quaint and picturesque. Any artist would go wild over them. Why not I? Back of the cathedral is the famous old staircase flanking a strange, old-fashioned court. To one side is the entrance to the famous Rose Garden of the Bishop, also an ancient institution. Major Bulger said that, as the hotel was full, I might have a little room up at their château. . . .[52]

So I had dinner at the Duc d'Acquitaine where many of the correspondents ate. Went down with Herbert Bailey of the *London Mail*, and it being Cory's birthday, this 16th of July, we had a little dinner to ourselves and, as he wanted to honor her and me, he insisted on providing the champagne. . . . And I was glad to have remembered and celebrated the occasion so, and hope that the cable I sent her had arrived to greet her at the same time.

Who should drift into Meaux that evening but Floyd Gibbons, his first appearance since the wound at Montreuil. After dinner, the three of us took a walk around the old bridges and the cathedral doing them honor and praise. . . .

At last to bed. Waited for a time for the sound of the Hun, but he didn't come. Nor any shells.

July 17, 1918
※

*N*o chance to get anywhere today with the press cars, and Lieutenant Delaney is quite, and unnecessarily, curt about any responsibility in getting me anywhere. Don't quite understand this, for here we are captains in the Army attached to the Intelligence Section, of which the Press Section is a branch. We are further assigned to the Press Section for duty. In order to meet our needs, one car is finally assigned to us, with the use of the press cars to help out when we can be fitted in, it seems, but not otherwise. Eventually, we are to have two cars.

Finally, this afternoon I found that Thomas M. Johnson of the *New York Sun* was going out to the 1st Pursuit Group at Saints. So I take my belongings and beg a ride out with him. This was my first objective anyway, so I am happy. Report to Major Atkinson, who gives me the freedom of the field, if I won't expect them to assume any responsibility for me. He turns me over to Major Geoffrey Bonnell of the 147th, a Nieuport Squadron, who, by the way, was the one who recruited Henri into the RFC.[53] He has a billet that I can have, that of Cassard, one of his men who has just been lost. Takes me in his car to his HQ, introduces me to a number of his pilots, and one of them takes me to my room. They assign me a batman or striker to look after my leather, show me where the mess tent is, and welcome me generally to their crowd.

I find the family where I am billeted most interesting. Name has gone already from me. He has been a professor in a university. Science. Has a

"Sketch, One of Our Aviators in His 'Teddy Bear.'" *Courtesy of the Smithsonian Institution, NMAH, Division Armed Forces History. 46451.*

most interesting library, has traveled so much and so far in books, as have so many of the educated Frenchmen, that he began to tell me lots of little things about my own country that seemed strange coming from such a quarter. . . . He explained at great length why he was living in such a little quiet spot. Tapping his forehead, he would have me know that he was a bit *"toqué"* now from too much study with his books. It was pathetic to listen to the poor old fellow, his wife and daughter listening as he tells of it. They seem quite a happy family. There are two children — father in the war. He shows me lovingly and touchingly, a collection of very rare and ancient coins; there are also mounted insects and butterflies and moths. They take me into the family at once, mourning tho, as for a son lost, the going of Cassard. We try to assure them that he may yet be found, or maybe is only a prisoner, but while they appear to take hope, we know that they sense the truth. And it's a genuine grief they show me later.

I clean up and go to supper where I meet such of the men as are back from patrol. Later they all come in and I meet the lot. What a fine lot of fellows they are, too. But I have always found this so from the first visit I made to Henri at the Camp Borden field.[54] It is most interesting to listen to their "hangar flying"; the gossip and experiences told and recounted; the badinage or persiflage that flies like a shuttlecock from one to another. They radiate wit and humor and fellow-feeling and sympathy. . . . Major Bonnell seems a wonder, and how the boys all worship him. Of course, I knew his old record in the RFC and the trouble he had had in getting his squadron over here and into the field on account of the opposition he met from the officials here who had their own men ready and resented the fully American-trained men beating them into the game. They made it hard for him, but he, who had been fighting so long and so well with the British, wouldn't let them tell him that his men weren't trained for combat; made them swallow their words, as it were, and with Major Hartney, got their men out, and have been giving a fine account of themselves with practically no losses. They know how to fly and manouevre the Nieuport 28; have brought down sixteen machines, I believe, with only loss of a couple of men in the month they have been fighting. No other squadron in the other groups can equal this, or rather has not, to date. But still I know from conversations I have had with Colonel Mitchell, and also with Major Atkinson, that he is not liked. I think they resent the RFC spirit that he has developed in them. Perhaps they resent what they mayhaps consider a lack of discipline, insisting that the aviation branch must be managed with as stern a hand as the infantry, for example, instead of being a thing more or less apart, as in the British service. He certainly has his fellows well in hand tho, in spite of his catering to them as he seems to do. He seems to understand them; that undoubtedly accounts for the work he gets out of them.[55]

July 18–20, 1918
〜

These to me were wonderful days—in the very heart of a life that for me had always been the height of adventure and interest, and now that the war had brought combat in the air, the supreme sport. My heart has been so much in it that it has been the keenest regret to me that I am too old for the flying service. I have always loved the aeroplane as a spectacle too, the wonder and the mystery of its conquest of the air, and then its own beauty of form, a beauty built, too, on necessity, which, making its aesthetic appeal even higher, has always fascinated me. And here I am in the midst of them to spend a few days making drawings of their loved forms, albeit sad that they are all single-seaters, fighters in the 1st Pursuit Group. The 94th and 95th squadrons have Spads; the 27th and 147th having still the Nieuport 28 that they are so fond of and believe in so thoroughly as a fighting machine.[56] I am with the 147th, Major Geoffrey Bonnell in command. Major Harold Hartney has the 27th, Captain Kenneth Marr the 94th, and Captain David M. Peterson the 95th.

What a lot of flying talk I heard these days. How much of the excitement of combat flying or patrolling I experienced, too, as I spent my time with the fellows at the hangars and out by their machines as they were getting ready to leave. Watching the idiosyncrasies of the Gnome engines as they tried them out, or the patrol out on its way; some of them would have to come back thro engine trouble, cursing their luck that they had to miss what they knew would be a fight. And if by chance the boys did come back signalling that they got a Boche (by tipping slightly and rapidly from side to side or by the staccato blare of the engine as they cut it off then on full force), how much more they bemoaned the fate that left them behind. For they didn't dare risk engine trouble over there over the Boche lines with a seventy-five-mile wind against them to come home in and the archies shooting under their tail as they sat over them trying to beat them back. Possibly, too, a Hun after them in the air, tho they found that, in order to get a fight these days, they had to go way back of the lines to find them. Sometimes they went in as much as twenty to thirty kilos in order to get a scrap, and this was at a risk, if they had done much patrolling

"Victor and Vanquished." *Courtesy of the National Archives. 111-SC-56917.*

before they found them, for the Nieuport carries about enough gas for 1¾ hours flying. And it's a long ways home and . . . the wind . . . these days is blowing hard into Germany. The fellows are getting two patrols a day now and every third day they have three. Of late, they have had to stay up till a late hour to get their orders for the following morning's flight, so that they have been dead for sleep, surely bad conditions to fly in. I think I heard something about Major Bonnell having refused to send them out on one flight order, thinking that they were being worked harder than some of the others. I am not sure of this, but I think it's in things like this, perhaps, that he has incurred the displeasure of the powers that be. But he surely does seem a live wire, and he has certainly been kind to me.

I was surprised and interested to hear that their mess, figured absolutely on cost basis, cost them fifty francs per week exclusive of the cost of their help. Everyone in that part of the country seems to believe in squeezing them. And they didn't seem to be in a position to deal to any great extent with our Quartermaster. It seems a shame that it should cost them so much. It developed, too, that none of them had received any flying pay, tho they have been fighting here on the front for some little time. There are a number of the fellows who already have three and four Huns to their credit.

The RFC men come over from a neighboring field often to see and drink with them or to play cards, and the visits are returned in kind. Or they may all be invited over there to dine with the British. Major Freeman, in command there, is an old flying mate of Major Bonnell's. He seems very fine. They are like a couple of small boys together and have the best of times. Major Freeman stops often in his Sopwith "Camel."[57] One was struck with the speed of the Nieuport when the two of them flew from here over to the English field. At the altitude at which they flew, 1,000 metres, in order to stay back with the Camel, it was necessary for Major Bonnell to fly all around, zig-zagging the way over. At a greater height, of course, the Camel may speed up a lot, for many types of machines are so, as, for instance, the D.H., such as we are building, which I hear is fastest at 15,000 feet.[58]

It is great fun to watch the English winging their way home from a patrol, for as they get to this field here, they come up in wonderful formations wing-to-wing almost, which they are able to do with their motors that can be throttled down to any speed.[59] Then of a sudden they may break and start to stunting, or split-assing as it is now generally known, over the flying fields. They are great at this. Their skill in the air no one thinks of questioning, save the professional British hater, of which, sad to relate, there are still a number in our army, tho thank Heaven they are fast disappearing.

Word has just come that in a new lot of pilots that are being sent out here is Pat Maloney, Henri's best friend. They may arrive on Sunday the 21st. Hope I get to see him; there's so much to talk about. Also Lieutenant Robert W. Donaldson, a friend of his and of Henri, who was recently in the hospital near Chaumont, struck by a "prop," is one of them. The different commanders drew lots for the men. Pat fell to Captain Marr of the 94th. Donaldson to Captain Peterson of the 95th. Major Bonnell got Lieutenant James P. Herron who is supposed to be the pick of the lot.

What a busy place the field here is. On one side of the field is the range for the lining up and testing of the mounted guns. There are always a number of machines out here, their tails propped up on a special jack so that the guns will point strait ahead at the target. And the row of machines out there are continually spitting long tongues of flame like some fiery dragons at the target over in the clay pit. Every third bullet is a tracer bullet which leaves, even in daylight, a line of fire and a trail of smoke. At night it is brilliant fire. This serves in a conflict to check up [on] the range for the pilot or the gunner, so that it becomes not unlike playing a hose on a moving target, and it is not so necessary to use the intricate sights so much. One is not in the dark as to how close he is to the enemy or the vulnerable parts of his machine, for the trail of fire or smoke checks it all up as it passes or hits him. Then there is a gun with incendiary bullets also when they want to fire a petrol tank or for work against balloons.

It's very exciting when the machines are all lined up for a patrol or, better yet, when they are answering an alert, for then they are all rushed into place, tho the chances are that they are already there in position for just such an emergency call. The pilots rush into the machines. The mechanics are at the propeller and others are holding on to the struts, standing back of the wings. . . . As the motor is swung over at the pilot's word "contact," and the motor catches and begins to "rev" and finally is roaring . . . the machine strains to get away. It's for all the world like a frantic horse straining at the bit and held in leash. Here's a long line of them roaring and chafing to be off, like anxious runners. The chock blocks are drawn from the wheels at the pilot's command; the men let go or run along directing it out onto the field, and they are off and instantly in the air, one after the other like a flock of birds. . . . Soon they are out of sight, save that one or two of the fifteen . . . has to come back with engine trouble.

Then one forgets them for a time till instinctively one feels that they are about due back and goes searching the skies for a Nieuport. They are easily distinguished. First, one is seen, and soon there will be several, and later some stragglers who have had, one wonders, what vicissitudes out there over the lines. One speculates who the first one is, and some of the fellows know from the way they fly, or make their try at a landing, before their numbers are visible. They are down and everyone rushes out to hear if they saw Huns and where, and did he get one, or have a fight. They are interesting tales they tell sometimes. What excitement when they have gotten one and it's talked over and over. A story never old. Or one of the fellows . . . late to return, has had a forced landing. . . . Or perhaps here comes Jim Healy, fine pilot they say, but watch him land, they ask you, and they wager that, as he comes down on the field, he will lose his own hangar and go, likely as not, taxiing strait over to a Spad hangar before he discovers his mistake. And true enough he does.

I call on Captain Marr and meet Captain Peterson. They are fine fellows both. Also I meet Rickenbacker who is in the 94th. Pat Maloney will be in his squadron. Perhaps he will arrive tomorrow, before I go back, for I have been expecting Captain Morgan to call for me as he has promised, and can't understand the reason why he has not arrived. But will not wait longer, for the offensive is rolling up into a great victory and rout. The boys had come in from patrol in which they told of the wonderful sight that the battlefield made with the bursting of the shells below them in the dim light of the morning, and the lines of troops that they could make out on the move.

July 20, 1918
※

*W*e all went over last night to the RAF [Royal Air Force] town to see them and tonight they came over here to Saints and we were all in Major Bonnell's room till quite late. They played poker, drank and the British sang their RAF songs for the fellows. They are a remarkably good lot of songs and they sung them well. They show a spirit, these songs, that must be worth considerable in the flying corps. There is no doubt that the RAF (once the RFC) is a remarkably efficient organization, and no one denies that it stands head and shoulders above all other Allied flying in the matter of the efficiency of its work and its personnel. When one hears the fellows sing, one gets a hint of one of the reasons . . . for they have cultivated, or there has grown up a camaraderie or group spirit, that is bound to count and make, too, for personal achievement as well as group excellence. The songs are in many cases of literary merit. Some are tremendously amusing; some are extremely salacious.[60]

This is the 20th — our anniversary — and I write Cory a letter tonight. How strange it seems to be here in this secluded spot so many miles away on this day. And here I am among these flying men whom I like so much and whose work is so near to my longings in this war, and I'm here with a mission and, while I would so like to be there with them as they so well know — yet how happy I am here. And I know that Cory understands this too.

July 21, 1918
※

*T*hings have been progressing rapidly at the front, tho we get very little actual news at the field, save that we know absolutely where the line of operation is at all times there, for the fellows are working over it all the time and the map is kept up to the minute. They bring in lots of interesting observations, tho there are none of the stories of . . . human interest that [go] always with the infantry and [make] it all so interesting to follow.

Not knowing just what to make of Captain Morgan's not coming for me as he promised he would . . . I will have to get back to Meaux to get somehow into the game there and to try to locate him, so they manage to find a sidecar that is idle and back I go.

CHAPTER 3

THE AISNE-MARNE

The Aisne-Marne offensive was a joint French-U.S. operation launched by the supreme Allied commander, Marshall Foch, on July 18, 1918, and lasting until August 6. Eight U.S. divisions were engaged, particularly in the Château-Thierry area. By the end of this offensive, the Allies had eliminated the German salient threatening Paris and flattened out the line in that area from Soissons to the battered cathedral city of Rheims.

Townsend visited some of the U.S. troops participating in this operation, including members of the 26th or "Yankee" Division, commanded by the popular but inefficient Major General Clarence R. Edwards.[61] He also spent some time with the 3d Division. He toured sites of battles fought in late June and early July, such as Belleau Wood (which had been captured on June 25 after bitter fighting by the 4th Marine Brigade of the Second Division) and Vaux (captured on July 1, by the 3d Infantry Brigade of the 2d Division, after a short but intense and effective shelling by U.S. artillery). He also visited and painted Hill 204, a prominent battleground between Vaux and Château-Thierry.

Townsend kept in touch with his friends of the 1st Pursuit Group, which had been at the little town of Saints since July 8. The group moved to a field near Rembercourt on August 22, in preparation for further operations. Townsend temporarily operated out of press headquarters at Meaux and then returned to Neufchâteau for more sustained work at his studio.

Neufchâteau was not without its dangers, however, and Townsend experienced at least one air raid there, a not uncommon occurrence at this stage in the war. That the flu was already present to a serious degree in the AEF by late summer of 1918 is obvious from the artist's account. And the fact that war produced casualties had begun to register on the doughboys and the artists alike, resulting in a noticeable change in attitude. For the

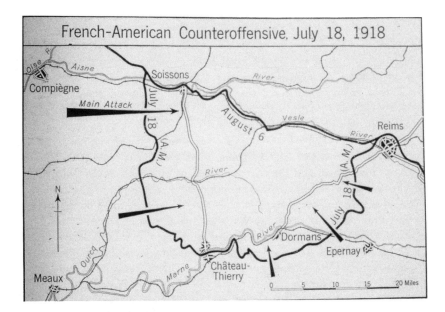

French-American Counteroffensive, July 18, 1918

painters, this also placed new obstacles in their way as they attempted to get their pictures completed. But despite the flu and growing numbers of casualties, there was a new spirit in the air as preparations began for further Allied operations. Townsend and his colleagues, getting hints of these, hoped to follow the doughboys into action. They soon learned that what was in the offing was the St. Mihiel operation.

July 21, 1918

... *This* morning the Boche were driven out of Château-Thierry! To think that at last they have been cleared out. Some of the correspondents had been in the town in the afternoon and talked with many of the inhabitants who have been prisoners for so long. The town, they say, is a fright, what with the pillage and destruction by the Huns as they left. Cleared at last! What a feeling it must be to the poor folk who have been held there so long. And our troops have freed it. And there will be a warm spot in many hearts for our boys . . . for the French people do not forget, bless them!

July 22, 1918 — A.M.

ᘏ

*H*aving told Lieutenant Delaney that I would like if possible to get to Château-Thierry, he found a chance for me to go there in the car with Henry G. Wales, of the International News Service, and Burge McFall, of the Associated Press. The trip there thro Trilport, then on to La Ferté, is a very beautiful trip. We found it a slow one owing to the great numbers of troops and amount of material going up. There seemed to be American troops everywhere and the Marne seemed to be full of them in places. They seemed to relish the chance to not only get a bath, but to have a real swim as well, and every fancy diver in the AEF seemed to be on the job that morning. What a contrast was . . . this young, enthusiastic American youth enjoying himself in what seemed his element, to the Marne a little farther down filled with the dead Boche killed along its banks and even on its bosom. La Ferté we found simply packed with Americans. We saw the wreck that the German raiders had made of the R.R. [railroad] station there with their bombs, but troops and supplies were still being unloaded there, for it's a very important and necessary point at this particular moment.

Then on up thro Montreuil-aux-Lions that I knew so well thro my stay there during the Marine's fight early in June. How different now. Still filled with our men, but now reserves, or on the way only, whereas then it was a storm center indeed. Passed the spot where I figured Floyd Gibbons was when wounded, on past Ferme de Paris and then over the brow of the hill into the most wrecked place I have yet seen, Vaux, of which I have heard so much, for it was one of the spots that is to stand in the history of our troops . . . thro the nature and intensity of the fight there, and, too, thro the achievement of our artillery, which we are told by various sources was so intense that Vaux was wrecked as we now see it practically in twenty minutes of gunfire. The Boche threw a few shells into it after our men gained it, but only a few, so that we were looking at our gunners' handiwork. And it was truly an amazing sight and a sad one, for from the evidence still left here and there in fragment or pieces of shells of houses, one could picture it as a beautiful little town, and not so small either. But there was nothing left now, and it was beyond all thought of repair.

Then on under the R.R. bridge past the house that gave our men so much trouble with the machine gun nests left in and around it commanding absolutely the road under the bridge as they poured thro in pursuit and also commanding the skyline as our men rushed or fell over the R.R.

embankment in their wild chase after them. So that it cost us many, many men, we are told, before this house was finally spotted and cleaned out.

The trees lining the road on both sides of the town are mute witnesses to their sufferings, too, from the shells. Great trees torn off at all heights. Some clean cuts; others sort of torn off, leaving an effect on the end of the bruised stump not unlike a frayed-out broom.

On the next crossroad we turn to the left. At this corner we . . . see our first dead American, tho there were many Boche still lying around that house back by the R.R. We pass thro a long line of our 155s on the right of this road just spreading out their split trail (or tails is a better word), and getting ready for more strafing. In fact, some are already at it, and there are three or four shells fired while we are passing. I wish I might have been here on my own and could have stopped for a sketch or two, and there is the disadvantage in our using the press cars; they are always at the beck and call of the particular correspondent one is with; you are really his guest without the other courtesy a guest might get. The ride and the chance to see whatever the correspondent sees is all one can expect. But that is a lot if one has no other means of travel, of course, but it seems a shame to pass such interesting stuff without a chance to do it.

From here we hunt and pick our way over very bad roundabout roads to the HQ at the farm.[62] What a bustle and air of importance this old farm had but also what a feeling of a sort of suppressed presence the whole place manifested. . . . Soldiers lay around on the grass on the edges. Never a word they seemed to speak. Officers walked rapidly from building to building with a glance upward at a passing aeroplane . . . and with never a word to another passing officer, popped into a building. We hid our car as other cars were hidden, by merely making it as inconspicuous as possible alongside a ruined wall. We skirted the buildings partly ruined and now filled with an astonishing assortment of supply wagons . . . with mute boys in attendance; passed a farm implement shed and hay cover that sheltered a group of officers seated around tables at which they worked hard; then were directed to the old cow stable where the officer we were looking for had his desk. While the correspondents were talking to him, I discovered Major Washburn who was the old Russian correspondent and who had come over on the *New York* when I did to join the AEF. Here he was in the 26th Division with General Clarence Edwards. I talked with him a while. . . .

Every stall in the old barn had an occupant; indeed, they were crowded. Each was a busy office with comings and goings. Here men seemed to feel freer for they actually talked, tho, as they said, they were expecting to be spotted by a Hun plane any minute and shelled. They had moved there in the night and had just arrived, in fact. Discovery would come any minute.

A couple of the stalls had groups of boyish-looking German prisoners in them who were being questioned by the intelligence officers. They all seemed more or less composed and satisfied, as do practically all the prisoners one sees. . . . Always, tho, there are some among them who wear strange faces, long, distant, wistful looks, a bit of fear, perhaps, or anxiously wonder maybe at what his fate may be. And being more or less human (more I am sure than our campaign of Allied hatred would like to have us admit), there are thoughts or anxieties for loved ones at home, even fears for their fate when the Allies reach them as they must at times imagine at least possible. Thoughts . . . like these cloud faces that might otherwise be content. Yet one doesn't waste much sentiment on them, 'tis true, and it's as it should be, for at the present the power and might of Germany can only be crushed by striking down her manpower and we are striking now as hard and as fast as our gathering hordes will permit.

General Edwards comes thro smiling as usual; he always seems to wear a smile, tho I'll wager he can be a stern master to his officers and men at times. A few words with him. He expresses satisfaction with the way our boys are keeping contact with the Germans as they run, and that they will likely have to move HQ, they go so fast.

Then we start back. Find Frank Sibley, correspondent for the *Boston Globe* who is attached to the Yankee Division.[63] We take him with us to drop him at a certain place on our way. We drive down thro the balloons on the road to the left, pass a 77 left by the Huns, edge around thro Lucy-le-Bocage and Bouresches, then alongside of Belleau Wood and thro the fields where there was such bitter fighting earlier and again now is evidenced by the shellpock over the hills and in the ripened wheatfields all along.[64] A long artillery train passes us here on its way forward, the boys singing, astride the great guns. One of the boys wore a silk hat he had picked up somewhere, another a ladies hat, and another carried a broken parasol over his head. What fun they seemed to be snatching out of their running fight! They carry the spirit of eternal youth it seems, and the French remark about this often. What an asset it is . . . for them.

Lucy seemed to me the loveliest sort of a village, beautifully ruined, if one dare say such a thing of a French village. Then into Meaux, but I didn't see Château-Thierry after all, and will have to try again.

July 22, 1918 — P.M.
⫯

*A*gain Lieutenant Delaney found a seat for me in a car going Château-Thierry way with Henry G. Wales of the International News Service and Burge McFall of the AP. They set out to see the HQ of the 3d Division at Gland. They found the château practically deserted, HQ having just this morning moved across the river right up under the edge of our advancing line. . . . It wasn't certain that we could get across as the pontoon bridges were just being gotten into shape and were terribly congested. But we decided to try.

In the meantime, some major, hearing that there were some correspondents there, came asking if Don Martin of the *New York Herald* was one of them. When he learned that he was not, he vented his spleen on the two that were, I hanging onto the edge of the zone of fire. The 3d Division has, for a long time now, believed that they had as great a part in the stopping of the Boche in his drive on Paris as anybody. There has, for some time, been a censorship restriction preventing the mentioning of any of the units of the Army being specifically designated in the press despatches. But unfortunately for them, this restriction, for some reason, has never applied to the Marines. And fortunately for the Marines, for they have gotten full measure and running over for all their magnificent efforts in turning back the Hun hordes. They sure have given them hell, as the boys put it. But of course it's true that, after all, in spite of a certain esprit de corps that they undoubtedly have, they are more or less off the same piece as the million or more other boys over here in the same game of strafing the Boche. Now as everyone knows, an awful lot of the very dirtiest work in bucking up the French and of hammering back and straitening out the line has fallen on the 3d Division, and they naturally want to square things up with Martin who fills so much space in the *Herald* with the Marines.[65] We listened to the major. Wales had an answer for him, commiserating with him, of course, tho I imagine he was just as guilty, tho what he writes doesn't get read over here so frequently.

Then we went on. It seemed strange to be going over the same old road again in approaching Château-Thierry now that we had tried to approach early in June when we met our movie friends, Hatrik and Hubbell, followed by the German shells that were trying to climb into their old Cadillac. How much more comfortable it was to know that the Germans were going as fast the other way now with our shells after them!

The bridges into the town were, of course, out of commission, and we had to follow on down along the river till we came to the pontoon bridge that the French had hastily thrown across for our troops to cross on. And what a mass of troops and artillery we found piled up there waiting to get across. As we were edging our car down thro to get near the river and the bridge, a lieutenant came hurrying up to me to ask my advice. Said he had orders to bring up his artillery on the road there and to meet his Captain not later than 4 o'clock. There was no one there to meet him and it was half an hour over. The guns were needed; what ought he to do? What should I say? I thought a minute, said that he might wait a few minutes more, then if he knew where they were to go, to proceed, at least on into Gland, where there would certainly be an artillery operations HQ. He seemed to think that a reasonable answer. He went back to his train and we went on to the bridge, got across with our staff car at once and on into Gland, I wondering just what would happen to the lieutenant, and if I had given the proper advice, for I found the roads on the other side of the river and in the town of Gland itself most frightfully crowded, tho everything did seem to keep moving once it crossed the bridge.

As we crossed the bridge, we were conscious that shells were bursting up the river. . . . In fact, it was over Gland, the town we were headed for about a kilo up the road. One thought what a fine place the pontoon bridge was for the Boche to drop a few shells, and one wondered just how long it would be before the thing did commence. You can bet that everyone watched the air and every motor that hummed by overhead was a possible Hun. There was very noticeable, in the whole atmosphere of the region there, a certain nervous tension lest the inevitable happen earlier than they wanted it to, for that bridge and road were bound to be shelled soon. But the French were busily getting another bridge ready a one hundred metres or so farther along the stream.

We hurried into Gland. This didn't look very good to me, for the noise from the bursting shells over the town was both annoying and extremely menacing. . . . The streets were crowded — traffic going forward at an excited speed, for the Germans were on the run a few kilometres ahead, and they were after them as close behind our contact as it was possible to get. I wondered again what the lieutenant with his cannon would do if he should come on into Gland. He certainly couldn't block the streets there and would have to move on.

I kept my mouth shut tight to keep my heart somewhere near its right place, and followed the fellows on foot to find 3d Division HQ. An MP directed us up the street and into a courtyard where we were further directed down into a cellar. This proved to be a subcellar, even. We were ushered into a veritable dugout; it seemed certainly well out of danger. In a dim light we could make out figures seated around tables pawing over maps. But they were all Frenchmen. Then we noticed that even the soldier we had passed at the door was a *poilu* [a French doughboy or rank and file soldier]. It was a French HQ. So we left and were directed to another place down a side street and almost at once we ran into our objective, the American HQ. The contrast was startling, and I give it with no real intent of drawing comparisons with the French HQ's concern as to safety.

As we went on to find our HQ, we stepped . . . gingerly and lightly over the broken tiles and crumbled stone that filled the streets of this ruined town. . . . We tried to be calm when a shell burst with a great raucous bang that seemed near, but we watched the sky from under cover of our tin hat just as intently as we could for its whereabouts, and we listened just as keenly for the patter of falling fragments as anyone would who hadn't been born and raised under it all and, at that, we didn't appear to be any more perturbed than many of our boys who passed, nor than many of the French soldiers who have not, in spite of four years of war, learned to entirely disregard or be insensible to danger.

We arrived at HQ, which, to all intents and purposes, was right there in the open under the big gate that led to an interesting old house which probably did bear a divisional HQ sign. But I will testify, to the everlasting credit of Major General Joseph T. Dickman, and his Chief of Staff, Colonel Robert H.C. Kelton, that that afternoon, at least, the real HQ was there in the open, and the town was being shelled at that.[66] But, from the extreme concentration the General was giving a large map spread over his knees, following the finger of a captain who was tracing locations for him which he would immediately spot with his thumb, to the nonchalance with which Colonel Kelton received me, listened to my demand and granted his permission to work anywhere in their sector, one would never have guessed there was reason for the slightest anxiety, tho the air was full of it. . . . I shall never forget that little group there in that interesting setting. What an interesting painting could be made of it, too. And how well General Dickman's helmet becomes him. The fellows got apparently what news they came for. Having made the briefest sort of a note of the situation, and having found the colonel a much more agreeable man than some of the fellows had led me to believe I'd find him, and having received a most cordial and gracious permission as graciously as I could, we departed. We drove back thro Château-Thierry on that side of the river, and looked around a bit at the ruins and the litter the Huns had made of things.

Then the correspondents decided they wanted to go back up to see General Edwards, or rather the HQ of the 26th Division . . . where we had found them just moving in in the morning. It had seemed to be moving day all around. We were nervous going up the road on the crest of the hill past Hill 204 which looks so utterly used up and abandoned, past our batteries of 155s that lined the right side of the road, their enormous split tails spread out and usurping the road, almost, in places. They were keeping up a steady fire it seemed, and while they evidently had been located, for the Huns were throwing back at them a few shells, still it wasn't quite so dangerous as it had the appearance of being, tho there is never any telling when the one dreadful one, which one fears, will arrive.

We arrived at headquarters and found them all feeling a bit more settled than in the morning and a bit more comfortable, for they apparently had not as yet been discovered, and their boys still had the Huns on the run so that they didn't know but that they would move on a bit, with the HQ. We saw General Edwards for a minute. He seemed very happy as he had every reason to be. Then we return to Meaux, passing great lines of French troops coming up into reserve positions, and bringing up armoured cars to help us chase the retreating foe. Also their cavalry was being brought up for some sudden need.

July 23–30, 1918
꒰

These were hectic days what with begging for a ride and being sat on by the transport officer who declines to assume the slightest responsibility for me. Finally, I take the train into Paris to the repair shops on advice of Major Bulger who seems to think that that will be the easiest way to settle my auto question. A car is promised to me absolutely in two days time at the most. . . . So I go back to Meaux with my confidence restored. And on the following day, I get a ride to Vaux with McFall, one of the correspondents who is also taking along with him Delahaye, a French artist who, thro some arrangement, is doing work under a Committee on Public Information permit, I believe.[67] He was quite a genial old fellow, and he lost no opportunity in getting out a handful of postcards with photos of his famous paintings to give me one. Some of them are simply awful war pictures. I chose a quiet Morland-like subject and told him I liked it.[68]

I was dropped at Château-Thierry . . . and caught a camion there, but decided to get out at Hill 204 and made a drawing there, then walked the rest of the way to Vaux. What a sight 204 is; simply shot to pieces, and scene of a most terrific bombardment. There is quite a fine group of

"Hill 204, July 23, 1918." *Courtesy of the Smithsonian Institution, NMAH, Division Armed Forces History. 46437.*

German officers' graves there on the side of the hill just off the main road, with elaborate crosses and flowers planted on them and shrubbery of some growth. There were great quantities of munitions and a 77 left along the road here and the trees are cut off cleanly at all kinds of heights. I got to Vaux finally, establish pleasant relations with the French town major who has just moved into the only house that is at all habitable. This also shelters General Champ, in command of the 52d Cavalry Division of the French army. Was introduced to him and he was very interested in my work, as was Captain Lambert, the town major.

Well, I set to work and had just gotten well into a drawing when I was startled by a tremendous explosion near me and apparently in or back of the General's HQ. Pieces of rock, and as I imagined, shell, were falling all around me, as well as dust from the ruined masonry. The only thought I had, naturally, was that the Germans had thrown back a shell into the town as they could easily do, tho I hadn't heard any shell screech. . . . A group of Frenchmen, who had been working up the road, seemed as excited and frightened as I was. I left my easel where it was and made for the house, thinking it had struck there, and wondering what fate had befallen the general. They all there seemed to think it was a good joke on

"Vaux, July 23, 1918." *Courtesy of the Smithsonian Institution, NMAH, Division Armed Forces History. 46456.*

me, for they had forgotten to tell me that they were setting off all the duds that they had found in the town, some seventy-four I think they said, all sizes from 75s up to 240s. This had been two 75s they had laid side-by-side in the court back of the house and less than fifty yards from where I was working and only a low broken wall between them and me. They were quite alarmed then, when I showed them my things where I had been working. So they asked me to wait for a half hour while they finished up a number in that vicinity. I had the pleasure of seeing them dig a piece of shell out of the cheek of one of the lieutenants there who, with the rest of them, had gone on the other side of the house into the street to be protected from just such fragments . . . while none of them had hit me, fortunately. . . . They insisted that I eat the lunch that I had brought with me in their dining room, and as I ate, the Captain and the General came in and talked to me. It certainly seemed good to run into somebody as sympathetic as they seemed to be.

There are some very stirring pieces of ruin in Vaux, and there is a piece of a great and quite remarkable tunnel revealed in one place which appears

"Vaux. Shapeless Mass of Masonry." *Courtesy of the Smithsonian Institution, NMAH, Division Armed Forces History. 46457.*

in one of the drawings that I made. I haven't investigated its history but will in time. But there is little standing, the place is so badly shot to pieces, and there isn't the slightest thing to indicate where the church once might have been that I could discover. Just back of the General's house there is a tremendous hole made, so the French said, by an aerial torpedo, and that it was the largest they had ever seen. There are certainly some tremendous shellholes there in the town. Most of them are partly filled with dirty, yellow water from mustard gas, and many of the walls that stand are stained a bright canary yellow where they have been hit by mustard shells that were thrown into the town. While all ruined towns of that size look much alike, Vaux seems different, and there is something very strange and weird about the bits that stand, and the yellow stains add to it.

I found two American boys from the 26th Division who had been left behind to guard some trench mortars and who moved about like ghosts in the old house and yard where their guns were. What types they were. They had been thro hell, all since the old days at Seicheprey, and now thro this long fight they had had here driving the Huns back, and you could read it in their eyes, too. They looked like creatures of another world with a strange, wild, hunted look. I've heard some men say that the boys go thro all this like doing their day's work, and that it makes little impression on them, but I don't believe it, and I noticed the same thing in the faces of many of the Marines who had been thro the mill in June. The boys here in Vaux were quite worried yet murmuring little because they had been promised a relief the following day after they were left, but no relief had come, nor any food, and all they had was what they could get here and there till the cavalry arrived and now things were better. They showed me the potato patch where, when they held the town, . . . the Germans had shelled them so hard they had had to steal out in the night to dig them, where they could find a vine that hadn't been uprooted by the shells.

I explored the town and looked over carefully the old house on the far side of the track where our men, in driving out the Boche, had encountered the nests of machine guns and had paid so heavily there. Saw, too, over near the little station where so many of our boys were killed and where some of them were still lying, the German, who in chasing our boys, had gotten hit with a grenade and he had tumbled forward into a shellhole, dead, with his feet sticking up into the air. He was still there.

Have made arrangements to leave my things as long as I like in the Captain's room there, and so decide to quit and catch a car or a camion back. But am told that next day I must not come till after 11, as they were taking the early morning to finish the duds and the road would be closed. I manage to find a French troop truck bound for La Ferté. Here I get a supper and then find that the train I had been told I could get for Meaux was not running now. So finding that there was not a place in the town where I could get a room for the night, I have to go to the main crossroad in the hope of catching something going to Meaux or to Paris, for Meaux is on the Paris route. The French MP stopped most everything that passed, trying to find something that would get me there; he was graciousness itself. But his willingness was in no wise a promise of a car, for it wasn't till 10:30 that an American aviation car came along. When he stopped it, I gasped, for it was apparently full, but no, they were going to Paris, and they did have a seat and would be glad to drop me at Meaux. So at about 11, I arrived tired out, and hunted the little room up at the Press chalet. Here I have a cot with no sheets and only one blanket and I about freeze but I won't suggest that they might have the maid put sheets on it and hunt up another cover, for they have them there. They just simply are not interested enough to think about my not having them.

July 25, 1918
⁊⁊

No cars going in the direction of Vaux, so I can't get back there. Nor does any telegram arrive that the car is ready in Paris. So I simply lie around thinking and disgusted. They refuse to run me up in a little Dodge they have at the Press. I offered to beat my way back as before.

July 26, 1918
⁊⁊

Still no cars going to or near Vaux. And they are all filled so that I can't get a ride with them if I should decide to ask for one, which I am determined I won't, because of their attitude. Hear today of Lieutenant Walter L. Avery's first Hun. He shoots down Captain Meierkopf, who is one of the crack Huns with twenty-six to his credit. This happened near Château-Thierry. The Hun was not wounded and they rode away in an auto together, victor and vanquished, with the vanquished smiling until he learned that it was Avery's first victory, when he is said to have turned to stone.[69]

No word of my car and no way of telephoning to the repair shop. . . .

July 27, 1918
⁊⁊

And still no cars going my direction nor is there any word from Paris and I am getting desperate as I know they will be wanting the car at Neufchâteau. . . . I explore Meaux a bit.

July 28, 1918
⁊⁊

I go out to Saints again today, with George H. Seldes, of the Marshall Syndicate. O'Neil had been over one night from the 147th Squadron and had dinner with us and told us about Major Bonnell being taken away from them and sent to England, because, as they said to him, . . . he was inefficient.[70] So we met Captain James A. Meissner there today; he is now their commander and, from what the boys say of him, he ought to work out well.[71] He's young, tho, and so much one of them that it seems an older fellow would have been better.

It was raining and was the kind of a day for hangar flying and we sat around all afternoon and listened to their tales and I made a number of little detail drawings of the Nieuport, a machine that I guess is about thro as a fighting machine. Their squadron is the only one on the front that uses them now and when they are gone, they will have Spads too, and Meissner is very partial to the Spad. They wash out a lot of Nieuports there on the field and . . . when the few extra engines that are yet at the depot in Paris are used up, it's goodbye forever. I'll be sorry to see them go and there is no other machine I know that looks as dainty and so meant to fly, . . . save perhaps the Boche Albatross, whose lines are a lot like it. They prevailed on us to stay to supper, which we did, and had a very delightful time with them. They are a wonderful lot of fellows. We learned also of Major Freeman's death over at the RAF field.

Tonight Macdonald brought out the car from Paris and I am free again.

July 29, 1918

Off early to Château-Thierry and Gland at which place I make a study of the old gateway under which I found General Dickman and his staff that morning when they were so close to the Germans and under shellfire. Then back to Vaux where I buckle down to work. In the afternoon I started a large sketch in oils which I think will be a good sketch, and I like the place as it lies there wrecked in the sunlight.

Finished today at my lunch table in the General's house the bottle of wine which I brought out before. In the General's presence I poured out the last of it, and along with it came seven or eight flies that must have been in an old unwashed bottle. It was almost too much for me, having drunk it all. I bought it at a good store and paid a good price too, and the General was all for my going strait back to the shopkeeper and also for having her reported. I promised to, but of course I won't. They did seem to sort of take it for granted that it was one of those cases where something was being put over on the Americans; said there was too much of it going on here and that it was a shame, taking advantage of us with all that we

"View From a Ruined Garden, Vaux." *Courtesy of the Smithsonian Institution, NMAH, Division Armed Forces History. 46458.*

were doing to help the French people. And that the matter ought to be taken up in this case. I think the General said, too, that steps were being taken by the authorities to put a stop to the unnecessary raising of prices merely because they knew the Americans would pay without protest. But I've seen little evidence of their work as yet.

Have felt miserable with a sort of grippe for the last two or three days so that it has been as much as I could do to work or keep up my interest. Then, too, the dead around are beginning to make their presence felt and a number of them are still buried in the debris so that one doesn't quite know what the odor is at first. The three dead Americans that had been lying in an old house here were buried today by the French. Why not by the Americans I don't know, for they had gone thro the fields and gardens of late cleaning up and burying their comrades. This morning I found three of our boys burying one of their own particular crowd who had fallen just as he was climbing the embankment by the station chasing a Boche up the hill there. A shell fragment, straying that way, had done him in. There's plenty of sentiment among all our boys as I have seen numbers of

73

times. There were almost tears as they told me of this incident, and their voices were near the breaking point one felt, and yet you knew they wouldn't quite do that. I have been interested and a bit surprised, too, in looking at the dead on the fields to see how very quickly they have discolored, turning black in some cases in a couple of days, and an officer told me that in cases of lacerations under gas that this sometimes happened at once.

July 30, 1918

⅍

*B*ack again today, tho I didn't feel quite up to coming this morning. But I know I must get back with the car soon or the fellows will raise a fuss. And I must finish up the things I have going there. But the smells are almost too much for me. They turn my stomach as it is, and I am forced to vomit a couple of times, while I was working on the oil sketch. Finally a *poilu* who is burying as he finds, discovers a Boche about ten feet back of me and pulls him out and leaves him while he digs, so I pack up my things and decide that my sketch is finished!

Today they discover a French woman of about forty-five in the cellar of one of the houses. They think she must have been here thro the German occupation and all thro the shelling, of course. She had been dead only about four days, the French doctors thought, not longer, and that she had starved to death, tho fright had probably helped. What a tragic fate to have lain there and finally died when her rescuers . . . had been in the town. . . .

Today too, some refugees came back digging around in the ruins of their old home. But Vaux is hopeless, and the officers said that it was not to be rebuilt and was to be left as it is. They said that many of the towns were going to be left just as the Huns left them, and that they would probably, in some case where the site was advantageous, build new towns near the old.

Wonder when I will get back in this part of the country, for the Boche are being driven on so fast now that they are having difficulty in keeping contact with them. Was loath to leave the General and Captain Lambert. I shall never forget their kindness in trying to help me, nor their concern in the incident of the "dud." Nor today at noon the calm of them all there and the matter-of-fact way in which they took the matter of one of our ammunition trucks that took fire just in front of their dining room . . . while I was at my lunch there. One of our loaded ammunition trains was passing on its way to the front, hurrying along, when suddenly we heard a shout and one stopped and we saw flames coming from the engine. The boys, who jumped off, knew just what to do, too. One hurried back down the road; about four trucks back, he held the others but ordered the ones in between to shoot on past. Meantime the other soldier, and the men from the French kitchen, were putting out the fire as best they could, and it took them some little time. But there seemed to be no alarm on the part of anybody, which I couldn't understand, for only about six kilometres back the other side of Montreuil-aux-Lions we have been seeing for a week all that is left of a similar truck that, charged with a similar load, took fire and blew up. Some of it is still there. But there was no great concern on the part of anyone here at the burning truck save poor little "me" and I didn't dare show that I was anxious for weren't the General and the Captain leaning out of the window beside me watching the thing burn most calmly? There was a truck and it was filled with 75s loaded and ready for the Boche, and the truck was afire and burning merrily at the front-end and it was directly in front of me in the middle of a very narrow street. And there seemed to be a merry party watching it. But the thing, the great thing is that they did put that fire out and there weren't any burned and twisted truck fragments left there for passersby to see as there were further down the road. Nor will there be as many graves along the roadside as there might have been. The Saints be praised!

But it is of such stuff that these Frenchmen are made, from the highest in command to the littlest *poilu*. And our boys show up well beside them, too, in cases of great danger, I am told, and I saw evidence of it today, though I was all ready to give a poor exhibition myself. But the General and the Captain saved me.

Just before lunch today a small detail of our men, one white in charge and two colored, appeared at the door while I was there and were shown to the General who, speaking no English, came with them to me to act as interpreter. It was a burying party sent out to lay away for keeps the many dead horses along the roads. And particularly three that were at the upper end of the village by the road there. And they wanted some *poilus* to help. The General was very gracious and called a Lieutenant there and had me ask how many they would want, and he doubled the number and they were produced. In a few minutes, we were all amused to see them up the road pulling and digging with their gas masks on. This was a new idea to the General and he was greatly amused. It struck me as a fine idea, and I am sure it was the same to our boys, for there is work around these battlefields that carried little glory with it, and this burying job is one of them. One dreads to think of the time when they finally get around to cleaning up Belleau Wood! If they ever do. Some say they are not to; others, that they will wait till it's old history then they can go in and get the identification tags. What a thought, tho now one can't approach the place, for we tried it the other day.

As we were at the foot of the hill and the woods the other day, deciding that we wouldn't attempt to go up after all, we saw a couple of our boys who were kicking and stumbling around in the ripened wheatfield there. A pal of theirs, who was wounded and suffering from shell shock too, had suddenly gone mad and broken away from the little field hospital up near Bouresches before they could get him back to the evacuation hospital. He was supposed to be dying with only a few hours to live, they said the doctors had intimated to them there. Their pal had fled down into this field; someone had seen him leave the road for it about an hour before, and now they were trying to find him, and they were so pathetic as they told us about him and how fine a pal he had been and how they wanted to get him before he died if he hadn't already. What an incident! Yet it's only a mildly pathetic one as compared to some of them.

Packed up my things and got back into Vaux quite late.

July 31, 1918
ᆋ

Start back for Neufchâteau this morning early, stopping at Saints on the way back as it's just off our route via Coulommiers. Lieutenant Mangin had called up to ask if the car was fixed yet so I take it that the fellows who wouldn't come up with Morgan are now getting anxious and think I have been having the car too long. If they only knew. But still those things don't matter to them and there will be no sympathy even showed by them for they aren't that sort. Queer crowd that was sent over here when it comes to human sympathy. Good artists and good fellows but all for self, it seems. This doesn't apply to all but it does to most all.

We arrive at Saints at a good hour. I look up Maloney first thing in 94th Squadron but he has only just arrived at the camp, it seems, and has his new Spad out for a trial flight and will be back any minute. So I will see him after all. Everyone seems glad to see me at the 147th. They are just starting a patrol; I call on them all as they are getting into their machines. There is a signal, the props are jerked over, there's a clatter, then a buzz, then a roar, and chock blocks are pulled and away they go out over the field, one after the other, into the wind and off. . . . It's Doc Rablo leading and his Nieuport lifts off, swings up into a stiff left bank and then like something mad, slams down hard onto her nose with a terrific crash and rolls over. And before one can get his breath and start toward the wreck, and the surely smashed-up pilot, No. 2, with Abernathy in the office, takes off, goes up on a stiff left bank and over, for all the world like "follow the leader," and buries her nose in the wheatfield and then rolls over.[72] Doc Rablo has climbed out of his machine cursing bitterly and swearing that some mechanic has tried to do him out. And now Abernathy climbs out of his machine, with that winning smile of his, and swears that he can't account for his accident, save that his controls would not work. He is so tall that when she turned over, his straps let him down just far enough so that his head hit mother earth. Otherwise, there is nothing hurt but pride. And there is disappointment, for there was excitement expected on the patrol, and there is always hope of getting a Hun, and now, too, there are two perfectly good Nieuports washed out and they are that much nearer Spads which they dread.

Soon Maloney is in. I have a nice visit with him as he is out on the range setting and timing his machine guns, getting ready for his first trip out to meet the Huns the next day. I can't help thinking what a serious business this is, taking a new machine that you are not yet acquainted with, taking new guns and helping mount them and test them yourself to thoroughly know what your life is going to depend on, and knowing that tomorrow, you may run into Richthofen and his Circus and your engine or your guns may go back on you or both.[73] Of course, there is always the thought . . . that you may do as so many of the Allied aces have done — get a half dozen fat birds out of the flock and then come home with your own tail feathers plucked. . . .

And then home. It was a wonderful trip down. And I arrive to find that another car had been added to our crowd and the fellows had been out for days and that I need not have come back. If only they had phoned me so. And there is no thanks for thinking of them. They had just come back and were so full of their trip that they didn't even say "too bad, old man, we are sorry and we ought to have let you know." Not they. On the whole, it has been a very disappointing trip, tho I did get a lot out of the trip to the 1st Pursuit Group. And of course I did accomplish something at Vaux, but for the time I was away, I did little because I was unable to get around, and because the Press Section would take no interest or responsibility for me.

※

"The Light Tank at the Tank Center." *Courtesy of the Smithsonian Institution, NMAH, Division Armed Forces History. 46428.*

Townsend made no diary entries for the month of August 1918. However, as he noted in his official report, submitted to the Chief of G-2-D, GHQ, AEF, on September 1, 1918, he had visited the AEF light tank center at Bourg, near Langres, in August, observing tanks on maneuvers. In addition, he stopped at several aviation fields for yet further studies, and, according to a list of pictures and sketches that was also submitted on September 1, he completed ten works in August. (These documents are in Record Group 120, Entry 224, Case 70, Drawer 3, Folder 2.) By early September, Townsend was at work in Neufchâteau.

September 4, 1918

After a more or less quiet day yesterday with a good dinner at the Club, and a shake of the dice for a coffee afterwards in the cafe, with my usual good luck, I sauntered home. Sat on the *terrasse* for a time with all the Bathos [family] and watched, for some little time, the play of a number of *projecteurs* (searchlights) over to the northeast in the direction of Toul, then went in to the dining room where we were looking over some new magazines I had gotten. Doors and shutters were closed, as is our custom now since the raid of August 15th. At exactly 8:30 there came, in quick succession, what seemed to be three violent explosions with considerable concussion. The house was shaken violently and it seemed that we could sort of hear or feel the falling of little particles on the roof or on the *terrasse*. There was no doubt but that the Boche had, without any warning, save perhaps the distant play of lights that we had watched, paid us another visit. There was no alarm on the part of the Bathos [family], having been thro it all many times before. Thro their calmness, there was no nervousness on my part, I am glad to say. A moment or two afterwards, or rather a second or so, a couple of light noises, as of the closing of doors loudly, were heard. We had discussed the advisability of going down to the *arbi*, but instead went back to the *terrasse* where we could hear the sound of the motor going away into the distance.[74]

There seemed to be sounds of considerable excitement around. Mr. Godin, the soldier who sleeps in the rear, said that there were terrific flashes of light which, of course, we missed with the doors and windows closed. The Bathos [family] decided to risk a later attack so went to bed, and I sauntered out on the street to discuss it all with the MP stationed there and to see if they were getting any information. They had heard the machine approach and circle the town. Then they say they had distinctly heard a hissing, as of a dropping shell, then, of course, there came the bursts, and all they could say was that it seemed to be over back of our house but not close.

Well, today I have investigated. Eight bombs were dropped in a strait line, the first one falling just across the railroad back of the Club, in the yard of the house which is also directly back of us, a matter of 150 yards from where we were sitting when they fell. Henri has all day been finding pieces of the shell in our garden. The first bomb dropped at a corner of a house, tearing off the porch and stairs, and causing great cracks in the end wall of the house, without breaking any of the glass, strange to say. The one in the garden directly back of the house was the largest of all, tearing out a tree. The others were all small. The fragments of the bombs show that they were less than an eighth of an inch thick.

One is at a loss to understand how any pilot could risk a trip so far back of the lines as this is, having a perfectly clear field with no defenses here, have a whole, closely settled town for a mark with large railroad yards with their lights lit, and too, at the particular moment he was here, to have a trainload of troops on the track at the station and then to display such poor ability as a marksman. One wonders what sort of a glowing report he will turn in to his CO [commanding officer] on his return.

The boys say that they were still at the Club when the bursts came and that the ones who happened to be leaning against the wall, felt a very decided heaving and pushing in of the walls. That . . . all the French officers who were there, with the exception of a very cool French aviator who was with a party of Americans, got up in great excitement and rushed out. But that the Americans remonstrated when the lights were suddenly put out, protesting that if they were going to get one, they would in spite of it, and why spoil a perfectly good game. Also they said the girls who serve there grew very excited and threw themselves close on the floor. This is in no way a criticism, merely an observation of the effect of the raid on the people here. There always seems to be difficulty in keeping the Americans under shelter, a fact which I have noticed both in London and in Paris during raids there. . . .

September 5, 1918
ᔰ

This has been a dull day, save for the constant passing of French supply trains and many American camions, as well, on their way toward the front. Sergeant Howard, MP, dropped in to see if I had use for him and said that during the night numbers of our infantry had gone thro toward the Toul front in camions, and also American cavalry, and a number of batteries of French 75s. And they were hurrying thro madly, as tho things were at stake. This all goes to confirm the suspicions that . . . we are getting ready . . . now to pull off a big offensive of our own down here on what has come to be thought of . . . as our own front, tho it will likely be in conjunction with Allied offensives up the line. . . . How wonderful is the news from the British front! And now with our men up on the Vesle too!

It has been raining most of the day. But it is clear tonight, tho I doubt if there will be a raid this night.

September 6, 1918
⅔

*N*othing of importance this day. Began painting — "Air Battle Over Sausage." Great troop movement all day in both directions, French as well as American. In the night also, and at 3 in the morning, was awakened by the sound of men marching and all whistling "Yankee Doodle." These were on the road to Mirecourt and Épinal probably, tho only going up into a more advanced rest camp. They seemed in fine spirits. I went to the window to watch but it was cloudy and still too dark to see. Why the movements are all made in the night, or largely so, even of this sort, seems strange, tho I suppose it's all in line with the idea of covering everything as completely as possible from enemy intelligence.

September 7, 1918
⅔

*T*ook the car, picked up Captain Morgan and went over to see Colonel Niles at Domèvre-en-Haye — stopped at Colombey-les-Belles at our air depot there to take a good look over the machines there and to see Colonel Jones in command to get a permanent pass so that I might drop in at any time to make drawings. Was glad to find that an RAF pilot had just landed with a D.H. 9 — the type dear old Henri was flying when he was killed. So his "Diana" was like this.[75] Perfectly beautiful machine of a sort of a refined super type, and, although delicate and intricate as it seemed, it was very compactly and substantially built. It seemed somehow as tho I were looking at the very machine he had and loved so much.

We saw a D.H. 4 — Dayton-Wright built — come in, make what seemed a perfectly good landing, then strike one of those rough spots in that terribly rough and dangerous field that they have there at Colombey-les-Belles, smashing the undercarriage with the impact, as well as one of the uprights, throwing him over to his left, swinging him around with the wind then up on his nose, where, tail in air and his nose yet off the ground, he rested on his propeller, which, with the end snapped off, stuck in the ground. He poised there for all the world like a big dragonfly with his nose searching the ground for sweets. How lightly it seemed balanced. I was told by a guard that this is a common accident there, and it certainly does seem that that undercarriage is not heavy enough for so heavy a machine

— it doesn't seem at all as heavy in comparison to its machine as the carriage on the Spad, or Salmson or Bréguet.[76]

Had stopped on the way to our Handley-Page field, but machines had not yet arrived.[77] The RAF, which was recently bombed out of Ochey, are using it now and for a time, I understand, will share it with us. Our bombing now, day and night, is being handled by D.H. 4s.

Stopped at Le Comédie in Toul for lunch. Six francs. Good. Saw Lieutenant George A.S. Robertson and Lieutenant Thomas J. Abernathy and some new pilots of the 147th *Chasse* Squadron, 1st Group, come in, so called them to our table where there was space. They have just moved down to Rembercourt, above Bar-le-Duc.[78] They have only lost one man since I left them at Saints on July 20th. Lieutenant John H. Stevens has been killed, but no others. Quite a record.

How differently we found things over back of Ménil-la-Tour from the earlier summer. It's all feverish activity; the railheads there on the way over to the front, skirting Royaumeix, piled high with supplies, food and ammunition. Troops and artillery everywhere. At Domèvre, Colonel Nile's HQ, we found things busy, too. Up on the hill back, they were busy getting tracks ready for railroad guns . . .

Took Morgan then back thro Toul to Evacuation Hospital 114 just outside the town on Nancy road to see Miss Barclay, an old friend of his. . . . She is a nurse there. . . . Start for home at 9. Pitch dark and no raids, but lights not allowed, and all the way back we meet long lines of our men and trains of supplies going on to the front under cover of the night. They are packing them in thick up where we were today, hiding them in the woods. We are simply forced at times to turn on our lights in order to find the road or make turns, but it was always met with a decided remonstrance from the marching men, who, in spite of the darkness and the rain that was beginning to fall, evidently were afraid of air raids. Two hours to make the trip home.

September 8, 1918

꙳

Still no mail at bureau for me. Conference at the studio centrale at 1 P.M. to discuss an important letter from Major Banning to Captain André Smith re the work of the official artists which had arrived to date in Washington.[79] This included the work of Morgan, Smith, Peixotto and Duncan, none of the others having yet arrived. The Committee on Public

Information, it seems, thinks that there is not enough dramatic or inspirational interest in the work delivered. Certain magazines, which were willing and anxious to run colored pages of the drawings, were frankly disappointed and in fact found nothing suitable. These magazines included *Ladies Home Journal, World's Work, Collier's, Country Life* and *Town and Country*. Also such editors and critics as Francis de Sales Casey, Charles Dana Gibson, Parker (of *Ladies Home Journal*), Allison of Keppel's and Leila Meichlin of the American Fine Arts Federation, also condemn them as unimportant and unworthy of the great opportunity, in fact, the greatest opportunity that has ever come, or perhaps will ever present itself, to a similar group of artists.[80] That the appointment of further artists depends entirely on whether or not we make good, for we must justify the use of artists here before they consider further appointments. This is all a bit in line with a letter sent to Captain Morgan criticizing the first lot. There was no doubt a basis for some of his criticism on the first lot, but apparently they are not trying to take into consideration any of the difficulties or circumstances here under which the first ones or even later pictures were produced. But to send such a scathing criticism as this Smith letter seemed entirely unjust, and then to name as the critics such people as he did name, and further to assume to try to have us believe that we are working entirely for the Committee on Public Information seems unwarranted, for we know it to be untrue, either as to our duties as outlined in the letter giving us our commissions, or from our orders delivered to us assigning us to post and duty. We do know that we are working really for General Pershing, that is, the AEF, which is the Army here in France. We have been told unofficially that our work was satisfactory to the Staff officers at GHQ and, like a ray of sun thro a stormy sky, came word thro Major Magruder who met us at the officers' club last night. He began at once to tell us what a great success our exhibit was; how surprised and pleased the officers were that we had been able so quickly to catch the spirit of the war and the men, and to grasp the little military details, and of how interested they were to see or get new material in the show each time, and he spoke particularly of the interest in the group of tank pictures which were mine. You may believe I was pleased at this after all this other stir.[81] Major General James G. Harbord, too, had seen it all and was much impressed.[82] We intimated then something of the criticism that was arising in the States and he asked us to pay little if any attention to it but to do our work as we felt it. That they would stand back of us to the end. Major Magruder is Colonel Dennis E. Nolan's assistant and Colonel Nolan is Chief of the Intelligence Section, G.2, to whom we are attached here in the AEF. We asked then what Colonel Nolan felt about our work, and he was happy to tell us that he was most enthusiastic; that at dinner after this last show, he had spent considerable time discussing and praising the drawings. It certainly put new heart into us.

Colonel Cabot Ward, Park Commissioner of New York City under Mitchel, came with Major Magruder.[83] We found him a most interesting man. He is to spend a few days here and seemed glad to find a group of artists here, for he is very appreciative and is a close friend of the Henri-Bellows group. . . .[84]

September 9, 1918

Mixed weather and mixed feelings too as a result of the conference yesterday. But the air was rather cleared by two good long letters from Cory and Barbara telling me how nicely they are situated in their new home. Also Cory has come to regard my possible flying as in the line of duty, so that, while she may do a certain amount of worrying, I can go into the work with a much freer feeling than I would otherwise have done. Have tried to paint today but accomplished little. . . .

Have heard today that Lieutenant Paul-René Fonck, the great French ace, is to be quartered here in Neufchâteau soon.[85] It seems that there is to be a great *chasse* field near here opened soon, with all the Allies flying there. The old French depot on the hill above us is already turned into a Bréguet bombing field — so these two facts account for the eighty French aviators who are here now. It gives promise of putting our town on the map, both in Allied circles and with the Huns, I fear.

September 10, 1918

Today has been a day far different to any of the others. There has been a spirit in the air, a subtle something like a premonition of impending events; of course, we are all keyed up and have been for some time waiting for it. But today, and more tonight, one has felt that at last the hour has arrived, or will very soon, when we will strike. All afternoon, and still at 11:30 tonight, an apparently unending stream of camions have been hauling the 78th Division past on its way up to the line or front. Commencing with American trucks, it soon changed into a line of French trucks carrying our boys, driven by Americans, then it changed to French trucks driven by Frenchmen, then it became French trucks driven by Chinese or Annamites, and they have been driving past for hours it seems, and they say will be, far into the night. What a spirit, too, our boys have had. They were a fine looking lot of fellows. Happy and singing or laughing, and they had the air of knowing they were going up into something big and important, but glad that they were. And a great crowd gathered to see them pass at the corner at the hotels. They too seemed to feel the thing, and one had a real thrill at it all. And we fellows also felt that it was like a call to us to be ready at a moment's notice to rush to the point of impact. For we have been waiting a long time, fearing to get out on any other work lest it break in our absence. There have been little rumors and hints given us for so long now at GHQ that we began to think it would never arrive — that moment that seems so imminent now. Tomorrow some of us are going up to 1st Army HQ at Ligny.[86]

September 11, 1918

ᘓ

. . . *Morgan* and Peixotto take Sibley, of the *Boston Globe*, up to the 26th Division near Verdun. I thought of going with them but changed my mind, and in company with Smith and Duncan, go up to 1st Army HQ as I have things to talk to Colonel Mitchell about in regard to my work in aviation. Found him in midst of a very important Allied air conference to do with the coming scrap. He has only a minute for me, and says that for the next two or three days, while the big battle is on, there will be no chance of my getting into the advanced fields. Positive orders against and all that, which I don't quite understand, for it's against all rules so far that we be shut out of the important action at the front. Two Colonels have been severely jerked up for denying us privileges that General Pershing in our orders asks that they extend to us. We know all the details of one of these cases and his reprimand was most severe.[87] So that this coming from Colonel Mitchell, who is more or less of a friend of mine, and is particularly interested in my devoting myself to picturing aviation, was something of a blow to me. But his adding to come back in a few days made it hard for me to take the matter to HQ. Nor do I want to with Colonel Mitchell, but I intend to somehow make him know how important our job is considered at HQ, and that we are trusted at the front even in most vital moments.

Afterwards, we drove on to Bar-le-Duc which I had never seen. It is a most wonderful old town, and has suffered much in the earlier days of the war, and bears . . . the marks of recent raids. It builds finely up and up to the top of a commanding hill where the old town lies. Place St. Pierre there is something like a dream in the beauty of its old houses with their wonderful faces, with all the character of as many beautiful human beings. What taste and what exquisite and delicate carvings. What aesthetically moving arrangement or disposition of the details of doors and windows and carved panels. And the delicate changes of color in the stone greys. The church has a fine interior. We were disappointed to find the carved skeleton of Louis duc D'Orange, so famous, had been removed. I must visit there again to see more of the place. I know that it impressed me more than any other of the old towns we have met in our travels.

On way back stopped at a village for water for the motor, and White, our driver, let the bucket get off the hook in trying to draw it from a well on the street there. We tried to pay the woman from whom it was borrowed, but no, no, her husband would get it out when he came. I mention this as reflecting the spirit of most of the French one meets. But they are not all so, sad to relate.

CHAPTER 4

ST. MIHIEL

Following the French-U.S. successes in the Aisne-Marne area, the British struck along the Somme River on August 8, 1918, initiating a series of blows that continued until the armistice on November 11. At the beginning, the U.S. 33d Division was involved in these actions, but it was later withdrawn to participate in the Meuse-Argonne operation. The 27th and 30th Divisions, which served throughout with the British, were used in conjunction with Australian troops to break the German Hindenburg line at the tunnel of the St. Quentin Canal, beginning on September 29 and completing operations on October 20, 1918.

Meanwhile, on August 18, the French, under Major General Charles Emmanuel Mangin, began the Oise-Aisne phase of the Allied offensive. Starting at the Soissons-Rheims line, which had been established on August 6, the French had pushed forward almost to the Belgian-French frontier by November 11. The U.S. 28th, 32d, and 77th Divisions participated in the early phases of this action but were withdrawn by September 16 for the Meuse-Argonne offensive.

Other U.S. troops were engaged at different times in British operations. The 27th, the 30th, the 37th, and the 91st Divisions took part in the Ypres-Lys offensive, which began on August 19 and continued until the armistice.

On August 10, the U.S. 1st Army was established, and a new phase in the U.S. involvement in the war began. Under General Pershing's personal command, the 1st consisted of I Corps (commanded by Major General Hunter Liggett and made up of the 82d, the 90th, the 5th, and the 2d Divisions), IV Corps (under Major General Joseph T. Dickman, with the 89th, the 42d, and the 1st Divisions), and V Corps (under Major General George H. Cameron and composed of the 4th and the 26th U.S. Divisions and the French 15th Colonial Division).

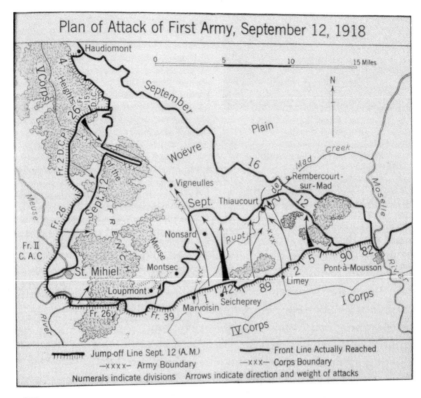

The 1st Army's initial venture was the Battle of St. Mihiel, September 12–16, 1918. The battle involved the reduction of the St. Mihiel salient, which formed a triangle between the Meuse River on the west and the Moselle on the east, with the lines intersecting Verdun on the north, St. Mihiel on the west, and Pont-à-Mousson on the east. The salient was approximately twenty-five miles across by sixteen deep and was one of the quieter zones along the western front. The Germans had had four years to construct formidable defensive works, but being a salient, the area was vulnerable to attacks from the sides. In the first full-scale operation planned and carried out entirely by U.S. staff officers, Pershing hoped to wipe out the salient, creating a new line, Verdun-Pont-à-Mousson. Unknown to the Allies, the Germans planned to evacuate the area and were in fact caught in the midst of their withdrawal.

The matériel and personnel buildup for the battle was considerable. The United States employed 550,000 troops; the French contributed

110,000. The French and British made available much artillery, many tanks, and numerous aircraft. Some 267 French light tanks were used, 113 with French crews and the remainder manned by U.S. tankers. A total of 3,020 pieces of artillery, almost one-half of which were served by Frenchmen, were utilized. Major General Sir Hugh Trenchard brought in the Independent Bombing Squadrons of the Royal Air Force to bomb rear areas. The French contributed an air division of 600 aircraft, and the United States had in place a new aviation section, which contributed to Pershing's total of 1,300 aircraft. In charge of the 1st Army's tactical air operations was Colonel William Mitchell. The tanks were commanded by Brigadier General Samuel D. Rockenbach, the AEF's chief of tank corps, aided by Lieutenant Colonel George S. Patton, Jr., his key staff officer and a tank brigade commander.

The battle began with an intense four-hour artillery bombardment at 1:00 A.M. on September 12. The troops advanced at 5:00 A.M., making rapid progress. I and IV Corps attacked from the south, while V Corps joined the battle from the west. French forces were extended around the apex of the triangle. On the following day, when the 1st Division of Dickman's IV Corps linked up with troops of the 26th Division of Cameron's V Corps at Vigneulles-lès-Hattonchâtel, the major part of the battle was over. The Allies had won a relatively easy victory, sustaining about 7,000 casualties while capturing over 400 guns and at least 16,000 prisoners. Because the Germans were in the midst of evacuating the salient, the Allies had to contend mainly with rear-guard troops.

Ultimately, the salient was reduced, the Germans had retreated, the French regained territory that had been in German hands since early in the war, and the Paris-Nancy railroad was opened. The battle also demonstrated that the U.S. Army could plan and carry out an operation of some magnitude, and valuable lessons were learned, though some of the mistakes would be repeated in later U.S. actions.

The St. Mihiel battle was rapidly terminated on September 16, as the U.S. troops began to move hurriedly to the northwest to participate in a far larger operation, the Meuse-Argonne campaign. This offensive would last from September 26 to November 11, 1918, when the armistice brought the conflict to an end.

During this period, Townsend hoped to observe air operations in the battle, but Colonel Mitchell would not permit it. As a consolation, he was allowed to follow the tanks as far as possible. He once more had difficulties in obtaining transport — a perennial problem that produced continuing friction among the artists. But throughout the action, the haunting beauty of war scenes attracted Townsend, and he recorded his impressions, both on canvas and in his diary, of various aspects of the conflict, elated that the Allies were making clear progress toward the war's end.

September 12, 1918

*W*oke this morning to find that the big offensive was begun by us in the night, heavy artillery beginning at 1 o'clock and infantry at 5 on a sector to the north of St. Mihiel, and on the sector between there and Pont-à-Mousson. And with great success, tho there seems to have been practically no resistance. No artillery reply to speak of, and no Hun air activity. It was too windy for balloon observation, several of ours breaking away, and one was last seen at 10,000 feet sailing toward Germany, one observer only dropping in his parachute. The tanks, presumably our light ones, made great strides. When the last communiqué came at 10 tonight, Montsec, that has always been thought almost impregnable, was in our hands, taken without resistance, and the French, who were advancing in the middle sector directly against St. Mihiel, had their patrols there at the end of the day. In some places the advance was as great as ten kilometres, averaging eight for the entire line. In leaving the fields here at Neufchâteau today, French planes lost heavily because of wind, two coming down in flames here at the field at Neufchâteau. Aviators killed. The enemy is surrendering in great numbers and readily. Low casualties in our forces. Our light tanks, commencing at Maizèrais, take objectives easily, followed by crawling infantry, against machine gun fire. At 1:30 P.M., our troops were an hour ahead of their schedule. In 10:30 communiqué or news summary, they were twenty-four hours ahead of the objectives set for the day. We have arranged for cars to go up tomorrow.

September 13, 1918

Captains Smith, Duncan and I set out for the battlefields, going up by way of Aulnois, Jouy, and Gironville to Rambucourt, Beaumont, then Seicheprey, and the ground there where the fight started. We had an early lunch at the Yale Mobile Hospital #39 at Aulnois, so spent the afternoon getting around over the ground in the vicinity of Seicheprey, walking over the ground, for it was difficult to get around in the car owing to the very heavy congestion on the roads. Such activity. As one looked across the country forward or back, as far as the eye could reach, and not only on every available road but on many new ones built by our engineers, were the same long, toiling lines going forward to the fight in hot pursuit. Here and there were lines of troops coming out for relief, having driven way beyond their objectives. What a mass of ruins these old No-Man's-Land towns were. Between the two fires for the past years of the war, they showed the evidence. Seicheprey was interesting to see, after all our boys have gone thro there since they came over.

While we were there, they brought in a large number of prisoners who were taking off their heavy coats to begin work fixing the roads thro the town. They were a healthy-looking crowd too, and seemed in no way depressed. We found many tanks, the light Renault type that we use, stuck in the mud and in shellholes.[88] Later, I found Captain Baldwin whom I had met at Tank Centre who was salvaging the tanks now in the field. I think he said we had 144 tanks in the operation, with some thirty out in the fields, stuck, tho none up to then had been shot out of commission.

We had made arrangements to spend the night at the hospital. Got there for a late supper. A Bréguet two-seater French aircraft, attacked by a squadron of Huns, had had its gunner shot, and its pilot had managed somehow to get away from them, and had just landed at the hospital for aid for the gunner as we arrived. He had been badly wounded in the hip and in the leg. Had bled profusely. Died in the night. Pilot was not touched.

We spent the evening in the various rooms at the hospital watching them prepare the wounded men for their operations, then . . . we spent some time in the operating rooms. It was all very interesting work. I managed better than I thought that I would, tho I had to go out into the fresh air a couple of times. We were finally put in one of the wards to spend the night. On my side of our group was a wounded Boche lieutenant. On the other side of Captain Smith were three Boche soldiers; all had been operated on, as had all the Americans in the ward, for it is strictly a surgical hospital. It was very interesting to hear the conversation of the orderlies with each other and with such of the wounded as were able to talk. And the surprise registered on them when they heard that there were Boche there was amusing. The tenderness of the orderlies, and their understanding and interest in trying to get the men comfortable, was touching, for they are enlisted men who have been wounded at the front, and for a time, at least, are doing this sort of work till they are fit to go back.

September 14, 1918

Up early after really a good night's sleep. Heard in the early hours a discussion between a nurse, who was evidently counting and checking up on the patients, and the orderly who was trying to tell her that there were three officers only spending the night, as to Duncan's status. Because he was perpetrating a peculiar rattle and murmur as he slept, she insisted he must be one of the wounded, for it was the very sound of many of the others. This struck me as very funny. Too bad they couldn't find some reason for waking him to give him some medicine or attention. Would have been a good joke on him.

Had a good breakfast; then went out to look over the Bréguet in the field nearby. It was truly beautiful in the sun there with the wonderful hillside beyond and the beautiful town of Aulnois down below. For all the world like some insect that had alighted for a fleeting moment on the grass. It was a tragic sight, tho, knowing the fate of the poor observer who had given his life, as have so many others, for the great cause. One wondered that the pilot had escaped, for there was a bullet hole directly thro his pit or office that must have passed only an inch or two from his body. The machine was badly scarred from the bullets the Huns had succeeded in putting into it so that one shuddered to think of the veritable inferno they must have been in for a time. There would have been a perfect rain of fire around them . . . all the while. What a strange warfare is that of the air, and so unlike anything the world has ever experienced before, and beyond their dreams, in its wild combat up there in space, beyond the gaze of the earth below.

We started out soon for Xivray, by way of Apremont. Here was a town that has been right in No-Man's-Land for these terrible years. It was the picture of absolute ruin and desolation, tho its houses were not so badly demolished as many others, but it has been little more than an advanced post for the Hun for a long time. Old, rusty barbwire everywhere to prevent the French from coming thro. The finest old house there was lined with wire to prevent entrance to, or passage thro. We found a new concrete pillbox that was still damp from its making that guarded the main street from three directions, tho I am sure it found little use. The work of the shells, our barrage, in this section, preceding our infantry advance, appears to have been terrific. How the earth has been churned. The roads were in very bad condition, tho they were being rapidly made passable for the long strings of supplies and troops that must go up on them. We had expected to go thro to Montsec when we reached Richecourt, but this was impossible owing to the congestion and the condition of the roads which were scarcely one-way roads as yet.

I shall never forget the sights along this road thro a country that for four years now has been in German hands. The fields that in other times were so carefully cultivated by the French, adding to the beauty of their fair France, bore now the look of long neglect. Far back of the Hun lines, perhaps the Hun may have cultivated them. Not so here. And now in driving him out . . . we had pocked it with shellholes till it had a look that was terrible to think of. How well . . . our guns had searched out the road across. Our Pioneers — the 57th Engineers — were now at work trying to fill up the holes so our men could get thro with their incessant trains.[89] Holdups were many and progress seemed slow, tho I think that it was pretty fast for the conditions. Once in a line of traffic . . . one must stick in it, for there was no turning out or back. Here and there were trucks that had come to grief thro having slid off the road in the mud into a great shellhole at the edge. This danger faced one often.

We picked our way to Bouçonville, then Xivray, Richecourt, Lahay-ville, St. Baussant, Maizèrais and then into Essey. It was a wonderful trip up this far watching the different outfits working their way along with all possible speed and passing . . . the ones coming back to rest positions. Here and there were balloons in different stages of inflation getting ready to get into the air for observation, and here were batteries of 155s getting into new positions along the roadside to strafe the retreating Huns. The towns all bore evidence of Boche occupancy, for all the signs were in German, and the streets all bore German names, of course.

Essey we found a very interesting place. The church there is a very beautiful ruin for, after all, a ruin can have all the elements that make for beauty even though it may not be consciously created. The interior was particularly fine in its calm resignation. Here I found Lieutenant Sewall of

"A Tank Surprises and Cleans Up." *Courtesy of the National Archives. 111-SC-57035.*

the tanks, acting as liaison officer between the American and French Tank Corps. He told me something of the great work the tanks had done. Said that their HQ with Colonel Patton had been there but had just moved on to Pannes. Says if I will stop next time I'm up, he will take me over to the French tanks to make some drawings. The Boche had shelled Essey in the

94

morning, and as we were there, another round came into the edge of the town. I imagine that the minute there is the least halt in our advance, they will get their artillery to work, and make it uncomfortable along the roads we had gone over today and in these towns that have now become HQ towns. One thought today what havoc a few shells could work there.

Then we went back to our right to Flirey. This was a difficult but very interesting trip up over the hill thro the Bois de Mort Mare. Here the German trenches and positions were literally torn to pieces by our shells. And it was necessary to entirely rebuild the roads. Great gangs of colored troops were at work at this, along with the Pioneers. Finally, the delicate skeleton of the church at Flirey was in view. What a lovely but sad wreck has been made of it. Here I found the fine old bell of the church mounted at the rear of the church with a big clapper beside it for a gas alarm. A battery of our 155 cannon had just moved in and was getting ready for work. The houses were pretty well demolished but there was that about the ruins that appealed to one as big; the masses and proportions were such as the artist delights in, and these things are not found in every ruined town that one sees. Just what chance it is that makes for this I can't imagine, unless it be that there is much in the original character or substantiality of the houses themselves. This, with the degree of destruction, may account for it.

We came home on the road thro Ménil-la-Tour, passing thro a perfectly amazing mass of munitions and supplies for our big drive. One can understand now why it has taken such a time to prepare all of this mass of sheds and dumps and get the stuff there and camouflage it all. We had to prepare, of course, for a big resistance, which it seems Fate decreed we were not to meet just yet. But we were ready if it had been, and now it will all have to be sent forward again, I suppose. What a busy road this was too.

Somewhere between Ansauville and Royaumeix, we come on all that remained of a big ammunition dump of ours that had been burned, set on fire by an air raid. We have heard that the explosion and shock was so terrific that the people in that neighborhood thought that the end of the world was at hand.

At Ménil we saw great crowds of refugees who, now that there was soon to be shelling in all the fought-over areas back of the advanced Hun lines, decided to move back to avoid it, also to get a look at their friends and renew their acquaintance with the France they used to know.

Neufchâteau at last. We find a news summary at the Press saying that at noon today the number of prisoners counted and verified was 15,397, and sixty-six light cannon, twenty-one heavy cannon, forty-three mortars, thirty boxcars and many trains of ammunition trucks.

"Mopping Up." *Courtesy of the National Archives. 111-SC-57034.*

September 15, 1918

ac

. . . No excitement here at Neufchâteau, save great flocks of bombing planes go over all day. Then in the afternoon I went down to see Tom Stevens's Joan D'Arc Pageant at Domrémy, played up on the steps of the chapel on the hill, built on the spot where she had her visions.[90] The road leading up is on the old path up which she brought her sheep. It was a pretty good performance all around. . . .

Later communiqué says our patrols hold Woel and Wadonville. . . . One of our Corps has taken 8,000 prisoners alone.

Slovak prisoner said that when he was taken, he was surrounded by automatics. Was so frightened he could only splutter in Slovak. At once, his six captors greeted him in Slovak and gave him money, cigarettes and food.

A Hun Major and his staff were led in today by his grinning orderly, to the great amusement of the other prisoners.

Vandières is taken. Clemenceau called at Corps HQ today and offered congratulations on the great success of the Americans in releasing St. Mihiel.[91] The Americans have already cleared over 150 square miles of French territory that has been held by the Hun for four years. No small thing to do in three days. . . .

A German 240 R.R. gun is reported firing into the Vosges sector.

September 16, 1918

ac

With Captains Duncan and Peixotto I started for the front today. Hadn't felt very well last night, but we had planned the trip in spite of it. This morning I wasn't quite myself, and when they came with the car, I plead a certain lassitude, but they were sure I would feel fit when I got out, so we set off. Wonderful day too. But what a different country we voyaged thro, tho it was the same route we returned by on Saturday. Whereas the roads from Ménil-la-Tour on up thro to the front were simply packed with movement, there now was comparative quiet. Many of the ammunition dumps along the way had been entirely removed. All the big guns had moved on, and even the 155s that they were just placing at Flirey, had done their work and gone farther forward. There was practically no moving of divisions to the rear . . . as before, for rest.

What a difference we found at Flirey. The Pioneers, who are repairing the roads, have gone in there, and to get stone for roads, have begun to tear down many of the houses, or rather walls, that were standing there after the bombardment. It was quite a remarkable ruin, Flirey, and now it is disappearing, tho I imagine that the wonderful remains of the church will be left; at any rate, I hope so.

We had stopped at the officers' mess at Ménil for lunch and saw all the correspondents who had come down there as the only available place to eat in the region. There was Herbert R. Bailey, Thomas M. Johnson, Edwin L. James, Newton C. Parke, Arthur Ruhl, Don Martin and a couple of others.[92] Bailey was most enthusiastic over having seen Metz from some advanced observation post.

The Boche now had their artillery working, or at least some of it, for they had begun to shell . . . the areas in the rear of our lines and were sending over a heavy shell here and there near our roads. As we were going across No-Man's-Land to Seicheprey, we saw three or four break in the fields over near the Xivray road; while we were making a sketch here, one fell nearer us, and as we were leaving, one broke with a tremendous roar back and to the side of us near Beaumont — I didn't . . . like the feeling of having them drop like that — tho one's chance of being hit in that way . . . was pretty small. But I was feeling miserable anyway, so that it didn't help my condition any. As it was getting late, and there was no time to go on farther and get any work done, we decided to come back here if need be. They will start out again in the morning at an early hour, and if I feel fit, I will go along.

On the way home, we were treated to several exhibitions of aerial acrobatics by RAF men who were returning to their fields after what must have been very successful trips over the lines, for there was every evidence that they were exuberantly exalted in spirit. One was struck by the very likeness of a bird's control of the air as they whipped and wheeled and looped, dropping and winging aloft again. To think that poor, dear old Henri once did this; that he was perfect, too, in his mastery of all the tricks, and that he had worked out several new manoeuvres that were quite his own, and then to lose his life thro some break in a petrol tube, perhaps. But he died in his duty, and got his wounds besides, over the Hun lines, from their shrapnel. So Glory to his name and to his memory. And that on the way home from his raid he should have his engine go into flames from wounds that it too had received, and to have this happen over his own airdrome and to fall from 100 feet just as he was trying to land with his own wounds for help — seems a cruel fate for even War to deal him. But, after all, we mustn't murmur or cry out in our grief. And he did get into the big fight for all he was worth, whereas many . . . give their lives before they have even tasted the wine of war in the air.

There have been alerts sounded here the past two nights. No bombs have fallen, tho they have visited airfields nearby. On two occasions recently, bombs have accidentally fallen from French bombers as they were leaving the fields here. One fell in a garden of a little town on our edge. War has its dangers from friend as well as foe. . . .

Today at Flirey a sergeant there showed us a copy of a newspaper that the Boche is printing and leaving, so he said, in the abandoned trenches for the American soldiers to find. It's propaganda. It's called *America in Europe;* well-printed, on good paper, with typographical taste. It had an artistic cartoon design on the cover by possibly Gulbransson of *Simplicissimus,* tho it wasn't signed.[93] Its policy was to discredit the awful tales of German brutality . . . and to show them up as human and to be admired. There was a picture carefully and well-taken, a half-tone, well-printed, of one of the first groups of American prisoners. They were all smiling and looked in fine condition; it gave all their names and organizations. One wonders about the design and the method perhaps in caring for this particular lot of prisoners, at least until the picture was taken, then one wonders what happened to them after having served this purpose. There was also an extract from some published account of an RFC pilot's fight with a certain German pilot. This had been published in England, and he had paid his respects to the valor and the skill of his fallen adversary. While they admitted it to be rare — such praise from the English — they did want to publish this particular tribute as having the more value thereby. Will try to get hold of some of these.

To bed early tonight trusting to feel better in the morning, for I am losing out on this offensive thro the three boys having selfishly taken our only available car, as they knew, and going up to the battle leaving three of us helpless here. Conduct scarcely becoming officers, let alone friends. At that, with three vacant places in the car. Little friendship there. . . .

September 17, 1918
❧

*N*ot up to going today with the boys. Will stay home and try to collect my scattered thoughts, do some necessary reading and work out some ideas for pictures. . . .

All enemy airdromes were heavily bombed during the night, with direct hits doing great damage, so that there was little enemy activity in the air. . . .

Noon. . . . Total prisoners of one corps is 4,953, of which 111 are officers. Prisoners speak of great discontent in Austria and of the great bitterness arising between Germany and Austria. And now here is a great appeal being made by Austria on behalf of the Central Powers for a peace parley, even with no stopping of hostilities, assuming that the Allies are averse to that. And on the same night, a horde of Gothas (last night) made a raid on Paris, and from the way the Paris papers state that the loss of life and the material damage was great, undoubtedly means that it was a bad one.[94] Tho ordinarily they don't state that there was loss of life so willingly as they have done this time, it was undoubtedly authorized to show up the hypocrisy of the demand for peace discussions.

I have heard that [it] has been observed that in the hospitals, when under the effect of ether, the Hun officers almost always mutter the numerals in their order instead of babbling secrets. That this is part of a plan to avoid any such revelations, and that they are heard to begin this counting when they go under. It continues then during that condition. Will investigate this later.

September 18, 1918

No excitement here and not much news from the front. . . . Last night Lieutenant Frank Luke, Jr., and Lieutenant Joseph H. Wehner of the 1st Pursuit, arranging for a night landing, left at dusk for a trip back of the Hun lines. In thirty-five minutes, they had downed three balloons which could be seen burning from the American hangars. This is Luke's ninth balloon in three days. That's doing pretty well.[95]

The Hun has now got his artillery going and uses it nightly now on the towns back of the lines. . . . St. Mihiel was again bombed on the 16th. . . . They seem to be revenging themselves now on the town that they were forced out of. Also one hears that they are preparing strong defenses for Metz. Last night they made unusual observations with low-flying airplanes, dropping illuminating bombs over St.-Dié and the roads. He seems to be getting his second-line trenches in shape now.

September 19, 1918
※

... Our bombers dropped ten tons of bombs on troops at Mars-la-Tour.
... Lieutenants Luke and Wehner go out again, and Luke gets two more
balloons, making eleven in four days. He also attacked an enemy plane
near Verdun and brought it down, following it down to make sure, then
landing also, to prevent escape of the pilot.

A French girl has come into our lines saying that on the evening of the
attack, the 12th, German officers were at her home, Souleuvre Farm, and
that when the battle had reached some headway, two battalions were
ordered to take Bois Gerard. After repeated attempts and failing, they
absolutely refused to advance again. . . .

September 20, 1918
※

Lieutenant Luke says that in addition to the two balloons and plane
reported yesterday for him, he is sure that he downed two others that he
fought, and his superior officers are inclined to confirm this. Lieutenant
Wehner, who always seems to accompany him, failed this time to return.

French patrols encountered a new type of enemy plane, extremely
manoeuverable and not unlike the English Bristol Fighter. In attacking
three enemy machines, one of them was driven down out of control, and
the observer was seen to jump out and descend with a parachute. The same
thing was seen on September 13th. . . . [96]

Some Boche movie films have been captured. One is a Charlie Chaplin
film — "*Charlie ist bereit*." The others were "*Bilder aus dem Kaukasus*" and
"*Der Antiquaar von Strassburg*.". . .

After weeks of waiting, our other car is at last repaired and one can get
out again. What a relief it is, for without it, one is really helpless now, tho
I don't imagine the discontent in Washington on the part of some of the
anxious ones there will admit that as an excuse. But with the car shortage
and transport difficulties as acute as they are here, it is a verity. One is
blocked absolutely, and with eight men to be served with even two cars
means that, with all their different ideas and desires, it's hard, then, to
really accomplish what one would. Well, soon I'm off to the Services of

Supply for a change, and it won't matter then for me. Then to the aviation fields, and once I'm there, I need not worry about them, for a time, at least. But I certainly was the loser at the time of the great attack thro there being only the one car, and the secretiveness and the greed of the three of our men, who slipped quietly away in it, leaving three of us here cursing — for they could have taken two more with them. Oh well! Such is Life! And War! And it's so that the human ego often works! But how can there be a real scoop in art, I'd like to know, and they surely know better.

It's a wonderfully brilliant, full moonlight night, perfect for the raid that all are expecting, and expecting will undoubtedly get. I wonder. But to bed just the same.

September 21, 1918

*And sure enough! Sleeping the sleep of the "bien fatigue," tho I never heard the two or three bombs that fell fairly near us here, I awoke suddenly conscious of excitement and to the put-put-put of machine guns which seemed to move, for they seemed near, then to recede. If I had heard the sound of a motor that I listened for, I would have believed that we were being machine-gunned like a trench by a Boche — however futile it would have seemed with the streets deserted as they were at this 11:30 by my watch. But hearing no telltale hum, I was at a loss.

I went to the window and saw a couple of officers hugging the tree trunks there in front till the guns should stop. The Bathos [family was] up; they had been awakened by the bombs. I don't understand their not having dislodged me, for I'm a light sleeper with noise. They had heard the machine . . . whisk away into the night, and they had watched the flight of the tracer bullets after them from the machine guns on the hill back of us. What Ho! And here I was right after all! For the Hun did machine gun our streets and also some of the houses, dropping also the two bombs in our fair town, and there has been great excitement in the place, and the natives, I hear, talk of taking to the fields these moonlit nights. Also we hear that anti-aircraft 75s have been asked for several days ago and that it will be a matter of eight days yet before they can be delivered. This seems strange that there should be such a delay, and it is, of course, only a rumor. There is a rumor, too, that one man was hurt by the bullets but none by the bombs, which did but little material damage, they say. I have not hunted up the wounded gardens this time. After all, it seems to me now the ideal way to take these air raids, if only they come no nearer. For there I missed the anxious excitement of alarm and expectancy and fear that comes, in spite of all, to one who hears an alert! And here I slept unsuspecting, or rather, forgetting the possibility that the moon brings, and there was for me only a certain morbid, but keen, curiosity as to the thing that happened, and the more or less certain morbid delight that often comes with contemplation of deeds that thro their horror awfulness, one surely deprecates.

With the danger apparently passed, I could regard the excitement on the streets in a more detached manner. If I had known then absolutely that it was Hun guns mopping the streets, I would have understood better the two fellow officers who were hugging those trees so tightly. Bad enough to have to dodge spent bullets from the sky which fail to find their mark there. But to have a machine gun strafing your street for its full length from the air, playing like a hose, as it were, and no telling but that the stream turns your way next, is yet another matter. I never get the picture quite out of my mind, the strafing of the Hun from the air as told by the pilots at Saints at the time of our work on the Marne battle. Of how, catching the Huns in their little holes dug in the ground each for himself, and just deep enough to protect him from rifle or machine gun fire, and to afford a degree of protection against flying shrapnel, they ran along the lines of these poor creatures, pouring onto them their streams of veritable liquid fire. And I can imagine how well they would do it too, these fellows who have become so skilled with their guns that they can catch the wary, darting, humming Hun. Somehow, dragonflies with bean shooters would seem an easy game for them. And I can imagine how those Huns there in their little shallow cups in the fields must have felt as they writhed around, knowing their utter helplessness, no place to hide, and how they must have longed even for a trench to dodge about in.

But the fire ceased, the officers hurried on. I walked out on the *terrasse* and watched the sky for a minute and listened well, then went to bed, and listened to, and wondered at, the people as they passed, for it seemed, an age afterwards. . . .

Yesterday and today there has been a constant line of funerals, it seems, passing my windows here for the military cemetery. About evenly divided — French and American. As I've been told, the ones buried here are only the ones who die in the hospitals here from sickness, since they have no surgical cases or cases from the front. One is always hearing the volleys of the guns there over their graves.

Tonight comes an order from Major James, our Chief, to confine our efforts, until further notice, to action in the Advance Zone with the accent on the action, it seems.[97] So it looks as tho, either he had not seen the correspondence between Major Banning and the Historical Section representing Smith, also the contemplated letter from General Nolan, or he has disregarded them for some reason.[98] Which all goes to prove that some of us have been right in our contention that [because] Smith and Peixotto [have] flooded the people in Washington with their profuse and none-too-carefully edited SOS drawings . . . when some of us . . . were supposed to [and] would like [to] make drawings there from an entirely different point of view, we find the game has been spoiled for us. They have been told pointedly that their drawings were not satisfactory, so that I don't quite understand why some of the rest of us shouldn't be allowed, now and then, judiciously to go back to do a few, for there are certainly many things with human interest which the aforesaid two never attempt, that the folk back home would like to see, aside from the fact that pictorial records in color would supplement the photographic records to great advantage. But perhaps all in due time.[99]

CHAPTER 5

THE MEUSE-ARGONNE

The Meuse-Argonne campaign brought the U.S. 1st Army its greatest challenge of the war. Its weaknesses and failures were to be amply revealed; nevertheless, it was able to contribute in a major way to the end of hostilities. The supreme Allied commander, Marshal Ferdinand Foch, ordered two armies into action in the campaign: the French 4th and the U.S. 1st. Specifically, the goal of the operation was to cut the Sedan-Mézierès Railroad, to break the formidable German defensive lines in the area, and to destroy the sizable German military forces. The attack generally was to contribute to the overall Allied plan of attacking the Germans at numerous points along the western front, keeping them off balance with no time to rest or regroup. Hoping to force the Germans to commit their last reserves, planners believed the sustained Allied operations could well cause Germany to sue for peace. Such proved to be the case.

The U.S. forces were concentrated from the Argonne Forest to the Meuse River. They consisted of I Corps, led by Major General Hunter Liggett and made up of the 77th, the 28th, and the 35th Divisions; V Corps, commanded by Major General George H. Cameron, with the 91st, the 37th, and the 79th Divisions; and III Corps, under Major General Robert L. Bullard, consisting of the 4th, the 80th, and the 33d Divisions. East of the Meuse, the French XVII Colonial Corps and the U.S. IV Corps, under Major General Joseph T. Dickman, were to cooperate in raiding activity and artillery support. West of the Argonne, the French 4th Army was in place.

The Air Service of the 1st Army, under Colonel Billy Mitchell, had 850 French and U.S. aircraft available. Some 189 light tanks, under Lieutenant Colonel George S. Patton, were to assist.

At 11:30 P.M., on the evening of September 25, 1918, 4,000 guns

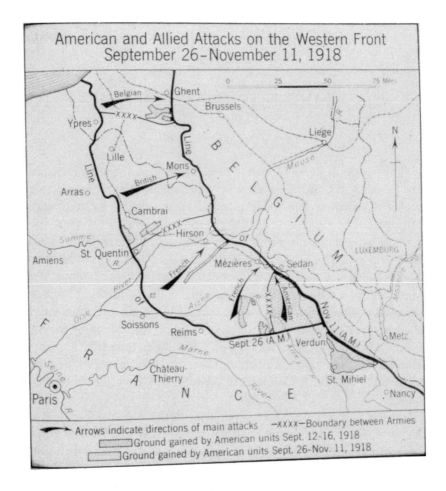

American and Allied Attacks on the Western Front
September 26-November 11, 1918

began firing, continuing through the night. At 5:30 A.M. the next day, the infantry started forward.

The Meuse-Argonne operation consisted of four phases: The first lasted from September 26 to 29, when the 1st Army ground to a halt. After some initial successes and rapid advances, confusion and congestion soon prevailed, especially behind the lines, and the attack became mired down. This was in glaring contrast to other Allied advances along the western front. In addition to the Meuse-Argonne offensive, Foch had ordered an attack by the British on September 27 in the Cambrai sector; a combined Allied assault in Flanders near Ypres, beginning on September

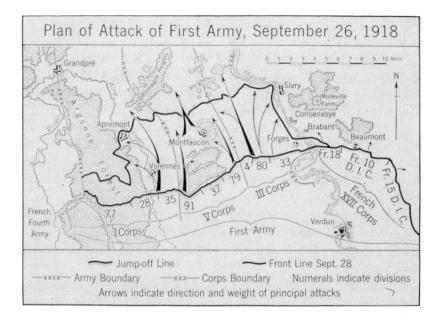

Plan of Attack of First Army, September 26, 1918

28; and a combined Franco-British operation near St. Quentin, launched on the following day. These were going well.

By October 4, the U.S. 1st Army was regrouped and resumed the offensive. In I Corps, the 1st Division had replaced the 35th. V Corps went into action with the 32d and 3d Divisions, replacing the inexperienced divisions used initially. III Corps retained its former makeup. After hard fighting and heavy casualties, I Corps had cleared the Argonne Forest by October 10. Nevertheless, the advance experienced major difficulties, especially with transport and supply, and encountered strong German opposition. Another halt was required by October 10, bringing an end to the second phase of the campaign.

On October 14, the 1st Army once more resumed the attack, under new commanders and with reshuffled units; most of the changes became effective on October 12. Major General Charles P. Summerall replaced Cameron as commander of V Corps. I Corps was taken over by Major General Dickman, former commander of IV Corps, with Liggett given a higher command. Dickman was relieved by Major General Charles H. Muir. Bullard, also promoted, was replaced at III Corps by Major General John L. Hines. The corps's organizations were once more altered: III Corps now consisted of the 3d, 4th, and 5th Divisions; V, the 32d and the 42d; and I Corps, the 77th and 82d.

As before, however, the attack did not go well. Stiff German resistance continued, and Pershing ordered a cessation of operations along a broad front, concentrating upon limited goals. There were some successes: The Kriemhilde defensive positions were breached, for example.

During this period, Pershing made other command changes. He dismissed Major General Beaumont B. Buck, commander of the 3d Division, on October 18, replacing him with Brigadier General Preston Brown. On the same day, he relieved Major General John E. McMahon, of the 5th Division, turning over command to Major General Hanson E. Ely. In the most controversial dismissal of the war, on October 25, Pershing relieved Major General Clarence R. Edwards of his command of the "Yankee" division — the 26th. Brigadier General Frank E. Bamford took over.

Other major changes came in the midst of the Meuse-Argonne operations. The 1st U.S. Army obtained a new commander. With over 1 million men in action along an eighty-three-mile front, Pershing's army was too large and unwieldly. On October 12, he therefore created the U.S. 2d Army, placing Major General Bullard — soon to have the rank of lieutenant general — in charge. It was sited in the St. Mihiel sector. The reconstituted 1st Army continued on the Meuse-Argonne battlefield, now commanded by Major General Liggett, who would also soon be a lieutenant general. He took over on October 16. Pershing accordingly assumed command of the U.S. Army Group, consisting of the two armies, with headquarters at Ligny-en-Barrois. He was now equal to the French commander-in-chief, General Henri Philippe Pétain, and the British chief, Field Marshal Sir Douglas Haig, and responsible only to the supreme Allied commander, Marshal Ferdinand Foch.

Meanwhile, General Liggett's immediate task was to once more revitalize and regroup the 1st Army. I Corps, under Dickman, now included the 78th, 77th, and 80th Divisons, with the 82d in reserve; V Corps, with Summerall in command, consisted of the 2d and the 89th, with the 1st and 42d in reserve; and III Corps, under Hines, included the 90th and the 5th, with the 3d and 32d in reserve.

Two hours after an intensive artillery barrage began at 3:30 A.M., on November 1, the largest U.S. army engaged until World War II began the

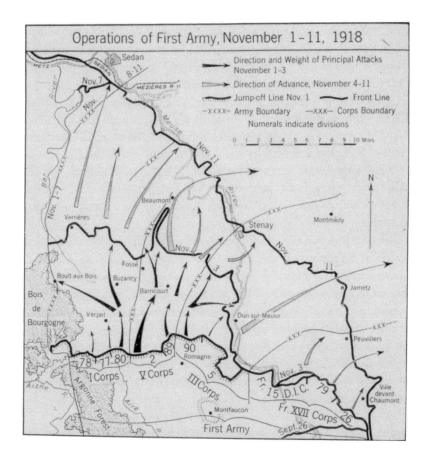

Operations of First Army, November 1-11, 1918

Direction and Weight of Principal Attacks November 1-3
Direction of Advance, November 4-11
Jump-off Line Nov. 1 — **Front Line**
—xxxx— Army Boundary   —xxx— Corps Boundary
Numerals indicate divisions

0 1 2 3 4 5 6 7 8 9 10 Miles

final phase of the Meuse-Argonne campaign, involving over 1.2 million men. From his headquarters at Souilly, Liggett followed the successful advance of his forces. Though the supply problem again became critical, the armistice prevented another collapse of U.S. logistics. The 1st Army was supported by the 2d when, on November 9, Bullard's forces began offensive operations, bound eventually for Metz in German-held Lorraine. It made only limited gains, however, in the time remaining before hostilities ceased on November 11.

At the end of the four phases and forty-seven days of continuous action, the Germans had incurred great losses. The U.S. forces also sustained over 120,000 casualties, including over 26,000 dead, while capturing 150 towns and villages, more than 26,000 prisoners, and

almost 900 large guns and thousands of machine guns and other armaments. During the Meuse-Argonne battles, many renowned engagements
and operations occurred: the clearing of the Argonne Forest; the capture
of Montfaucon; the breaching of the three heavily fortified German lines
— Giselher, Kriemhilde, and Freya; the incident of the "Lost Battalion";
and the exploits of Sergeant Alvin C. York, the Congressional Medal of
Honor winner who single-handedly killed twenty-eight Germans and
captured 132 others, as well as thirty-five machine guns.

The bitterly fought campaign ended only with the armistice. The U.S.
goals had been largely attained, except for the capture of Sedan, which, as
a consequence of a series of debacles, was left to the French to enter as
conquerors.

Townsend missed out on the initial operations in the Meuse-Argonne
because of his preoccupation with air operations and his failure to realize
the importance of unfolding events. But, making up for lost time, he was
soon closely following the U.S. advances, especially noting the tank
operations. He also spent additional time in Paris, making two trips there.
His diary gives an insight into the improving Allied prospects, though he
grew impatient, asking on one occasion, "But oh when will the end be?"
He did not have long to wait, and he recorded the collapse of the Central
Powers as, one by one, they asked for armistices, culminating in the
German overtures for peace.

September 22–24, 1918
❧

Barren of interest, these days. One works on at the regular task of getting
his material together into pictures for the monthly delivery. . . . This
morning of the 24th, we get a tip that there is to be another offensive or
drive by our forces, due to break at any time. That we will get word when
Major James leaves GHQ, which will be time enough and also proper
warning for our cars to start. . . . And now it's to decide who is to go. A
number of us are in the midst of work that we ought to finish before
starting other things or getting too many impressions or ideas in our
heads, and it doesn't seem necessary that we should all go up. For it's by no
means the last engagement our men will figure in. And at the present it is
more important that pictures be gotten to Washington than that all of us

should rush up into a small sector just to see an engagement that will be like the one we have just finished. If a few of the fellows go, it will answer. For my part, I am in the midst of some aviation stuff. Everything seems to conspire against my getting really into the flying work, and I simply must not let my interest in all the other activities usurp my time that must be given to the aeroplanes and to flying. It seems to rest with me to do this end of the AEF, and they are crying for pictures of the Farré type in a recent letter from Washington.[100] However, we are all to be let know when the word comes.

September 25, 1918

At 1:15 today, word is sent that our cars must leave promptly at 1:45 to meet Major James at Bar-le-Duc or to look for his car there. Our meeting with him hangs on our promptness in getting there, as he is not to wait for us. We are to run without our General Staff sign on our car, as they want no appearance of unnecessary movement of officers which would portend something to any scouring Boche in the air, or for that matter on the ground, where they also are, unfortunately.

But I decide to stick here, and then in a day or two to get up to the flying fields, in the meantime getting over to Colombey-les-Belles to see Brigadier General Benjamin D. Foulois, with a view to finding out if there is going to be the same opposition this time to one's being around while the attack is on.[101] I go up to see our transport officer if he can get me over there. Not a car in the place. Also I learn that the Press Section has moved today to Bar-le-Duc, which sort of accounts for that as the meeting place for our cars. What a fine, old town that is, and hearing that the press is now there, it sort of makes one wish that we might move our crowd there too. But that will only be temporary with them, of course.[102] For the work of our army is really to lie in the other direction, and this can only be one of these sudden moves helping the French push in the line there as they are undoubtedly going to the north in unison with the English. Our work mainly seems to be down in the Alsace country. All our preparation . . . points to that.[103]

I finally get to Colombey-les-Belles in a Red Cross sidecar which an MP picks up for me as it's on its way to Toul to get a message from the 5:30 train and return at once. Nothing finer, and he will stop for me on the way back. I saw Colonel Aleshire instead of General Foulois. I wasted my time. To get anything out of the Air Service, it seems one has to resort to second-story methods. If I continue to have as much difficulty put in my path as I've had of late, I'll feel like throwing up the game. He insists practically that if I want anything, my chief, General Nolan, must take it up for me. That would be his answer to all my questions. Pleasant, to be sure, but there seemed to be no show of interest. But it's all put in such a way that I can't well take offense. I could go to GHQ with it, but if there was any unpleasantness over it, it could easily be made difficult for me to get what I want, even with wide-open doors, which there will never be, I am almost convinced. He did say that Colonel Mitchell was the man to go to, which seems strange, as he is only Chief of the Air of the 1st Army, while General Foulois is Chief of all the Air Forces of the Zone of Advance. So I am still in the dark as to where to strike. But it will work out.

It was a fine ride home cutting the air as we did in that bouncing, rollicking old motorcycle. At 5:30, a terrific barrage, including what seemed all the heavies we have, began somewhere down back of Toul, it seemed. Even the boys at Chaumont noticed and spoke of its intensity. I wonder if it is to divert the Hun's attention as we begin the other. Or perhaps there's to be work there too.[104]

September 26, 1918

❧

*H*ere is a summary of just what was let loose on the more or less unsuspecting Huns. We started the attack with a terrific artillery barrage; in fact, it is said by those who are in a position to make comparisons, that it was the most intense artillery fire that the world has ever seen, and its effect on the material and morale of the enemy must have been terrific, and undoubtedly accounts in great degree for their lack of stamina in the fight and the alacrity with which they have surrendered. This withering and literally world-shaking fire began . . . I believe about 2 in the morning, and at 5, the boys went over on a front of twenty miles between Rheims and the Meuse. The communiqué tonight reports an advance of about seven miles, which is really faster than the advance in the recent St. Mihiel offensive. . . . A glance at the map reveals the depth, and also a possible strategy, in the direction our troops are biting. Our summary states that we were surprised at the ease with which Vauquois was taken, as it was the strongest point in the region, and they had looked for stiff resistance there. From documents captured earlier, they knew that orders had been given to hold it, even to the death. As before, our troops were everywhere ahead of their schedule. The Germans retreated with great speed, and our aviators reported that they had observed as many as sixteen columns of the enemy, including their heavy artillery, passing to the rear. They were burning bridges and dumps as they went.

Orders have been found on officers which would indicate that an attack was expected either at Metz or in the Champagne.

Colonel Mitchell reported that his aviators had found a breach from ten to twelve kilos wide between a point north of Montfaucon and Brieulles-sur-Meuse. But with what seemed a centre of resistance at Romagne-sur-Montfaucon. But no resistance was offered here, it seems.

III Corps is way ahead of its objectives. It captured twenty 77s in the advance near Cuisy. These are plentifully supplied with ammunition so they were turned on their former masters to good effect. An officer they captured said that they knew of the attack four days ago. This seems doubtful, tho.

General Liggett's troops, comprising men from Pennsylvania, Missouri and Kansas, are reported as figuring in the fight. It is an excellent idea, it seems to me, reporting the participants so, and will mean so much to the folk back home and in no way reveals any information to the enemy. Save that now the next time they hear there are these troops in the line, they will at least understand what they are up against, or better, they will know just why they were hit so hard!!!![105]

It has been discovered that the 5th Guard Division, which we met and defeated at Château-Thierry, are being held in reserve behind the line. They, at least, are in no doubts as to the work before them. Austrian divisions have also been found in the line.

I Corps, at 2 o'clock, had reached its evening objectives. It had very few casualties and was opposed by the 1st Guard Division which also retreated. This is one of their crack divisions!!

Great numbers of tanks are in the operation and, as in the recent fight, they starred brilliantly.[106] There is little doubt but that a great part of the credit for the apparent break in the morale of the enemy, and rapidity of our advance, is due to the effect both of the fire and the dread of these Juggernauts of Behemoth! American tanks took part in the capture of Varennes and Montblainville. Many tank traps were discovered and many anti-tank guns. But in practically all cases, these were avoided and fired on by our artillery and destroyed. A number of our tanks were bogged in the marshes to the left of the river Aire. But this is a loss that has to be expected. In the St. Mihiel affair, of the some 150 tanks we used there, we had about forty to salvage. Many of these I saw in the fields, stuck in the

"A Six-Ton Camouflaged Tank." *Courtesy of the Smithsonian Institution, NMAH, Division Armed Forces History. 46429.*

mud or half buried in fresh shellholes that, half full of water from the rain that fell during the early part of the fight, had turned them into veritable quicksands as far as any possibility of pulling them out was concerned. But this loss was in no way excessive, I was told by Captain Baldwin, head of the tank repair shops at Bourg, who was in charge of the salvage.

It seems in the fight now, that Colonel Patton, Tank Commander, was very severely wounded, and was relieved of his command. I wonder who has taken it and if it is any of the men I know? Poor Colonel Patton. He was a most interesting man, and most enthusiastic and active and

"Camouflaging a Light Tank Under Observation." *Courtesy of the National Archives. 111-SC-31705.*

progressive as a Tank Commander. I shall never forget the ardour and joy with which he pulled off the tank manoeuvres there at Bourg on the 16th of Aug. This was, in fact, to give the more or less doubtful members of the General Staff an idea of just what the possibility of the tank was. For it seemed they had to be shown. General Rockenbach had told me at great length, just before this, of what a lot of detail proof they had had to collect from the British, who so far had used them most effectively, to prove to the American officers their value as an offensive weapon. The manoeuvres seemed to impress them too, and I remember how happy Colonel Patton was after it. How enthusiastic and pleased he was . . . to have an artist picture them and their deeds when they got into action. And here, so far, I haven't had a chance to see them. But I will soon, for I shall make a point of getting at some of their most striking and picturesque achievements. But how I wish I might have gotten that portrait of the Colonel before this happened, for he will be disappointed that I wasn't in on the action.

It seems that all morning our aeroplanes were prevented from making much observation on account of heavy ground fogs, but in the afternoon they got out and, flying low, fired into troops, and later the air cleared and there was intense activity on the part of both our men and the enemy.

The day's bag of prisoners has been heavy. As many as 5,000 by our men, and an equal number by the French who, on our left, have been advancing with much the same success as we did. There are very few commissioned officers among the prisoners in this affair which is in striking contrast to the recent debacle. Non-coms seem in charge of the troops who are left behind.

There has been very little artillery reply to our heavy fire; our casualties are very few. Practically none were wounded by shell fire, machine gun nests causing most of the casualties.

So much for the battle — what tomorrow? Today a couple of big French naval guns passed my studio on the road to Épinal. One wonders where they are going. One of them was named "*Sans Pitié.*"

September 27, 1918

The night seems to have been quiet on the front. It seems that this morning our prisoners number 7,000. Several . . . divisions went forward in the night, we were told, and this morning at 6:30 the I Corps attacks, under cover of the fog. Meanwhile, there has been no enemy activity save that he bombed and shelled all our back areas. In the latest report tonight, we hold Montfaucon, another of their strong points, Ivoiry and Epinon-ville. And there has been severe fighting all afternoon on the edge of the Argonne Forest.

September 28, 1918

Found the fellows at the office this morning. Had a very exciting time. Captain Morgan says he heard that Colonel Patton, poor fellow, was fatally wounded, tho this isn't confirmed. I hope it isn't true. Also he reports having seen the new anti-tank shell in use against our tanks. They break in the air above, with a very dense smoke cloud which tends to project upward. Its color is much like the sulphury, reddish-purple smelter smoke. The burst of the shell fire is conically downward, a brilliant flash of pale yellow-red in daylight. This has interesting pictorial possibilities. He heard of no casualties from it, tho.

The British have entered Bulgaria and are fighting and pushing forward with the sureness they have again manifested on the Northern Front. And poor Bulgaria, the old traitor of a Tsar-whipped kid who, at last, as he should long ago have been, is now crying, enough, and begging an armistice that there may be peace parleys. He had a good answer from the French commander-in-chief. They will talk with their representatives, but they will not trust their sincerity, and in no wise stop the operations that are now in full swing.

Meanwhile, on the North, the British are biting into the Cambrai sector with a ferocity that is sure to devour it in short order. Oh how good the news is! And just what does it all portend? Will there be an immediate collapse? I think not. But how can they be foolish enough to keep on? And yet, when they read the speech of President Wilson at the opening of the 4th Liberty Loan Drive, what is there for the German leaders, built as they are, to do, but fight on to their own destruction — throwing their poor deluded pawns into the game to be swallowed up — into the maw of that gigantic military monster that we have been forced to breed and rear and throw into the field here to stop the depredations of their blind, mad God? What will become of them; what their fate if they give in after having sacrificed their peoples so mercilessly for their own ends? No, I've an idea they are too deep in the mire now to extricate themselves from what would be also a sure death at the hands of their own people, or worse than death to them, should they give up, having gone so far. Not that the German people wouldn't welcome peace tomorrow at any price; there are certain observers who are sure they would, no matter what the price, if it were left to them to say. But the powers that be may prefer to go to their end fighting; it seems to be the life they have chosen and led, and disappointed tho they may be, they are as apt as not to fight to the last ditch, unless there should arise suddenly a social revolution that would deal with them summarily. But somehow this seems impossible in Germany; the people seem to have been under too long. But oh when will the end be?

September 29–30, 1918

These have been quiet days on the front but there has been much excitement and discussion among the officers over a rumor that Bulgaria has asked for an armistice and wants to quit or means to at all costs. This is certainly good news, for with them out of the game, there is no doubt that it will open up the way to the Austrian frontier for the Allied armies in the Balkans. Then the rumor is confirmed, and the papers are full of it, and one wonders what the state of mind is at home these last two days since this new situation has arisen. Everyone was pleased at General d'Esperey's answer in regard to the armistice; what other answer could there be?[107] Then late today, we hear further that Bulgaria accepts all the Allied conditions. That we are to have free access to her country for the movement of troops and supplies and I believe that no real settlement as to her future is to be brought up till the general peace conference. So she seems to be in a pretty penitent state of mind.[108]

The papers have made much of the brilliant feats of the English in the North. And particularly of their remarkable crossing of the Canal du Nord. How in order to get across it under the extreme fire of the Germans, they got out some of their old tanks which were practically out of commission, rigged up a platform on their top that their light tanks and their troops might cross over on, then called for volunteers to man them, run them over the edge into the canal and so make a bridge that their forces could cross on, for it had been found impossible to throw a bridge over on account of the watchfulness of the foe. Volunteers, it seems, came in great numbers and the feat was accomplished. . . . It was a wonderful performance and showed a resourcefulness on the part of someone that deserves every recognition. . . . I mean to investigate.

September 30, 1918
⅜

. . . There is a story of one of our *chasse* pilots who carried with him four light bombs for strafing the Hun lines. . . . Passing thro our barrage, a shell made a direct hit on his bombs or his machine. At any rate, horrible to think of, there was a terrific flash and explosion, and nothing but tiny fragments remained or were found later. This same thing happened, I remember hearing, along early in the summer in one of our other sectors. What a fate!

October 1, 1918

⁂

*Th*ings are moving. The Belgians are still advancing with little resistance from the Boche who, in fact, seem to be quietly backing out, and the Belgians are beginning to once again occupy their own little country. After such a time, it must be a particularly happy thing for them to really be winning by arms and pushing the invader back, both with slaughter to him and with losses in prisoners taken in great numbers, and in matériel which he has had to leave in his retreat.

Bulgaria has really accepted peace at the Allies' terms. One obstacle out of the way on the southern route to Germany. Things ought to move there now.

October 10–15, 1918

⁂

*D*ays spent on a trip to Paris purchasing material for the fellows. Captain Smith and Captain Duncan go up also. What a change we notice in the weather as we arrive there, coming as we did from the Vosges . . . where the air is already frigid by day and the nights often freezing. Paris was as mild as one could wish a summer night to be. Fellows coming down from there into our region had remarked often on the difference which, in a way, is remarkable when one considers the fact that we are in the same latitude and only 180-some miles inland, tho we are a trifle higher.

Paris we found so different . . . from my last visit of the 14th of July, for now she has quite her old spirit back again and her people. They, who had hid themselves away when the air raids and Big Bertha made their days and their nights troubled and anxious ones, have hurried back now that the menace is over. Over as to Big Bertha, tho possibly not as to the Gothas. But they are back, at any rate, and Paris is herself again. And crowded with officers . . . of all the Allies and what a business the cafes are doing. The Cafe de la Paix in its palmiest days never catered to such crowds, nor more carefree and good-natured ones. And it's so with the others, and one can't help thinking of the empty purses that go back to an SOS desk, or to the active front, when the leave is over. But the food is fine and the girls who crowd the place seem, for the most part, such a happy sort, practicing their English on every one, proud of it (and most of them seem now to be able to express themselves to the great delight of many of the boys), and they seem to be satisfied with a drink or a dinner paid for, apparently.

The old Montparnasse Quarter I found didn't show the change as much as the city itself. It still has the sad calm that has been so noticeable before. For its inhabitants are the ones who were permanent and they have gone — to the war — or those that the war left there perhaps sought their families in the country, or other departments, till their loved ones came home. And the city still shows this loss here. Many of them will never come back, no doubt. And yet it must show some change soon for the winter, one would think.

The Old Girl's Club, now a hospital, is a busy place these days, taxed to its capacity, I hear. Mr. Pattee, of the Paris-American Art Company, says that there is no increase as yet in his sale of materials which would indicate that there is no movement of artists back to the old haunts. We were interested in inquiring as to the possibility of getting studios for some three or four of the official artists for the winter months there and were disappointed to find that it is almost impossible to find them for rent. Which seems strange at first thought. But the artists who are mobilized, having no rent to pay while in service, have kept their studios, and while they would like to rent them for the sake of the rent for their families at home, they fear that by subrenting they would have to turn it over to the landlord, which would seem right too, so they have no interest in renting them. No doubt, there are many who would be glad to turn their studios over to us as official artists without rent, if they knew we were in need of places, but how to get in touch with them is the question. . . .

Tom Stevens having told me of the Theatre Michel and what a fine company he had found there, I decided to take a chance on whatever should be playing, so was delighted to find that Spinelli was there.[109] Now Spinelli has been the hit of Paris, I believe since 1914, when she was discovered or made her stellar appearance. I had heard of her often and here was my chance to see her. The play was a revue or farce of the broadest sort — "*Plus ça change.*" I got a seat in the fourth row at fifteen francs, for that was about all that was left at that late hour. The theatre itself I found to be one of the tiny *intime* sort, holding but a handful, which probably accounts for the reason that they seem never to advertise at all as there is no necessity. And why too, that there are probably no more Americans there than there were that night. For with the French theatres, if they don't have paid ads or paid reviews in the newspapers, they get only the publicity that comes from word of mouth. Yet for a playhouse of this sort, it's undoubtedly the best sort.

I was delighted beyond words with both the farce and its setting, and with the very consummate artists who played it. There truly was not a flaw to be found in it. Spinelli is the finest thing of her kind I have ever seen. And with the others in the cast, it made a combination that was perfect. It's a show that many, many Americans would delight in, and go again and again to. Lack of a knowledge of French is no bar to its enjoyment, for there are perfectly stunning girls in costumes brief enough to please the most fastidious, who can act as well. The songs and the music were charming; the pantomime was perfect, with a fund of humor that needed no words. The scenery and the costumes by a number of the daring designers, including Poiret, were beautiful. The dancing was fine, and Spinelli in the Lucifer picture, with her wonderful figure and the art with which she used it, and in the wild dance with Mlle. Josy, who was almost equally fine, made the whole evening an absolutely unforgettable affair, and I wouldn't have missed it for a lot!

This was Monday night. The car had arrived for us to take us back to Neufchâteau, so we gathered up our things and had a wonderfully beautiful ride down thro the autumn foliage and faint, hazy sunshine that seemed to turn everything into a blaze of color that was unreal. Had dinner at Provins, which is French GHQ We were delighted with Troyes, which we decided was one of the most picturesque old places we had yet seen. How old it seems and unspoiled by any modern touch. We covered the 192 miles down in exactly seven hours of travel, which for our heavy car was pretty good work. . . .

On the whole, we had had a fine trip . . . I accomplished most all the affairs I had gone up for, tho I would have liked to have had more time to myself, for I seem always to be so busy when I am there, that I veritably run my legs off, and am tired to death by night. . . . We were able to investigate the possibility of getting an etching press to use this winter in Paris, in case we should move our studios up there, and located one thro Mr. Pattee, tho they seem to want a bit too much for the use of it. Also Cabmel said he could find a lithographic printer for us. So there need be no difficulties about that now.

I had hoped to have the time to look up an old Roman amphitheatre on the Rue des Arènes, near Blvd. Saint-Germain and Rue Monge, that William Beebe wrote of in his article in the July *Atlantic*. But there seemed to be no time on this trip, so will have to save it for the next.

There seemed to be little enthusiasm in Paris over the prospects of a negotiated peace. To them General Foch should be the real arbiter. Tho they admire Wilson much!

October 16–26, 1918

*A*m informed on our return that the casualties in Neufchâteau from the Spanish grippe have been enormous — that it has approached a real epidemic, and everyone is more or less frightened over it, for everyone has a bad cold and feels that they are going down with it, so that it's all one can do to fight this universal belief. There is a steady stream of funerals passing my studio all the time, and alas many, many of them are American soldiers, too. The loss in the civil population, tho, has been very heavy, I am told, as many as three or four a day, they said, in the week passed. I have counted as many as three some days, since my return, and the military ones have run as high as six U.S. and three or four French in one day, and there's never a day goes by that there isn't the more or less regular count of them, so that it can well seem alarming to a people whose belief in sickness is already keen. The rumors, too, that reach us of the number of cases in our army at the front are amazing. But it's an epidemic that hits the enemy even harder than it's hitting us, we are told, so there is consolation in that, tho one has to feel sorry for our poor boys when he thinks of the way they are living up at the front now, with their little pup tents out in the rain and the mud, their bedding soaked and no chance to dry it out, so that there is little wonder they go down when a cold gets them. And with the . . . fear of the grippe in the air, they have little chance to dodge it. Our medical corps, I understand, are going into the thing hard, trying to discover the germ and a remedy, which the French authorities to date have been unable to do. In the meantime, our hospitals are overflowing with our boys, and many of them start West as a result of the ineffectual treatment. It's a hard death for one who has come so far, thinking at the worst, to die fighting the Hun.

There has been considerable excitement over the verbal exchange between the Central Powers and President Wilson as to peace. There seems little enthusiasm, tho, over the possibility of a negotiated peace, and it seems to be the universal opinion among the French and the Americans that the thing will probably have to be fought to a decisive end, and the military power and the Kaiser driven from control absolutely. There was real disgust at the German answer denying inhumanity, either in the

"On the Gas Alert." *Courtesy of the National Archives. 111-SC-56922.*

retreat or in their sub campaign, and at their protesting that now the German people were really represented in the Reichstag and they were now speaking thro their true representatives.[110] This was such a clear case of shoddy propaganda, that it fooled not even the most simple-minded French peasant, and a real reaction has set in with the French and with our boys, even, who had truly hoped there might be an end soon, and now everyone is determined to fight it out till they are not only brought to their knees, but truly rendered impotent. Wilson's reply is now . . . acknowledged a masterpiece by all, both in the clearness with which he presents the Allied point of view and the firmness with which he refused to deal diplomatically with any but the true German people; that for the Kaiser and his regime there can be none but a military answer of a most decided nature. It's unconditional surrender or a fight to the finish. This has made a big hit with the French people.

The Advance Section of the SOS has now moved up its HQ from Nogent to Neufchâteau, so that, while there may be a danger of their trying to get the artists' billets as did the 1st Army, there at least is now a chance that we can get wood supplied to us, which has to date been

"Soldiers of the Telephone." *Courtesy of the National Archives. 111-SC-57011.*

impossible, so that we have had to buy it at the extortionate French prices. And there will now be linemen here to put in electric lights as were promised us, and which we need badly, if we are now to get in full days of work.

Our 1st Army has struck a snag in its offensive north of Verdun, in that owing to the nature of the country there, and the fact that it's . . . such a vital sector to the Boche, he is throwing in all his available strength there to stop the American advance. These facts, and the fever, are a hindrance, but in spite of all, our troops make slight but steady progress. The Germans are launching ceaseless counterattacks, preceded by artillery fire, but we have been able, in all cases, to stop them, and generally to turn them to our advantage.

Our aeroplanes seem to keep up their good work. Their losses as to *chasse* machines are very light for their victories.

And now a light breaks from Washington on the work of the official artists. In a personal letter to Captain Morgan, Major Banning, in speaking of the dissatisfaction that prevails there over the first lot which arrived because of a great preponderance of what they seem to think useless architectural and SOS drawings, states that the second lot had arrived and that "they were more hopeful now of getting the sort of things that they felt they wanted; that the work of Captain Harding was enthusiastically received and that some of his — Captain Morgan's — and some of Harry Townsend's were liked."[111] As to the old dissatisfaction tho, it still seemed to prevail, for there was a hint of possible replacements among the artists, tho he said, without mentioning any more names, that there were five men in the lot that he had every confidence in. Well, I certainly am glad to have this indirect word from them there and, while he only says that some of mine were liked, it at least shows that it is possible for me to please them, and I feel as they seem to now; that, after all, much of the trouble would have been obviated if we had had more specific instructions from them there; if they are, after all, to be our bosses, instead of, as we were led to believe here, that it was the Intelligence Section with the AEF here in France. So now perhaps things will right themselves at once.

October 27, 1918
❧

More funerals today. Both civil and military. Captain Peixotto, who was suddenly stricken with a sort of a heart attack the other day, is progressing, and will be in condition, no doubt, to send up to his home at Samois in a few days where he will be with his wife and get better care than is possible here.[112] Today Captain Duncan is under the weather. So that the artists are hit a bit, too.

Great numbers of American aviators flew around and cut capers over the town today. All Salmsons, and it was noticeable, for it's the first time I have noticed them in particular, for it's always Spads or Liberty-powered D.H.s.

Papers tonight say that Ludendorff has resigned and that the Kaiser has accepted it.[113] Also a number of the German papers are quoted as suggesting that now that they have gone on record as having accepted all of President Wilson's conditions, they must see the thing thro, even if it means the abdication of the Kaiser in order for the voice of the people to be heard in the peace settlement. It looks as tho there was plenty of sentiment in Germany to justify Wilson in demanding a representative government.

The battle up on our front seems to have assumed a sudden fury that the papers say has not been exceeded in the war. There is much troop movement thro here by train again, and there are rumors that another big offensive is being prepared, tho there is talk that it is out of the question at this particular moment, on account of the fact that it is necessary for us to keep all our experienced troops up above Verdun, and that we have none but green men for a new attack. But I doubt it if that is a true condition.

Had a telegram from Captain Wicke's office telling me that the Boche planes, that are being exhibited in Paris, will be there about two weeks longer, so must not miss the opportunity to get there and make some studies of them. For it is impossible to find one down here along the front that hasn't been literally torn to pieces by the souvenir hunters of our army. Either that, or they are so badly wrecked or burned, that one can't reconstruct them easily.

October 28, 1918

꛰

Nothing of importance occurred today until 6:45 tonight when, just as I was on my way to the Club to dinner, the siren began blowing a frantic alert, the sort that is supposed to mean that there is immediate danger, or that the Huns are over the town. At first, I thought that they were merely trying the siren as they do each noon. But just as I arrived at the Club, it came again, so that I knew there was some reason in it. But somehow you couldn't make the town believe it, I mean the new American inhabitants, for the place is now filled with the men and officers of the Advanced SOS, who have never really been in the advanced zone before, and who only know what an air bomb is by hearsay. And they closed no shutters on their brilliantly electric-lighted windows, and they had all their auto lights on; in fact, they use them freely nights here all the time, and tonight it seemed to mean nothing to them. In fact, there seemed to be no MP instructions, after the alert, to darken the streets. This may be serious.

No Boche arrived here tonight, tho an aviator who had just come up to the Club as I arrived, said that a phone call had just come into the Railroad Transport Office as he was leaving that they had bombed Colombey-les-Belles. And I remember hearing and feeling a slight shock only a few minutes before I heard the first alert, but didn't think of it as such, for things have been so very peaceful in these areas here for so long now that one had almost forgotten the danger which, of course, is just as present as ever.

And now Austria has really asked for a separate peace, in spite of whatever may develop in the negotiations with Germany. This will undoubtedly please the Allies, and is just what President Wilson would like, I am sure.

October 29, 1918

Austria's note is apparently in earnest. She accepts unqualifiedly all of President Wilson's conditions, and agrees to an armistice on all her frontiers, without awaiting the results of other negotiations. How different from the last Hun note which merely reiterates that the Government is now truly representative, and that the military is subservient to the legislative, and that (how cool and collected she says it), the "German Government now awaits the proposals for a preliminary armistice." There can be but one answer to such a nation. Unconditional surrender! Then we will dictate, not discuss, peace. How can there be any other solution now to a government that has gone on record as desiring to crush forever the "French menace," as Bernhardi called it.[114]

Captain Peixotto is better and will go to Samois tomorrow. How wonderful the autumn is here now but it will only be a few days . . . till all the leaves will have fallen. Last night was very cold and it froze. There was a heavy, white frost on everything this morning that lasted way into the slow, pale sunlight.

October 30, 1918

Report comes today that our combat planes yesterday brought down eighteen Huns with a loss of only five of their own men who failed to return. Poor old Lieutenant Luke has at last been given up for lost, tho they think, from what they know of the case, that he was probably forced to land in enemy country and is a prisoner. I think, too, that they have finally established that Max Parry is also a prisoner.[115] How I hope that this is so with the two of them.[116] Parry is the son of D. M. Parry, the great carriage maker of Indianapolis, whom father used to know well in the old days when Parry was just building up his business and when he used to get out himself often and cover his drummer's routes. And I remember him from his visits to Camp Grove in those long-ago days when I was interested in the happenings at our cross-road emporium. And how well I remember Parry buggies. Young Parry has become quite a promise in the new theatre world thro his clever, short plays. He was connected at the last, I think, with the Washington Square Players. I have only now read that Stuart Walker is to produce one of his things soon.[117]

Another alert tonight, and a rumor came into the Club again that Toul had been raided. Nothing arrives here, tho.

One is sure, now, that poor old Austria is in earnest, and the new note sent direct to President Wilson this time is almost pathetic in its appeal. What is there left now for Germany to do but give in, if this thing goes thro with Austria, at once. And yet, how bitterly Germany is still fighting, in spite of whatever certainty she may feel as to just what she must do and soon, and I've a sort of notion that she is actuated as much by the desire to throw every energy and hurt she possibly can at the Americans before it is over, as by any real desire or thought that she can save the cherished resources in steel or iron that she now holds in the region she is protecting there. For she must feel now that no little or big piece of enemy territory she may happen to hold when the peace terms come, will in any way count in her favor, for the very tenor of all of President Wilson's Fourteen Points, which she has twice said she accepts, makes it unthinkable for her, surely.

October 31, 1918

Nothing of importance, save that the wood, delivered after much negotiation, will not burn. Too damp, and how they expect a fellow to get any heat out of it is beyond me. All they have, they say. No alerts tonight. . . . I wonder if they have discovered, these Huns, that SOS advanced HQ are here, or if they are going to care a lot about their being here?

November 1, 1918

Rumor has it today that we started something with our 1st Army up above Verdun with any number of divisions, and terrific artillery fire. As before, we were in no way given any tip as to the move, so were not there. And why GHQ continually does this is more than we can understand.

Today is the Fête des Tous Saints, and all morning people have been carrying potted plants and flowers to the cemetery for, as in most of their Fêtes now, everything revolves around their dead. There is to be a big ceremony there, and this is a tight holiday; not a store is open and no one, save the Americans, work. Tomorrow is Fête des Morts so that there will be more ceremonies in the cemetery. These are the two very big Fêtes of the year, I am told. Wonderful today. Explored Rabeval Barracks most thoroughly trying to find some models there, and finally succeeded in getting some boys from the hospital — convalescents.

November 2, 1918

*R*ain all day. Great news came in on the wires today that the Austrian fleet had sent an offer of complete surrender to the Allied Council with the query as to where they should deliver it. A prompt response was sent, signed by Colonel House, Clemenceau, Lloyd George and Orlando, naming a place, and asking when it would sail, and when they could expect the arrival.

Also, our new drive is part of a concerted one from the North Sea to Verdun, and in our sector, at least, it has developed into a rout, with the enemy fleeing so rapidly that, pursuing as we are with auto trucks, we can scarcely keep in contact with them. There are no other details, save that there are large numbers of prisoners. It will be interesting to get the verifications tomorrow. The boys are quite excited about our not having had any word of the expected move, which has been planned for some time.

Word has reached here now generally of the terrific ravages of the Spanish grippe in the States, particularly in the East, where it is said the deaths in Philadelphia have reached as high as 300 a day. And heavy losses in Boston, too. I wonder if it is really true? Have heard tonight, thro a Red Cross man, that the losses in one of our divisions (I think he said the 88th at Belfort recently) was averaging thirty-five deaths a day from the same disease, with pneumonia complications.

Had models today. An interesting boy from western Pennsylvania who was in machine guns . . . and was wounded in the third day of the fighting in our Verdun offensive. His talk was interesting, as he was quite a bright and observing fellow. Butler by name.

"Sketch, One of Our Boys." *Courtesy of the National Archives. 111-SC-20119.*

November 3, 1918

ɜʁ

Great troop activity passing thro here today, French in one direction and our men the other up toward Toul. We hear stories of the preparations that our 2d Army, with HQ there, is making for a heavy attack soon toward Metz, and a big pursuit field is being gotten ready over near Manonville, which will be about as close to the line as any field has as yet been put. Wonderful day and everyone is out for a promenade on the Épinal road, and this afternoon, as for several Sundays, the boys are over again with their Salmsons playing around low over town and doing modest stunts, tho nothing thrilling, tho I believe the Salmson will stunt as well as any of them.

I finish up my drawings today and tomorrow they are to go up to Chaumont.

The armistice terms with Turkey are certainly stringent ones and thoroughly to the advantage of the Allies in forcing the war to a finish quickly now.[118] And there is no doubt but that she will get her just deserts in the final settlement. And Count Tisza has been most dramatically assassinated. . . . [119]

November 4, 1918

ɜʁ

Took up the pictures and hung the exhibit at Chaumont. Had expected to see Major James and try to talk over the general situation of our work here. And Harding had several matters to take up with him, but as usual, he was away, for they keep him so busy with his many points to cover, that he has little time to think of us, and none to give us for discussion, and there are so many things that ought to be talked over. We find that our work of the month before has been held in GHQ for the entire month and it was still there today. How we are ever to get them to hurry them along is the question. It's always someone else's fault. This time it was the Motor Transport Office, which was to send them up by courier truck, it seems, and for the trivial reason that they weren't marked with a brush in big letters, they held them up waiting for proper marking. No excuse at all. And we suffer in Washington because none of our work gets back there. Last month Captain Viskniskki added to the delay with keeping them almost a week at his place.[120] These are questions that we can't answer. There ought to be a way out for us.

November 5–7, 1918
🎋

*A*ustria gives up; terms are signed and fighting ceases at 3 P.M. yesterday.[121] The Kaiser, in a speech, bemoans that the old order has passed but says ruefully that he is willing to do his part in a new order. But he doesn't abdicate just the same, tho it can only be a matter of a few days till he must, surely.

Our 1st Army, on a front of eighteen miles, has in three days, advanced twelve miles, so that now our heavy guns command the main R.R. line at Montmédy, Longuyon and Conflans.[122] This was up to yesterday the 4th, and they are still going strong. . . .

Wednesday the 6th, the German armistice delegates leave Berlin to cross the lines with a white flag to demand of Marshal Foch his terms for an armistice. This was the answer from President Wilson to the Germans.

Reports from home say that the Republicans have carried everything in the elections there. I wonder if the folk at home would be surprised to hear, particularly the Republicans there, that the soldiers and officers here, and even the out-and-out Republican ones, believe that the Republican Party there has chosen a most inopportune time for raising the issues they have for the people here, in view of the confessed ideals we are fighting for, and can't quite make out the reason for a political quarrel at this time. . . . And surely they say, and even you folk at home must admit, there is no failure in our prosecution of the war. Of course, you say that Wilson started it by demanding a return of the Democrats to power. Yet Republican that I am, I see little wrong in that as a policy, and as an argument for the Republican Party to say, very well, we will oust them all and put in our men, unless they can put their fingers on incompetent Democratic congressmen specifically, seems absolutely an unclean thing for me, for when this war is over, there is lots of time left to play the old dirty political game again.[123]

Our troops are approaching Sedan. Harding and Morgan are talking of going up Thursday the 7th. I can go along, but there are two things that worry me so much that I am sick about it, for I want much to go, and particularly with them. But in the first place, it isn't going to be an easy trip and my cold is bad, for I cough and sneeze and "*moucher*" all the time, and they are apt to run into gas up there, for the Huns are throwing a lot of it back at us now, and if we should hit it, I would be a casualty sure, for I couldn't keep a mask on two minutes. So that takes a lot of interest out of going.

Then as Captain Wickes wired me last week, the Boche planes are to be on exhibition in Paris at the Tuileries just to the 10th, and, needing material from them for pictures I have underway, it seems like an opportunity that I can't afford to miss. . . . After talking it over with Harding, and his promising to go up with me when I get back in, I decide suddenly to go, order the car for Chaumont to take the train there, and off I go at once. Happy to be going to see them, yet sad that I couldn't go along with the fellows, for I would rather go with those two than with any of the others.

November 8–10, 1918

❧

*P*aris — I arrived the night of the 7th, at 9:30, or 3½ hours late, and too late to eat and, as it proved, almost too late to get a place to sleep. At 8:30, cafes and restaurants cease to serve food, and they close at 9:30 sharp under orders. I went strait to the Hotel du Tibre thinking, of course, they would have a room for me, as they always have at least one or two, I've found. But no, the YMCA had ordered every extra room they had, to be held for officers arriving that night. I go strait to the Hotel Richmond, their hotel across the street, to investigate conditions, and find that they knew of nothing, and that they had taken all the available space in over a dozen of the hotels in town, which included all of them, from the very best ones down to the cheapest, for officers arriving, as they were coming into Paris on leave now by the hundreds every day. They phoned to a number of others for me, with no results; then they gave me a list of a few possible ones. These I tried to run down, and finally it grew late and I grew desperate, and was on the point of going over to the ole Hotel de la Haute Loire in the Latin Quarter where we used to stay, when I thought I'd go back to the Richmond, thinking some officers might have been missing in some of the parties. But no, they were determined to see Paris and had arrived. But they did think of another hotel, the Adelphi, not far away, and I went there and found they had just one little room on the very top at five francs, and you can bet I took it, and turned in. Dead to the world in no time. And eager for morning and a breakfast.

After breakfast, strait to the Tuileries to see the Boche planes. A wonderful bunch of them, and they are really beautifully designed machines and beautifully colored and marked as to their camouflage, too. Most of them were in almost perfect condition, visually, at any rate. But I found I would not be allowed to make sketches or photos of them without first getting a permit from the headquarters of the enemy division of Military Aeronautics. So this I set out to do, and after a long wait for Captain Delzace in charge, I got it, in the meantime, finding that I could get good photos of the enemy planes by picking them out in the proper bureau there, which I was glad to do, so that now I have a pretty complete collection of all the types.

By this time, it had begun to really rain hard, for we had found it was raining in Paris when we had arrived the night before. So hard was it raining, that one simply could not draw, for his paper became soaked at once, so I simply haunted the place and feasted my eyes on them to get familiar with their shapes and silhouettes. And I was glad to see so many of the different types of Hun cannon as they had in the Concorde too. . . .

Saturday morning found it still raining, tho later it cleared to a pale, sunshiny mist, so that I was able to take a few pictures, tho they will not be good negatives, I fear. Also made a couple of drawings. I am disappointed in having had the ill luck to strike such weather here, and will have to be contented with what I saw and the very good prints I got at their HQ. I also learned that I could go any time to St. Cyr, their enemy park, and arrange for permission to make sketches there, so late in the afternoon, I went out to investigate, saw the place and it will be a fine place for me later on, tho the commanding officer was not there at the moment. There were not many complete machines there at the time, but they were putting them in condition and the ones at the Gardens in Paris will go back there. . . . Got back late, wet feet, late supper, and early to bed, as I was determined to get back to Neufchâteau the next day, and the train left at 8 in the morning.

Was loath to go, for there was great excitement in the air over the way things were going as to the armistice, and it was plain to be seen that, with only till Monday at 11 A.M. for the Germans to sign, there couldn't be much more of the war, and everyone in Paris was already planning to celebrate, and, leaving as I was, it seemed almost foregone that I couldn't get back in time to get to the front for the last guns, and I would have liked to stay there for the great Fête when the great news came. But some invisible thread led me back, almost against my will. Even late Saturday night, there was a band out late in the night, and singing, as some rumor must have drifted in as to the end, and it woke me up.[124] I would like to have stayed, and the Ball Bullier and the other dance halls are to open at once for the celebration. But I got up and am away, *malheureusement,* to my train in a lovely, pale sunshine that is promise of a perfect day.

Great news in the paper which I read in the Metro on the way, of our boys' entrance into Sedan. There were stories on the street Saturday that two of our divisions were already quarreling as to which entered there first.[125] Rumors there were, too, that the German emissaries had agreed to all the conditions save two trifling ones, so that, while I could get no hint from anyone, there was reason to suspect that perhaps a true rumor had drifted in to account for the late excitement on the streets.

I found that early as I was, the train was simply packed, a dozen people already standing in each car. The prospect didn't seem good of finding anything under such conditions, and was on the point of stacking my things as well as I could in the corridor, when a YMCA man, in a compartment nearby, hailed me and said that one of the party he was conducting had not arrived and would I please take his seat. This meant, too, that I was to have his seat at lunch for the first service. I was certainly well looked after. His party included the Japanese General Hibiki and his son, who were on their way to Chaumont, both on a military mission, and the General, as head of the YMCA in the Japanese army, to attend a big meeting at the opening of the 1,500th hut in France with our army. The son talked very good English and is a Princeton student. The General talked fairly good French. They were very pleasant, the two of them. They gave us little silk Japanese flags and some Fuji postcards distributed by their YMCA.

Due at Chaumont at [about] noon, we arrived at 3:45 instead. Having phoned down for a car, there was McEnery there with one of the visitor's cars. Orders were to go back to GHQ to see Major James. There I found him busy as ever, too busy, in fact, to talk about any of the things I would have liked to talk to him about, but he handed me a letter that he had been putting in the courier mail for me in regard to doing some portraits at once, as the Historical Section was asking now for them, and thought with the war over, there would be opportunity now for them to pose for me. So now it's up to me, and I will have to begin at just the time when I want to be collecting other material that can now be gotten at. However, there will be a way open to do both, I am sure. . . .[126]

CHAPTER 6

PEACE AND A JOURNEY TO METZ

On November 8, 1918, Marshal Foch, representing the Allied armies, and Sir Rosslyn Wemyss, on behalf of the Allied navies, together with other officials and high-ranking officers, met a group of German representatives led by Matthais Erzberger in a railway car at Rethondes in the Compiègne Forest, northeast of Paris. The Germans were presented with a draft of a cease-fire document. The terms were severe, and the Germans protested, but Foch gave them only seventy-two hours for a final decision. In the meantime, the war would continue.

The Germans, obtaining a few insignificant concessions and concluding that they had no other choice, accepted the armistice terms on November 10. The document was signed at about 5:20 A.M. on November 11 at Rethondes, to go into effect at 11:00 A.M. the same day.[127] Germany's allies had already withdrawn from the struggle: Bulgaria on September 29, the Turks on October 31, and the Austro-Hungarians on November 4.

The terms of the German armistice were stiff, calculated to make it difficult for that nation to resume military operations, though this was always a possibility. Germany agreed to evacuate Belgium, France, Luxembourg and Alsace-Lorraine within fifteen days. The latter territory had been lost by France to Germany in 1871, a consequence of the French defeat in the Franco-Prussian War. The chief city of Lorraine was heavily fortified Metz, which now drew the French toward it, as well as some of the more adventuresome U.S. citizens who could find an excuse to go there, including the official artists.

In other provisions, the Germans were to evacuate districts they occupied on the left bank of the Rhine and a zone adjoining the river on its right bank, forty kilometers or so in width. They had sixteen additional days to clear the German areas involved. The Allies were to keep pace with the German withdrawal, taking up occupation zones. The Belgians moved into the area adjoining Belgium and Holland. The British zone centered on Cologne, with a bridgehead extending in a thirty-kilometer radius on the right bank. The U.S. troops occupied Coblenz with a similar bridgehead, and the French zone included the major Rhineland city of Mainz and an east-bank bridgehead.

Other terms provided that Germans outside the Reich were to return to Germany. There were also provisions for the surrender of armaments, aircraft, and naval vessels, as well as specified items on a list of goods and matériel. Financial clauses outlined reparation for damage done to the Allies. The armistice was to last for thirty-six days, with an option to extend.

Within a few days of the signing of the armistice, the U.S. official artists visited Metz. Being among the first of the Allies to arrive, they received the accolades of the restored Lorrainers. They found that the material conditions of the citizens there were much better than expected, and Townsend believed that the horror stories of massive starvation and suffering coming out of Germany were exaggerated. He regarded his Metz venture as one of the most interesting that he experienced during his time in the AEF, and his diary accounts add to an understanding of this phase of World War I.

November 11, 1918

*U*p betimes. After arranging my affairs, go up to the Press to see about the car and to see who is left here, only to find that Dunn and Aylward had taken it, and slipped away already, and they hadn't asked if I was back, as they had every reason to do, since they knew I was expected. I had seen Dunn the minute before I left and told him I would return. But it's his selfish way, and I was thoroughly mad about it, for with the only car left, they have no right to take it without seeing that the rest of us were provided for. . . . But no, they think only of themselves, till one is sick of it all. This pose of Dunn's of having seen more of the actual fighting than any one of the rest, and of being the only one who has really gone over the top, is unbearable, sometimes. When he goes back, of course, he will take the whole war with him! So after the effort I made to get back here, when I really would rather have celebrated the *victorie* in Paris than here in

Neufchâteau, and then having to lie around here and kick my heels and nurse a grudge, I'm in a bad humor tonight.

For the *victorie* has *déjà* arrived! The armistice was signed at 5 this morning and the firing was to cease at 11, and the Allies were not to advance beyond the positions then held till further orders from Marshal Foch. At noon, the bell began a joyful ringing that lasted for a full hour; everyone decorated their houses with the Allied flags and coursed thro the streets singing and dancing, for now singing and dancing is again permitted. Think what it must mean, what a feeling it must be, to feel truly free again, when you had really been in bondage for four years and a half. Two regiments of our boys, who were coming back into rest from the front, went thro town in camions at full speed, shouting and singing at the top of their lungs, and it seemed that the whole town was down at the crossing at the Providence Hotel to see and hear them and shout back. Soldiers about town were frequenting the cafes freely. And everyone talked of champagne for dinner. And I imagine it was the same throughout all France.

What must be the feelings of the *poilus* who at last know that the end, at least of their suffering thro hardship and battle, is over, probably for all time? I watched them much as they passed today. Happy undoubtedly they are, yet somehow they don't seem to express it as do the civilians. It's as tho they knew great things were in the air for them, but they weren't quite sure what it was, or being told of it, didn't quite know whether to believe it was true, tho it was pleasant to hear. And it must be hard for them, children that they are, to really grasp the significance of it.

And tonight there has been champagne for supper for us. And afterwards, I went with the family to the Place Jean d'Arc, where there was to be a gathering after a big procession in the streets, and some *cantatrice* from the Opera in Paris was to sing the Marseillaise. What excitement there was everywhere. And how strange it seemed, even to me, to see the streets all lighted, the first time since the war began, and no one had to close their shutters tight tonight in fear of the raiding Hun as he has had to do the full four years. So you can imagine it looked gay and it was all like some very pleasant dream come true.

Arrived at the statue in the square, but the ceremony was no ceremony at all, just a gathering in which everyone gave way to his feeling of joy and freedom. Two American soldiers, seeing an opportunity that the decorating committee had overlooked, climbed up beside Joan and gave her a French and an American flag to hold, also a Japanese lantern, then the *artiste* sang, and an Italian band played, and there was great cheering and it all broke up.

Coming home a roundabout way, we heard rumors of a dance which I understood was at the YMCA hut for the enlisted men. Mme. Guillaume, who was with us, asked us up to her little apartment to have a hot grog, then home and to bed. *C'est la victorie et maintenant?*

November 12, 1918
❧

*T*oday Captains Morgan, Harding and Duncan returned from the 1st Army near Sedan and had many interesting things to tell of all they saw there, tho it wasn't quite as exciting as I had imagined, nor as they had expected to find it. There was, of course, much interest in the final shots of the war, and the way the boys took the news, and the way the different batteries vied with each other to have the credit for the last shot of the war. But from all accounts, it seems that perhaps it was the Boche who really had it, and some officers, who were near a battery, say that the last shot the Hun flung over, right on the eleventh hour, made a hit on one of our batteries and killed five of our men. In some places, they threw over gas shells at the last, so they seemed to be playing their same old game up to what is to them, surely, the bitter end.

The terms of the armistice were published today and what stringent ones they are, and certainly now, since she [Germany] has accepted them, and if she fulfills them, there can be nothing but peace, for whether she likes the peace terms or not, her power is absolutely stripped off her. There is one ray of hope in them, tho, and that is that it seems the Allies have obligated themselves to see to the victualing of the German population. This seems like a considerable . . . promise, but it is made, and will be, no doubt, well done.

There is another instance of that strange reasoning on the part of the French military in that, instead of our troops occupying Sedan after they took the town as the papers stated, they were asked, after driving the Germans out, not to enter, but to stay on the other side of the river. And then they moved up French troops, and let them go in and deliver the people, as it were, from the Huns. This is something that our boys don't seem to understand. It was much the same way at St. Mihiel. We encircled the town, joining our troops behind it after forcing the Boche out, then the French move in and have the honor of entering and greeting the people who we delivered. Little, unimportant towns do not matter so much, and these they let us take or pass, but the big ones, with a sentimental interest attaching thereto, they are very thoughtful of, but there can't be anything but the proper credit and gratitude later when the people really know.

Also the boys said that for over a week, on account of the congestion of the roads, and the length of time that it takes to get from Press HQ to the front there and back — a matter of forty-eight hours or more — the correspondents have not been near the front, or seen anything but the official communiqués and written their stories from them, and whatever they could pick up from anyone that went thro who had been there. . . . They eagerly pumped them for all they could get, and there was much that the boys had seen. It seems that the roads were in such frightful condition that they had difficulty getting around up there, and that one afternoon, it took the entire time to go five miles. Shellholes and congestion on such roads made it impossible, almost, hence the long time they were overdue in getting back.

The Kaiser flees to Holland, leaving his wife behind.[128] There he will be interned, I suppose, and well guarded from assassins. Rumors are that the Crown Prince wept copiously when he signed away all his rights to the throne. But there seems to be a strong feeling that there is something suspicious about the new government, and those at its head, since they are friendly to the old regime. But I imagine the Allies are clever enough in their plans now to block any later attempt of any party there that may rise up to get the Kaiser back at the helm again.

Rumor has it, too, that the Crown Prince has been shot by his own soldiers but this not yet verified, thou it comes from many news sources.[129]

November 13, 1918

The world still seems to be rubbing its eyes to see if it is awake or still dreaming of a time long way off. But they smile as they have never done before, and they laugh as they haven't in four years, too, and some of them weep as they haven't in four years. . . . The tears now are not of suffering for dead ones on the field of honor, nor of suffering thro personal contact with the Hun, but tears of joy. And there are many kisses thrown the Americans these days, and no doubt as in Paris the other day, so throughout France, there are many real kisses bestowed on our boys by women and girls out of real gratitude and love. For I know that the French do love the

Americans, and they have no hesitation in telling us that we have truly saved them. That without our coming, as we did and when we did, they were defeated, that the Germans had won — so that they look on us as their deliverers from a fate worse than death: German subjection. This they are sure of, and they name us in their prayers. This is something to have won, besides having helped to whip the Boche.

I've no doubt that we will get our proper credit, too, from the discerning Englishman . . . if they . . . get what they think they have deservedly coming to them from us in the matter of the work of their fleet. And there is no doubt in the minds of most Americans as to the glorious part that the British fleet has played in it all. For before we saved France, one might say that they had saved us. There is little doubt, but that for their fleet, the war would long since have been finished and with German victors.

Late tonight Dunn and Aylward get back from a trip up beyond Pont-à-Mousson. We went up to GHQ today to talk to Major James about the outlook for our work, and the kind of plans we ought to make to get the material as we felt we ought, and we found him in the midst of writing . . . to tell us that the Press Section was planning to move, and they were getting their own little army ready to go along with the Army of Occupation, and we were to pack lightly to move . . . with our two cars.[130] We are to hold on to our studios here so that we can have something to come back to at first, before we have to hunt up permanent new studios elsewhere later. We are to go Sunday; possibly will start on Saturday.

They have not yet found a location for Press HQ as a base, but it will be way forward near the frontier, and now we are wondering if we will get a chance to go up thro Metz, which we would like to, or whether we will enter Germany a bit further north. Think of it! We are going to either Mainz, Coblenz, or Cologne, the three cities that are to be occupied. We may get to all of them, who knows? But anyway we are to get into Germany with the Army of Occupation. No one knows how long before we get back here, and that's my problem, for the Bathos [family], with whom I live here, want to go back to their town of Cirey near the border, as soon as it is evacuated and clear, tho they don't seem to think this will be before the New Year. Surely we will get back before then. We are all excitement!

We have been asked also to make out personal memorandums as to how we think we can best go ahead to carry out our work properly, in order to get the necessary material, how long it will take and all, in case there comes any sudden word from Washington calling us home.[131] This . . . they would send on to them there, and stand back of us in seeing that we are allowed to complete our preparations reasonably. This sounds like good policy. . . .

A letter from London tells me that *The British Artists at the Front* has been discontinued before the fourth number by orders of the Government. Strange! One wonders if it was because they had been giving too much sympathy or publicity to the Moderns? Too bad, for I had hoped to get an Orpen number. . . . [132]

We are led to wonder often what form the publication of our drawings will take. For they have spoken of it several times, so that there seems to be a possibility that they will appear in some sort of a makeup. I, at least, want to have a number of paintings there before they begin with mine, I am sure. And we hear now that they are going to have an exhibition of our work in New York soon.[133] What a pity they can't wait, for our sakes, till an adequate amount of our things arrive there so that we won't be judged by that first stuff. We weren't in the war then, or hardly at all, for there had only been the Marines and the 3d Division at Château-Thierry around early June. This, and some raids in the Toul sector, was our part till then.

November 15, 1918

𝔽inding a car idle, and having heard me express a desire to get out on a trip, Captain Smith, who now has charge of our cars and assigns them to us to prevent any more injury to Lieutenant Mangin's feelings, assigned me the old car that was left, as he and Peixotto were going out in the other, and better one. So, while I protest to him that it is not in good condition, he assures me that as far as he was concerned, I take it this afternoon for a two or three day trip to Sedan, via Verdun, and Varennes, Montfaucon, Stenay, and on into Sedan. I planned to spend tonight at Rembercourt with the boys of the 147th Squadron.

At a point about six or eight kilometres the other side of Bar-le-Duc, my driver informed me that she [the car] was laying down on him, and that he didn't think that we could go on safely. So we go back to Bar-le-Duc where the Press HQ are now, thinking that we could get into their repair shop and, as White said, with three hours' work, fix it. When he finally decides that he can't fix it so that it could be taken on so long a trip as we planned, we plan to go home, if we can get there with it. But there was no way of getting Neufchâteau on the phone, as it was out of order, so there was nothing else to do. This took us three hours, by nursing the old hack along.

But I managed to get some good dope from Major Bulger as to our advance, and the length of our sector, or if one chooses, the width of our advancing army.[134] Starting Sunday, they are to advance for two days, ten kilometres a day, when they are to rest for seventy-two hours to allow the British to get up into line. Also I got word there of the expected entrance of the French troops into Metz, so I was determined to get the old car back and somehow patched up; to turn my misfortune into good fortune by getting over to Metz at the earliest possible minute.[135]

Mayhap the boys weren't surprised to see me back, but pleased, too, at the news I brought of the Metz affair, and at my plan to get them over there, surely on Sunday, as the troops were expecting to go into the town Sunday night. So Dunn has promised to go over the car himself, rather than let it get into the Motor Transportation repair shops, when there would be no telling when one would get it out. . . . [136]

November 16, 1918
❦

Car will be in shape, so Lieutenant Mangin and Captain Dunn say, for an extended trip tomorrow so we will head for Metz and from there, go on up into Luxembourg with our Army of Occupation, perhaps swinging around up thro Verdun and the battlefields there.

November 17, 1918
❦

Wonderful day and we are off at 8:30. We go to Metz via Toul and Pont-à-Mousson, stopping off at Flirey and at Limey to look over the old ground there. Saw the machine gun emplacements that the Boche had built up at the back of the church at Limey. Most unsuspicious-looking from a little distance and absolutely a part of the structure. Also in the graveyard at the rear of the church, a large wooden cross — French — had been shot away. This they reconstructed of concrete, even imitating the bark and grain on the old one, and thro its base they also constructed a pillbox or machine gun post. These two things are thoroughly characteristic, and are fine examples of the skill that has gone into their making.

The country from here on to Pont-à-Mousson is about the most characteristic battlefield on which we fought in the way of continuing all the marks and all the resources of trench and dugout and gun emplacements that are used, besides being very interesting and rolling country, with woods here and there. It's a fine place for material for the making of decorative pictures.

Pont-à-Mousson was a delight to us. The old square is very Spanish in appearance, with an arched or arcaded ground floor that makes it most beautiful. And these have all been barricaded or revetted up to protect the shops behind, thro the long years in which it has been under occasional shellfire and constant bombardment from the air. This revetting with twigs and sandbag and box has been as carefully and regularly done as a fine piece of masonry and it has been a thorough protection, too, from any danger of flying fragments of shells or from bullets.

The town we found full of colored troops and also we found the 329th Field Artillery there, a Wisconsin outfit. We had our dinner with them, and found Captain Lamar (Battery F) of Baraboo, Wisconsin, a most unusual and very inspiring sort of a man. A perfect type of what we like to think an American is or should be: big, finely proportioned, clean, wholesome and amiable; the kind of a man that will accomplish what he sets out to do. Like our Army, he will reach his objective, and ahead of time, too. What a wonderful mess they had. . . . Real American food. As Captain Dunn puts it, "Honest to God food."

After our lunch with Captain Lamar, we start for Metz, going up the left bank of the Moselle, but at Vandières we were stopped by a 2d Army major, who had orders to let no one pass without a special order from the 2d. The road up this far had been put in good condition, for this was all old German terrain. We passed branch roads that were marked "Mined," and also we passed a ruined house near where we turned back, at which were its former owners, back for the first time since they had been forced to evacuate it. And they were a sad party. How dejected and hopeless they seemed, father, mother and a little girl. He carried a basket, lunch, no doubt, and I am sure there were tears in the woman's eyes. They had evidently just that moment arrived.

We turn back and cross the river at Dieulouard below Pont-à-Mousson, and take the road on the other side which is held now by the French troops. We meet with no difficulty here till we reach Corny, where an American car in front of us is trapped by a guard and made to turn back. We are a bit disheartened at this, but whether because he knew ours was a staff car, or because of his mistaking our red, white and blue insignia for French, we will never know. But he passed us without so much as a suspicious look, and we sailed on.

It had been an interesting ride all the way up thro ground that had so recently been held by the Hun and shelled so hard by our guns. At Jouy, not far out of Metz, we were stopped by a sentry who was droll in the extreme as our big car came rolling up toward him, he all the time addressing us with his gun, backing away from the car in a frightened way lest he be run down, yet determined to face us. We stopped and a lieutenant approached. I handed out, not our regular American pass, which there might have been a doubt about in his mind owing to its early date, but our French pass, which may have had no present privilege with it, in this case. But it worked, and seeing it was French, perhaps, and bearing a distinguished French signature, no questions were asked, and we ran on into Metz, that historic city at which even the Americans have gazed with longing eyes for so long.

How often we have watched it bombed at night by the British aeroplanes in the old days, and how our artillerymen have longed to pay their respects to the Boche on its outskirts for so long, but restrained, . . . lest they might demolish too much of the city.

Little we realized, either, why we were stared at so curiously by the civilians that we passed on the outskirts on our entry, or the great enthusiasm that greeted us as we rolled up into the Grand Place Empereur Guillaume. Little children had, far back, tried to climb on our car as we passed. Everywhere there were waving arms and kisses thrown us, and cries of "*Vive La France!*" In a couple of instances, there were cries of "*Vive l'Amérique!*" But for the main part, we were hailed merely as part of their deliverers, for, not knowing we were Americans as we learned later, they knew merely that we must be Allies and probably English.

By the time we had stopped, there was a great mob of excited people around our car, till one could scarcely see where we were going, and we were afraid that we would hurt some of the children. There were plenty of hostile people in the crowd, too, and there were menacing looks. There were girls in the crowds who beseiged the car, shouting and ready to kiss us, but we were just alarmed enough at the situation, and the fact, as we had just learned, that we were the first of their liberators to reach Metz, and that the French had not arrived, and that they weren't expected till 5:30 (it was now 1:30), that much as we might have enjoyed their conventional and inevitable offerings, we had no time nor interest.

We were showered with attention from the time that they learned we were Americans, and they lost no time in telling us how much they owed to the Americans. They told us we were the first of the Allies to enter their town (this couldn't have been true, though we may have been the first that were seen by them, for I believe there were some men put into the hospital in the morning). We tried to learn if there were any French HQs, but there was none, and, as they told us, the Boche were only then leaving at the other end of the town. We asked if there were gendarmes there. They told us there was nothing but patrols of German revolutionary soldiers on patrol, and that they were leaving too.

We decided it would be best to keep moving, so we drove slowly around, picking and forcing our way thro the crowds which, as we got farther down to the cathedral, grew more dense and took on a different tone. Their looks gave them away. They were Boche, and they had evidently been seeing their troops away. And their attitude was decidedly unfriendly and, in a number of instances, menacing. We were spit at many times, and many a face was made at us.

Some of the fellows in our car were a bit restless under it all. For a time, I was, till the excitement began to get hold of me, and I decided the best thing was to see it thro as, after all, nothing could really hurt us, coming as we did on a peaceful mission to a freed people.

We edged round the town, and soon found ourselves back at the Place. So we pulled up in a corner, and the crowd had its way with us for a time. By this time, the word had gotten round that the Americans were there, and there was all the town around us by the time we were stopped. I talked to as many as I could at one time, answering all the questions I could. "When were the French coming? When the Americans? Were we going to stay and please do?" And with pointing fingers, they would show us "*sales* Boches" in the crowd around us. They had heard that a French general would arrive at 5:30 to set up a bureau near the Gare. We knew the French troops were not there yet, but we had passed many of them on the way up, and told them so, and that undoubtedly they would all enter the city in the evening. This pleased them, tho they were disappointed when we told them that the American troops were not coming.

While a couple of the fellows were discussing the advisability of pulling back out of the city to spend the night, as it was growing dark, and they were a bit afraid of a possible hostile demonstration when night came, owing to the frowns we had met with from the Boche, I was asking about a hotel. And finding a boy who seemed honest and absolutely Lorraine, and French Lorraine, who was willing to take me to it, with Dunn, I go down and find that another American car has just pulled into the city after us, and had headed strait for the hotel; this was Carter Harrison, one-time mayor of Chicago, and now in the Red Cross. They had just registered at the hotel, getting their names down ahead of ours, but first after a long and distinguished line of German high officers . . . as well.

We found that we could have rooms and a place for our car. So back we go, delighted. When we tell the fellows at the car of what we had done (for we had registered the crowd), and that these others had just arrived, Harding changes at once, and we are all united in our determination to stay and enjoy it all, too. For it took on now the possibility of a delightful, even if a slightly dangerous, adventure.

But what a difficult drive it was down to the hotel, short a distance as it was. Our car was simply hidden with the children that were draped over it, and we were fearful lest some of the smaller ones, mere infants, should slip and fall under the wheels. At last we arrived. Taking our things out of the car to put in our rooms, lest something happen to them in the night, we leave our driver, White, to put the car in the shed, while we are shown to our rooms.

The Grand Hotel Europäischer (Ancien Hotel de l'Europe) is the leading hotel in the town, and has been used since the outbreak of the war as a hotel for the higher German officers. It is quite imposing with its heavy iron grille that opens into quite a large court with the hotel an open square around it. Only this morning has the huge sign across its front been changed to French, though the smaller one on the very top has been left, probably out of respect to the sentiments of Herr Hafen, the *propriétaire.* How like the Kaiser he is, with his waxed moustache. How German everything was from the *garçon,* who with mighty efforts, finally got our things up to the rooms, which still had pinned on their walls the military billeting notices, which he tried at once to tear down. We were the first to enter the rooms after the Huns left, and they were not expecting us so soon. Taken unawares, they were. I rescued my signs from the floor where he had thrown them, and mean to keep them. When he found I wanted them, he decided to leave the others for the fellows to take down themselves. The rooms were large and comfortable. Four Marks was the price. They were piping hot. But the place showed lack of the ordinary care such a hotel would get in peacetime.

On going downstairs, we found that five French officers had just arrived. All captains but two, and members of the French Mission from our GHQ. They were pleased to see us, but a bit crestfallen, I am sure, to find that, after all, they were beaten into the town by us. They had no official mission there, they told us, but that the French troops were coming in the morning at 9, and that the Grand Revue was set for Tuesday morning. And that they were going to stay for it and would we? We assured them we were. They offered to be of any use to us they could. Said that the Boche were in a bad mood in the town, and advised us not to venture out on the streets at night unless we went together.

We found that they had decided at the desk that there was no place for our car in their stalls, and that we must take it, or rather be shown to a place, some five minutes away, that they assured us was perfectly safe. We didn't like this, not knowing what might happen to it in these strange and unusual surroundings. A couple of German soldiers came in on bicycles and, on opening a stall for their wheels, we saw that there was to be ample room left for our car. Talking with them, we found they were Lorraine and French, forced into the German army; that they had just been discharged in Belgium, and had ridden all the way down to Metz, which was their home. They saw our situation as to the car, and insisted that it be put in with their wheels. We saw the doors firmly locked and the keys back with the clerk, then we felt free, and mingled a bit with the curious, but enthusiastic, crowd that had collected in the court and at the gates.

We were surely creating excitement. So also the French officers, tho I am sure we had the most of it. Arranging to meet them at 8 to have dinner there with them, they went their way into the great crowd and in a moment we went ours.

How we were received on the streets, I shall never forget. Everyone saluted, tho there were whispered discussions here and there, and we would hear the words "*Anglais*," till someone would say "*Américaines*," and the word would be taken up in a wave and "*Vive l'Amérique*" would greet us till the line was broken, perhaps by a group of Boche, to be taken up again. Children and even grownups ran along, pulling at our hands for a greeting.

When we return to the hotel, we find a Major Stoppenbach and a captain there. They were a fine sort, and we went to the dining room anon. Hafen the *propriétaire*, speaking good English, was courtesy itself. He arranged a table for us, and showed us the card for the day. There was a party of happy men, who looked German, but from their happiness and enthusiasm at seeing us, meant them to be taken for "*tout à fait*" Lorraines. They insisted on ordering wine for us, and fine wine it was too. They drank it first to our health so, as the major said, "No poison there." And we drank long and deeply, too.

The Frenchmen didn't put in an appearance, so we ordered our dinner. The major ordered champagne and the Lorraines ordered more wine of the same mark for us. Hafen and Madame came often to see if things went well, and we were served by the strangest and saddest German girl that one could possibly imagine. Nervous in the extreme, she seemed to startle at everything. She must have been a victim of the same propaganda that was fed to the German soldiers by their officers, that the Americans were not to be trusted, and that they would victimize them when they came, for she seemed to have a genuine fear of something impending.

Hafen had to tell us of his pride in his house and all the celebrities he had had there, from the Kaiser and Empress down to the Crown Prince who, he assured us, was really a very fine fellow. Then he told us of the special register he had in which they had all put their signatures, and this he was so proud to show us. Everyone was there in the Imperial machine save Hindenburg, who was to have been there, but failed to come. He bent over me as he turned the pages, and as I looked up from time-to-time at him from below, I shall always think how like he was to many a picture one sees of his worshipped master, for we were all convinced from his talk and his sudden enthusiasms, which he couldn't control, that he was still a loyal subject, and, no doubt, a part of their secret service. There was no doubt but that he had been for some time an officer, and a high one, in his majesty's service. He counts on selling this book of autographs for a fancy price to some rich American, tho I think his chances of getting the $50,000 he expects were much better before the war.

We had a good dinner at ten francs.

Then we all take to the streets. The noise of the Lorrainers in their celebrations and their new-found liberty and their freedom to talk French again after so many years, was intense. They were tearing thro the streets in long lines singing the Marseillaise and shouting. At the cathedral, we were pulled into their crowd and went along with the rest, and maybe they weren't content to have us taking a part in it! When they would get to the sections that they knew were particularly Boche, they would end their songs with a decided "Boche, Boche, Boche" every other beat, and they would keep this up till someone started singing again. It was great fun. The girls were attractive, tho decidedly not French in appearance, and they bore as little evidence, as did any of the people there, of undernourishment.

The party broke up at a late hour, after dancing and singing around the large equestrian statues of Kaiser William and Kaiser Frederick, and the statue of the German soldier that looks from the Esplanade over into France so defiantly. There was talk of tearing these down, but no effort was made while we were with them.

When they broke up at Kaiser Frederick, we four found ourselves arm-in-arm at that time with a group that turned out to be a family party, tho we hadn't suspected it until they began to talk, and the old man who was along suggested that we go to a cafe near there where we had a good chance to see them all and talk. It was the cafe of a friend. One of the women in our party was a widow whose husband had been a German soldier killed in the war. Her sister was wife of the cafe *patron* and served us there. Their father it seemed, too, was in our crowd in the street, tho I hadn't seen him till then. The old man who led us in, a fine old fellow, most refined and most touching in his gratitude to the Americans, had two daughters in the party, who had been arm-in-arm with Dunn and Aylward on the street. The other girl in the party, Marguerite, was with me. The two sisters, very handsome, were also married, their husbands in the German Army also, tho they were out-and-out French Lorraine.

We had a nice visit and talk there, and it was most amusing to hear Aylward, who has a little French, and Dunn, who knows practically none, carry on a conversation with them all. From time-to-time, I was called in to straiten out difficulties in the language. It seems strange for me to be occupying a role of interpreter so often, as I seem to be these days, and while I know I don't talk it well, I am being told often directly and indirectly how well I get along with the French tongue by the French themselves. And I suppose they do mean a bit of what they say, at any rate, so that I feel a little pleased, and I found, tho, that what little German I knew was next to none at all when up against the real thing here, for everyone seems to talk German, so that I have to make them talk French. In the party here, even, it was almost true, for they have talked it for so long that it's almost their tongue now.

Just as we were about to leave, Madame of the cafe came up to me and suggested that it would be well to be quiet when we left if we went in a crowd, and not to sing, for at that late hour in that section, if we weren't a bit careful, we might attract a shot from some Hun; that the night before there had been several shots fired into singing crowds late in the night. The party all saw us to our hotel. We voted that we had had an interesting evening. . . .

November 18, 1918

❧

Today we do the town and a very interesting town we find it, too. We hunt thro the German bookstores for anything of interest on the war, finding a number of magazines and pamphlets that are of value to us. The camera shops interest us too, and I find a fine Erneman with Zeiss Tessar lens that is a bargain, but there isn't enough spare money in the crowd to get it, I fear, for I am low and I know the others are, so pass it up. There seems to be no shortage in camera supplies, particularly as to films, which certainly are scarce in all the Allied countries. Here there are all sizes in plenty in new emulsions. And most of the film packs are in tin cases, which is also to be wondered at, for there is more or less of a shortage of tin elsewhere. All the shops seem filled with supplies, and as we all remarked, one would never guess there was a pinch in Germany from the look of the people and the shops in Metz. Prices, tho, are terrific in most all cases. We found iron crosses today are a fairly low figure, tho they will go up at once now that the Americans are coming! We get a few.

We find also that some time in the night, the two statues, William and, I think, Charles something near it on the Esplanade, were pulled down. . . . Were sorry we missed this.

We see many prisoners, who are coming in great numbers now from the German prisons on foot, in all sorts of conditions, many barely able to walk, and some barefoot. All hungry. They are being looked after, and the hospital has been taken over by the Red Cross, we hear. Today a big truck of supplies arrived. The hospital was found in terrible condition, I hear. James Norman Hall was evacuated thro there yesterday afternoon . . . for Toul.[137] Wish I had known it so that I might have seen him for a time.

We talk with many of the prisoners. Accounts of their experiences vary. Some insist they were well looked after, save that food was scarce, even for the Germans with whom they came in contact. Others insisted that they had rotten treatment and were worked near the front. Others were in mines that were being raided all the time by Allied aviators. Some, who were wounded and bandaged up, said that they had no treatment for their wounds because there was a shortage of bandages and drugs. Many of them were dressed in captured Russian uniforms, black with a wide stripe down the legs. But they were motley and wore whatever they could get. They were all eager for news, too. They knew nothing of the world outside, or what was happening. They had suddenly been freed and told the direction to the rear.

Late this afternoon, we find the correspondents have arrived, a few of them. Also we find that the French, who have arrived today in great numbers and now begin to color the streets as they seem inevitably to do, have opened the *casernes* near the Place, and are letting the soldiers and officers have what they want as souvenirs. We go up and get a number of things we want for our official use including some Boche uniforms.

Having found a nice, reasonable place to eat with considerable character, the Hotel Stadt Lyon, we decide it would be nice to look up and ask the last-night party to dinner with us, the men included. So we run them down from the cafe, but find that they think it best not to, or difficult on account of their children, for one of the sisters has a little baby and the widow a little girl, but they will all be glad to join us later for the processions in the street, and they do, fathers and all.

Later we see the fallen statues. Dunn has his harmonica along, and he plays and we dance in the park there. We find a party trying to pull down the lone German soldier with a short cable around his neck. This looked so dangerous that we order them to stop, so seeing we were officers, they did. But later, on coming back, we found they had pulled down all the decorative wooden structure, that had evidently been erected behind it more or less recently by the Germans for some ceremony, and the pylons at either end were burning. If they had succeeded in getting him over with that short cable, there would have been a number of them injured, too.

There are no police of any sort in town now, and the city has absolute liberty. Yet there seems no disturbances of any sort. It has been very noisy tonight, but there has been order, tho one could only pity the Boche who tried to start anything. Yet what a lot of them there are here. In talking with the French sympathizers here one learns that the Boche number about half. I have talked with a number today who talk French. They all say they are glad the war is over, and they are glad to be free from Germany, but they most decidedly do not want to come under French rule. Others are plainspoken and ask why we came into the war. And they malign the French but say they like the Americans.

Late this afternoon, we meet the French Mission fellows and they give us a copy of the first French paper in four years; three papers that were suppressed at the commencement of the war had now consolidated and got out their first issue today. It spoke of the fact that yesterday, a little after noon, some American officers had arrived at Metz, the first sight they had of their liberators. A little later some French officers had arrived. That referred to us and the French were pleased to show it to us. So we go down in history. And what a history Metz has.

This morning, as we were buying some German papers at one of the numerous little kiosks, covered with German posters, this one down by the river, where we had been enjoying the row of old houses that hung over the water near the dam, an old woman, who had heard there were Americans there, came out to ask us could we please get word to her daughter in Brooklyn that she was now free and safe. She had not been allowed to write to her in four years, nor had she heard from her. She was quite overcome when we informed her that tomorrow, as we had heard, the post to France was to be reestablished.

November 19, 1918

*T*oday is the great Fête. General Mangin is to review the troops as they make their formal entry into the city.[138] The streets are filled with girls and women dressed in gorgeous Lorraine costumes in all colors. And they range from the simplest to the most expensive sort of materials. Everyone wears *cocardes* and everyone is as happy as can be. The revue is set for 11 o'clock, but it is two before the troops arrive. As they are waiting, there is great excitement in the crowd. Drawn up on either side of the statue of Marechal Ney, who, by the way, was a native of Metz, are all of the *citoyens,* most of them bewhiskered and all in long frock coats and well-preserved silk hats.[139] Among them is the old man with whom we have been these two nights, he of the two daughters. And quite distinguished he looks there. They all wear brassards on their arms, and they are to welcome the entry of the liberators to their city, and having greeted the General, with him to review the troops. Well, suddenly they discover in their midst a man whom they evidently know and they resent his being there, and particularly his wearing the brassard which makes him one of them. He's a very nice-looking man and really quite distinguished looking. There is a very old man, about the oldest in the group, with long, thin face and long, white whiskers, who discovers him. I happen to be near when he sees him, and he goes up to him and shouts at the top of his voice, "*Allez* Boche," looks at him with a long, keen glance, and then grabs at the brassard on his arm. Others take up the cry of "Boche," and soon there is pushing and hurrying around him, and finally the old man gives him a push and then begins to pound him, knocking off his hat. Not a word does the Boche say. And wise he is, for they were a rabid lot of old men by this time, and it was most amusing to watch such a scrap among such a group. But they were beginning to handle him pretty rough, and finally a cavalryman rode into the crowd and got him out and they led him away under their protection.

By now, the air was full of aeroplanes, wheeling and cutting capers over the heads of the crowd; about the first aeroplanes to fly over the town ever, that weren't laden with death and destruction for them there. Finally one flies too low, and catches a wing in the telephone wires over the Place, and comes crashing nose-down into the crowd in the Place, killing two little children outright, from all accounts; several died soon after, and there were a couple of people who will die, they say.[140] The pilot, one of the famous French *escadrille* "*Les Cigognes,*" was not killed but his head is badly injured and nose badly broken.[141] He is reported to be one of their big aces, tho I couldn't get his name.

A little later, a messenger arrives, and one of the generals who is waiting, and who has been in charge of the arrangements there, goes up to a little woman and two little girls that are in front of the statue and tells them something. He has informed Madame Mangin that her husband, the General, as he was entering the city, was thrown from his horse and wounded, tho not badly.[142] She doesn't seem to be greatly affected by the bad news, for she leaves smiling. I imagine that after a lifetime of stirring service, such as her husband has seen, things like that become matter-of-fact to her.

I have a good position now from which to view it all, for a place directly opposite was reserved for officers, and I am in the front row. And while I am waiting the arrival, I am entertained by a couple of colonels who chase away small boys who are getting in the front row, and whom they strike with their sticks and call Boche. Sure enough, one of them has a Boche cap on and the colonel knocks it off as he runs after him.

Soon we hear trumpets and then the troops come, Marshal Pétain in the lead, taking at once a position in front of the statue on his white horse.[143] He seems a very human sort, not nearly so military as many of the officers on his staff, but much more military, I must confess, than a couple of Americans who seemed to be attached to some of the officers; one of these was a colonel who chewed gum violently all thro the review. The other was a captain with his hair long and unkempt, who slouched on his horse, and who, horrible! also begins to chew gum later. Do all Americans chew gum? I'll wager that the French officers think so, at any rate. They must have noticed. It's really a fine lot of veterans that pass in review. What a lot they have been thro. And they look the soldier too, every inch of them.

At last it is over, and the crowd breaks, and soon it is dark. And the sky is filled with fireworks, for they are shooting off immense quantities of German flares that have been left behind. At the Hotel, I meet Major Hartney and Captain Lister of the 1st Group, who are there with Lawrence Driggs, whom I meet for the first time.[144] They are very friendly. They ask me if I know where they can get gas for their car, and having investigated for ourselves today, I am able to take them to the *mairie* to make arrangements. Driggs stays behind to meet and to hold Nungesser, the French ace, till we get back.[145]

At the *mairie*, we find that there is a big reception for the French generals. We are asked if we would like to go up to see the show and to have some wine. We would. And we no sooner step inside the door, than we are the centre of a group of those same leading citizens who were at the review, and they overwhelm us with their appreciation of all that America has done for them. So they do homage to us, and they call for wine for us and it's brought in, tray after tray, by girls in beautiful Lorraine costumes, daughters of the leading families, we learn later. They were very amiable and the wine was finest Moselle and Champagne. There was there also Commandant Maré and a French lieutenant.

After some little time, Major Hartney suddenly turned and said to me, "Wouldn't it be fun to take some of the girls out to dinner?" We said, "Fine!" So he asked one if it would be possible. Of course, she said, "No," that it wasn't possible. But the Commandant said, "Oh, we will ask Mama." This made a great hit with the girls, who immediately clapped their hands with glee and begged that it be done. So eight of them were gotten together, and a couple of French lieutenants were added to the party — everyone was loaded into the Major's big Packard, and off we go for a round of the mothers. This was very interesting, for it took us to the very nicest homes in Metz, and home after home was invaded and conquered. They were all delighted, and "What hour would we be thro, so they could come for their daughters?" And we had to name an hour and it was fixed, at a suggestion, at 9:30, and we packed off to the Hotel de l'Europe.

Here was Driggs. Lieutenant Nungesser had gone out for a time, but would be back later, tho he wouldn't have dinner with us. Soon he came, all covered with medals. He was certainly a handsome fellow, much finer looking than his pictures showed him to be. The girls had been told who he was, for you must remember that the Lorraines haven't had all the news of the doings in France. He was a name to them, but not quite so glorious a name as he should have been. But one look at him, and he was the hero to the full, and the applause that was given him from our table was taken up thro the room, so that he had quite an ovation, and he started with the nearest girl and kissed round the table, to their great delight. He talked a while, then left. Then Commandant Maré suggested that all the men ought to kiss all the girls on such a glorious day as this, and we had to do it in the same fashion. Bashful Major Hartney balked at this, but after all the others were finished, he was forced into it, and made the rounds.

We had a fine dinner with nice wine, then the mothers arrived and had coffee with us. And we sat and talked for a time. Everyone got everyone else's signature, then the party broke up. We suggested dancing once, now that the war was over and one could dance again. Then it developed that none of the girls knew how, for they were all seventeen years of age, and before the war started, they were too young to have learned. Luck, or the invitation from the Commandant to take the seat there, put me between the nicest and prettiest of the lot, if such a thing can safely be said, Carmen Willemin and Marthe Dorr. A number of them spoke English, as they had learned it in the schools there.

Dunn, Aylward and Harding were taking some German girls to dinner at the Hotel Metz across the street, and had asked me to come over afterwards. But they had disappeared before I got there. Dropped into the Bodega, a Hun cafe, to see if they were there, but found instead Lincoln Eyre, the *New York World* correspondent who I like very much. This was a very interesting little place, so I sat with him and watched the crowd, all French, who had set out to bait the crowd that run it, who were Huns. They were singing French songs at the top of their voices, and shouting "Kill the Kaiser," and "*Bas les* Boches," and one of the girls at the bar I noticed was crying as I came in, tho later I saw her dancing with one of the Frenchmen.

Soon the crowd tired of this and shouted, "To the Casino." This was another Boche place. So they got single file and went running and twisting their way down the street, singing as they went. Eyre went with them and I followed along, tho somehow I couldn't make myself get in the line with them. But I arrived as soon as they did, and here it was the same thing over again, tho there were more Germans there, and when the one who played the piano, a big, long-haired fellow, broke into a German tune, the leader of the Gang, as I called them, went over and slapped him on the back and made him quit, so he burst at once into the Marseillaise without a murmur. Later a German girl there started a song they didn't like in German, and they made her quit. I neither danced nor drank, but I did talk to one of the German women who ran the place, and had quite a little talk with her in French. She said that she didn't blame the French for carrying on as they did, and knew that they would have to stand it, only as she said, it was pretty hard. For she was Prussian, and she knew that there was nothing to stay here for now, nor did she want to, and that they would go back as soon as they could. A little later I saw her on the floor dancing and smiling and singing up into the face of the big Frenchman who led their crowd. And then I left.

Soon the fellows arrived and told of their dinner and all they had learned from the Germans. They were in for sociological and political research, it seemed!

November 20, 1918
ᴣᵉ

We look over the town in its oldest, most picturesque parts today. Harding and I take a walk out along the river to the northeast, when we came to an arsenal where there are numbers of cannon left behind. We made some photos here, then in looking over the place, found a number of field periscopes, one of which the French captain of the 505th Infantry, who was in charge of that group of *casernes,* gave me, so I carried it away, glad to have it. . . .

Coming along the street on our return, as a little boy ran up and tried to take our hands, a woman in a doorway called to us not to take his, and called him a dirty Boche. This same sort of thing has happened a number of times. They seem to have them spotted.

Eat at the Stadt Lyon again. It surely does have good food. And it's one of the few places I have struck where I can get good cider. At night we go to the Cafe Astoria, and then to the restaurant next door to it. On going back to the Astoria for our after-dinner coffee, we found that a new order had been posted by the new authorities forbidding the serving of drinks or food in any of the cafes after 8:30, so we had to go without. There was a notice in plain language posted there saying . . . that it was forbidden. The lieutenant, who had asked us earlier in the evening on the street where we were going and if we had yet seen the battlefields, was there, and he pretended to recognize us, and to explain to the proprietress that she could serve us all right, and that it didn't apply to officers. We told her they had just served us dinner next door at a later hour than the notice mentioned (20:30), so after a brief parley, she went out to see them there and came back and said, "All right," she would serve us. But in a few minutes she had thought better of it, so we didn't argue with her, as we only wanted a cup of coffee. But the French lieutenant did argue for us and urged her to serve us, which seemed, at the time, very decent of him. . . .

November 21, 1918
ᴣᵉ

We get away early this morning for Neufchâteau. Lo and behold here is the French lieutenant around in the court this morning. As the first night when we met him on the street, he asks us if we are going to Nancy, and would we have a place in the car for him. We tell him no, that we are bound to Neufchâteau. He seems to be interested, too, in all the junk that we have, and we see him also looking over the cars of the others that are there. Finally, he prowls around ours, trying to see inside. Walks away nervously, comes back after a while, looks around all the cars again, scanning the numbers, apparently, till we get suspicious. Finally, after a time, he approaches me again, and asks if I knew if any of the others were going to Nancy. And had we seen the battlefields? Finally, he carelessly walks alongside of our car, which by now, looks like a museum, opens the door, looks inside, and remarks on the car, how practical it is, and how much room there is in a car of that type, and walks away. We decide he has all the dope he evidently is looking for, for we have decided he is some sort of a detective, tho a terribly amateurish one. But we aren't worried, for all the stuff we have has been given us by the French officers, so we give it up. . . . Metz is out of bounds for Americans, and practically everyone there was without leave or without permit to enter, and MPs were being established to send them back. But we had passes, and were in a position to satisfy any curious MP should he hold us up. But it was strange. He seemed to give much interest to the hotel also. Perhaps he also had an eye on the *patron.*

We go around to the see the statue of the German soldier that we heard had been finally taken down, but we find it still there with the cable still on it, but still defying them.

We pull out for Pont-à-Mousson, taking another road for part of the way. Along this road in a field, we come across a dummy tank, of the French Renault type, made of wire on a wooden frame. The silhouette is exact; all the proportions seem correct. On each side of it are fastened two pieces of armor plate — one covering the gunner in the turret, the other covering the tank in the rear. It had marks of machine gun or perhaps anti-tank bullets on these plates which were marked with red spots. And it was undoubtedly for target practice. I took some photos of it as a curious and interesting detail.

Had lunch again with Captain Lamar at Pont-à-Mousson. Made some photos there and a sketch, watched the 75s drill, listened to the colored band still there, and came home.

They are cleaning up Pont-à-Mousson. Soon it will be a different place. It's a fine old town. The architecture of the Place there is decidedly artistic and the whole effect of it Spanish. This was verified while we were there by the mayor of the town, who saw Aylward sketching, and came out to talk a bit. The revetted protection in all the arches gives an interesting effect. These they have not yet begun to remove. Many of the shops behind them have notices against breaking into them. Others are open, and have been looted by our men. There was a bookstore there that had still many interesting books and other things in it. I had thought once of taking one or two, as so many others had done, but thought better of it, for I don't like the idea, and there's too much of it being done. Besides, if an officer were caught at it, even tho it were not *défendu,* it would look none too well.

We have had really a remarkable trip. I wouldn't have missed the experience at Metz for worlds. I took many photos which will be fine to have. I talked much with the people there, and got an insight into the situation there that I am glad to have. I think, too, that I got an insight into the working of the German mind as it sees their situation now with their failure in the war. And I am sure, from conditions reflected there, that the German people, as a nation, are not so badly off in the matter of matériel, and perhaps even food, as they would have the world believe. It seems that they are really squealing now and, as Solf appealed to Wilson to ameliorate the peace terms as much as possible, so, too, are they playing up to the Americans now, in the hope of making friends.[146]

There seemed to be plenty of coal in Metz. You would see load after load of it being unloaded in the streets and put away in the houses. The hotel was too hot, and the restaurants abundantly heated. There was plenty of loaf sugar everywhere. And there seemed to be plenty of meat. Shops had every appearance of prosperous peacetimes, tho, as I say, things were high, and they were taking advantage of their liberators by exacting the full exchange rate for Marks. This the French are putting a stop to, and many of the shops on the last day were asking even exchange: a franc for a Mark. . . .

CHAPTER 7

LUXEMBOURG AND THE RHINE

The U.S. force established to participate in the joint Allied occupation of the Rhineland was the 3d Army. Created on November 7, 1918, its first commander was Major General Joseph T. Dickman, who had previously commanded the 3d Division, IV Corps (beginning on August 18, 1918), and I Corps (as of October 12). The 3d's second commander was Lieutenant General Hunter Liggett, who had led the 41st Division, the I Corps(from January 20 to October 12, 1918), and the 1st Army (from October 16). He took command of the 3d on May 2, 1919, remaining until July 2, when it was dissolved. The U.S. occupation troops were then redesignated the American Forces in Germany — the AFG — and a new commander arrived, taking charge on July 8. He was Major General Henry Tureman Allen, who had brought the 90th Division to France, fought with it through St. Mihiel and the Meuse-Argonne, and later commanded the VII, VIII, and IX Army Corps. He remained in charge of the AFG until its withdrawal in January 1923.

The 3d Army began its long, arduous march toward Germany on November 17, arriving in Luxembourg three days later. From November 21 to 30, it proceeded through the grand duchy, arriving at the German frontier on December 1. By December 7, its first units were in Coblenz, the Rhineland city that was designated the headquarters of the U.S. troops in Germany. On December 13, U.S. forces crossed the Rhine, taking up positions in the bridgehead on the eastern bank and completing their occupation four days later.

The units earmarked for Rhineland service initially included the 1st, 2d, 3d, 4th, 5th, 32d, 42d, 89th, and 90th Divisions. Numbering about 240,000 men, the U.S. controlled a zone of approximately 2,500 square miles, extending from Luxembourg to an area east of the Rhine.[147]

However, the Rhineland occupation was soon the cause of considerable

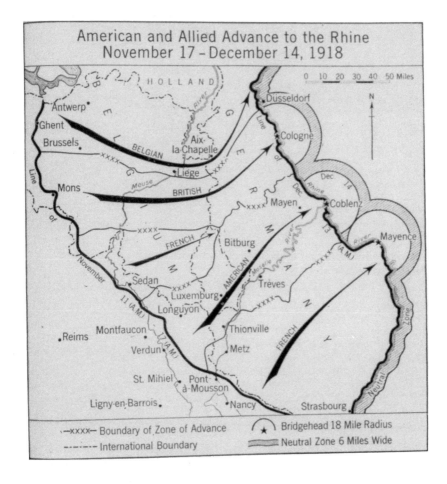

American and Allied Advance to the Rhine
November 17 - December 14, 1918

friction among the occupying powers. The French were fearful that the British and U.S. forces might not be sufficiently firm with the Germans. To ensure a greater French presence, Marshal Ferdinand Foch, the supreme allied commander, removed the southern one-third of the Coblenz bridgehead from U.S. control on December 8, placing it under French administration.

Another source of discord concerned the occupation of Luxembourg. Technically a liberated neutral country, it was the first nation occupied by Germany at the beginning of the war. The grand duchy was originally

Zone of American Army of Occupation, December 21, 1918

entrusted to the U.S. forces, but the French desired to move in. After numerous altercations, the U.S. troops retained full possession, though Foch obtained the right to maintain a secondary headquarters there.

The Germans were quick to exploit the antagonisms that surfaced in the Allied camp, which explains the friendliness toward the U.S. soldiers that Townsend noted. Subsequently, the U.S. forces retained their zone in Germany until January 27, 1923, but in the process, they withdrew most of their troops; by the time of their departure, only a token force remained.

It must have been a thrill for anyone in the 3d Army to proceed into Germany so soon after the armistice. The artists, with their freedom of movement, were certainly not to be denied the opportunity and attached themselves to the Army of Occupation. First visiting Luxembourg, both the little country and the city by that name, Townsend and some of the others did take time out for yet another hurried trip to Paris before going on to Coblenz.

Townsend's observations offer a unique insight into conditions prevailing in both Luxembourg and Germany at war's end. His account also provides some analysis regarding the attitudes prevalent among the French, the Germans, and the U.S. troops at this crucial time in their respective histories.

November 24, 1918

With Captains Dunn, Harding and Aylward, I start for Luxembourg with the Army of Occupation, the 3d Army. We go via Nancy and Metz. Starting late, darkness finds us at Metz, so we spend the night there and find the town quite a different place from the week previous. It is now filled with French soldiers and officers. The prices at the cafes have risen, taking advantage, no doubt, of the presence of so many officers with money to spend on food. At the cafe where we had had such a good meal before with real Munich beer, we found the prices so much augmented that we had considerable discussion with the *patron* over it. He had not only raised his prices for pay in Marks, which owing to the low rate in Allied exchange is no doubt necessary for them to come out even on their stuff, but for pay in francs they had also raised it, using the same argument which was, of course, absurd, and in addition, they were transforming the price into francs at the old pre-war rate — 1 = 1.25. We knew there was a French order . . . now fixing an even rate, Mark for franc, and many of the stores and the hotels had dropped to this before we left last time. So it finally ended in our demanding that he make us out a bill with the price in Marks, this also changed to francs at his rate of 1.25, then we insisted that he receipt the bill before we paid him. We had him pretty well frightened, and there were French officers there who backed us up, and said for us to go ahead, and then to turn it into the *Prefecture*. Of course, this was what we were threatening to do all the time, but having frightened the *patron* and having the Germans who were there also sort of uneasy over it all, and what they might well take for the sort of insistence on a square deal that henceforth was going to be demanded of them there in Metz, we did nothing further about it, for we were to pull out early in the morning.

After dinner, we went to the Astoria for coffee and cake. This was packed. We sat here and smoked and watched the crowds come and go. It's a sort of a Cafe de la Paix, and quite as large. Tonight there were numbers of girls all over the town in Lorraine costumes collecting money for some fund for relief of American wounded. There were a number of these girls in the cafe here, and among them were Carmen Willemin and Germaine Etienne, two of the very nice girls who were at the dinner party Tuesday night at the Hotel de l'Europe. Had a nice conversation with them; they had seen me first and were quite delighted to find me, apparently, and they seemed sorry to have to tell me that Commandant Maré had left Metz and was stationed at Nancy now, and that they missed him. I imagine that they were counting on him for more freedom as he was able to get for them that night with us all.

The new closing order has really gone into effect now, and cafes must close at 8:30. We went around to the Bodega but found it closed. . . .

Before I turned in, I took a long walk down the Nancy road to Montigny to Cafe Clement where I had a long talk with Mr. Clement who I had met before. This is the part of Metz that was so badly air-raided the last two months of the war, being near the car shops. He informed me that there was never a night for over two months that there wasn't a raid, and that they were forced to take shelter in the *abris*. He informed me also that yesterday the French had taken to Nancy to intern and possibly for trial, 400 Boche civilians that they had been quietly rounding up since they had gotten possession of the town. They have put the screws on tight, it seems. It is now out of bounds for our soldiers, and while they still flock here . . . AWOL, they are being put under arrest about as soon as they arrive by a very efficient force of our MPs. Officers are being arrested also, and either held for trial or reported. We have orders, tho, that will see us thro O.K. In a talk with one of the MPs tonight, I asked him a lot of questions about it all, but he never asked to see my papers, and I didn't venture to tell him that I had orders. But we weren't molested this day.

Walked around to see if the statue of the German soldier was yet torn down, but he was there as defiant as ever, tho he is now all decorated, most undignified too.

The *patron* at the Grand Hotel de l'Europe was as pleased as he could make himself appear to have us come back to him. I succeeded in getting my same room again. The others were not so fortunate and had to go higher up.

November 25, 1918

𝕒

*T*ook a little turn around the town this morning in the fog. Bought a few German magazines with war photos in them and hunted up a camera shop to buy a certain Erneman 9 x 12 focal plane shutter camera with a 4.5 Zeiss Tessar lens, that I saw last week at a bargain price. Alas, it has been sold. And I am desolate!

We head for Luxembourg via Diedenhofen, thro a thick fog. Could see nothing of the country on the way up. . . . As we passed Hespérange nearing Luxembourg, we saw Peixotto and Smith working there in the street. On the way in, we passed someone who looked like Captain Embury.[148] And later, when we were hunting the Press Section HQ, which was extremely difficult to find, we met Embury in the street. He was still with the 4th Corps with their HQ at Hespérange. Had lunch, Harding and I, at officers' mess with Lieutenant Grantland Rice and Captain Embury.[149]

Afterwards, we went over to Luxembourg proper where Dunn and Aylward had already succeeded in finding the Press and had lunched with them. Luxembourg is quite a lovely city. In the fog at least. Fine aristocratic houses, wide streets, wonderful-looking shops and hotels, and apparently no very poor quarter.

From the Press, we learned that their reception of the Americans had been almost too good to be true, a long, grand Fête, throwing open their houses to the fellows and treating them royally, charging them nothing for their rooms, and even feeding them and taking nothing for this service, so glad they were trying to make themselves appear. Some Americans pretend to think that a lot of this is really put-on, but from what I have seen of the people here, they won't go to this length of financial sacrifice to show it. At any rate, they have been doing all they could to make it pleasant for our men and officers. And our men admitted that it had been pleasant, too. There had been dancing every night, and a particularly lively party every night till then at the Casino, a Liberal Club that is opposed to the Royalist party here, demanding the abdication of the Grand Duchess, and having the unique distinction of having refused admittance to the German officers all thro their occupation of Luxembourg. . . .

We meet Morgan and Duncan on the street just starting back to Neufchâteau. They have a room in a private house, and as they are giving it up, recommend that Harding and I take it. Also want me to go around and act as interpreter for them as they settle up. She, Mme. Roeser-Thiel, #37, rue Joseph II, refused to take anything. Finally they insisted, with my aid, on five francs the night for the both of them. And we took it from then. They were a fine couple, thoroughly anti-Boche. And they were truly happy at the coming of the deliverers, for they, like many a Luxembourgois, consider that they have been delivered from something that has ever been a menace to them, and they credit the Americans with the deliverance, just as do the Lorrainers and most of the French people now.

We learn of the escapade of five of the correspondents, who against the terms of their agreement with the Army, slipped quietly into Germany by way of Belgium, and at the invitation of, or with the protection and credentials of the German Government, took a train to Berlin, sending their cars back to Luxembourg. This has caused a great stir in G-2-D, and there is high talk of meting out to them some dire penalty. Opinion as to what will happen to them is diverse. Everyone agrees that they are broken as far as their career goes. I don't quite think this, tho I do admit the gravity of their act as far as their relations with the Army are concerned, and they merit whatever the AEF sees fit to do to them which, after all, will probably be only the forfeiture of their bonds, $3,000 each. As for violating the terms of the armistice in crossing into enemy country, there can be no real thought of this, for from every evidence in hand, they went with the consent and thorough approval of the German Government. That they will get good stories and even much information that might be of service to the Army, there can be no doubt, but the censor has closed all avenues of communication with their papers for them. We await the outcome with interest. The men involved are Eyre, Corey, Seldes, Smith and Lyon.[150]

We look around the town a bit and find it all that it promised. Words will not do it justice, tho the postcards which I pick up will help to show its loveliness.

Have a good dinner at the Press mess. Afterwards we go with Major Bulger to the Grand Hotel, where we see one of the generals of the Luxembourg Army, glorified with a most amazing uniform. There was some sort of a reception and he was receiving in the foyer. He was tall with thin legs, trousered tight at the knees and wide at the bottom with a broad crimson stripe down each leg, with a swallowtail coat and a long sword that hammocked almost to the floor . . . and trailed on it. And over all was his pale, emaciated head with expressionless eyes and long, waxed moustaches, and then with the necessary monocle. I can almost see him now, as he swayed there before his guests, his knees together, his feet apart, and shook their hands, high, afar, and by the fingertips. He was covered with white trappings and silver braid.

Afterwards, we went to the Casino, but it was dead. No dancing this night. As the Major said, he imagined that their three days and nights of revel had been quite too much for them, and they were sleeping for another three. Worse luck for us.

The Army of the Duchy seems to be quite a pleasantry with our men. At the reception for General Pershing, it was out in almost its complete force: 250 men. Two hundred and thirty-four were able to be present, the others having the flu. The Admiral of the Navy was to have been at the review but, having lost an oar, was unable to get over with his fleet!

The people seem very friendly on all sides, but there seems to be a decided undercurrent of Boche looks, in spite of the protestations of the staunch ones.

November 26, 1918

𝕏

To Diekirch and Grevenmacher to see the frontier that our boys are now patrolling, with our army filling in behind them. We find the country very beautiful, but we are struck by the absence of livestock throughout. At the first, the towns thro which we pass seem nothing out of the ordinary, but as we get farther into the hills and nearer Germany and the Moselle and Sauer Rivers, things change.

We have a fine dinner at Diekirch. Ten francs. Bread is unusually good. Unlimited quantities of potatoes and there was butter and real milk.

The ride down the Sauer was like a dream. We drive on the edge of the narrow stream, on the other bank of which is hated Germany, with the lovely hills there patterned with tiny fields and with vineyards as one imagines the Rhine to be. Here and there are little towns nestling quietly by the stream, or else they cling above on the hillside. Ever our boys walk the other side, gun on shoulder, here and there a machine gun pointing a warning finger at any plotting thinker on the hill or in the town.

So down to Grevenmacher, its bridge guarded by our sentries, our men camped along the waterfront where, but for the mud, they would have an unexcelled drill ground. But it's a drill ground just the same. Field kitchens are up and there's the inevitable crowd of begging children, and more timid grownups, waiting till the boys are ready to hand them some coveted morsel of food, for all food looks good to the very poor, who are unable to buy what seems to be a perfectly adequate supply everywhere, save for the price. The stream is filled with wagons being washed and trucks being washed and harness being washed, and what isn't being washed, is being polished, for they seem determined to keep the boys at work, and, as one of the boys said, they hunt these muddy holes so that there will be something that needs washing.

Drove home thro Little Switzerland! No excitement tonight at the cafes. Home and to bed.

November 27, 1918

Today we go to Remich and up the river to Grevenmacher then back to Luxembourg. See more of the town as we drive in low along the river under the ruins. Take a walk at dusk down by the old dam and the overhanging houses. Then over the old wall to the ruins near the old stone bridge. Wonderful here, and what a lot of fine subjects to paint. . . .

November 28, 1918

Down at the office early this morning — Thanksgiving Day. Found Seldes there; had just come in on the morning train from the frontier. He seemed scared and dreading the arrival of the officers in charge. Have an idea that he lost his nerve there and beat it back to try to square up. Told us something of what he had seen of the revolution in Berlin; of how he had seen an officer shot near him; of how there was plenty of food and prices not too high, and how there was no opposition to their going into Berlin, and all-in-all, he wouldn't have missed it for the world. Little he knew, yet, of what steps had already been taken to stop their stories. We pretended to feel sorry for him, and told him how Major James was there hunting for them, and left him paler than ever.

We start for Diekirch this morning to go out from there to Vianden. We stop at Mersch on the way for gas. Find this the HQ for the 42d Division and find them with the Thanksgiving dinner for the Command's mess out in the street being photoed by their official photographers and by old Burr Mackintosh. In the group that was posing with the real roast turkey and the live goose and the mince pies was William Slavens McNutt, the correspondent who came over for *Collier's*. We had a talk with him afterwards. Then Mackintosh took pictures of the four of us, promising to send prints to us later. Then on to dinner at the little hotel at Diekirch.

Here we meet a very interesting man — Max Kuborn — son of the Chief of Customs of the Grand Duchy of Luxembourg. He himself has been chief of the Comité de Secours Français-Belge since the commencement of the war. Nine months ago, he was captured as he was home fishing from the bridge in the City of Luxembourg, his home. At that time, he weighed, so he said, 245 pounds. He now weighs 164, and has recently been very ill in prison. He had just been brought from the prison at Treves by one of our ambulances to this hotel, which is the home of his fiancee. Soon he was to go to his home in Luxembourg, of which we gave him the first news. He was surprised and gratified to hear that the American 3d Army had its HQ there. He knew well our landlady, when we told him where we were staying, and asked us to carry his respects to her when we returned. He sat and talked to me all thro our meal and, as we were going down to Grevenmacher later perhaps, he gave me a note to a very dear friend of his, a wine merchant who was living at a hotel there. He told us many things that he had seen and of his prison experience; of all that he had seen of Boche atrocities, and all the evidence he had collected in his official capacity. And it was for his bitterness and all the facts in his possession that he had been hunted down and persecuted by German authorities.

He spoke of having seen, at the commencement of the war, 400 Belgians lined up and shot at Arlon, because of sniping by some of the civilians at the troops going thro.

He spoke of his having had six trials since he was in prison, but that each time there was a disagreement . . . as to whether he should be executed or not, on account of his position as a Luxembourgois, which was a neutral state officially, and then he told how conditions had been a bit relaxed for him in the prison, and how they let him order and pay for his own food. This, for six francs each meal, was nothing more than a trifle better soup, he said, and some military bread, and now and then a vegetable.

He told of the contempt that he found the German officers had for the American army when he was first imprisoned. Also their contempt for the magnitude of our plans, which they characterized as boasting, pure and simple, to frighten them. But that at the very last now, in his talks with the officers, they were very frank and open in their praise of the Americans, both as to men and equipment, and as to their military tactics.

He had seen recently on the streets of Treves, which he says is absolutely the worst of all the Prussian cities, a French officer, who had been released from prison, shot on the streets by some unknown person. He feels sure that when the Americans arrive, there will be trouble. And he is sure that the war is not over, for it will be a long time before there will be a stable government there, and that there will be calls on our troops.

He has seen in the prison where he was, a French prisoner, for some offense or resistance, absolutely dismembered.

After dinner, we go on to Vianden, and are truly enchanted with this wonderful ruin and this lovely city, that clusters around the bottom of the high hill on which it stands. This part of Luxembourg was out of the zone of our army a bit, and in going up there, we noticed that on all the arc d'triomphes that had been erected, there were no American flags. Nor were there any on the arch that greeted you as you entered . . . on the little road that corkscrewed down to the village of Vianden. A few children shied off the streets and looked at us strangely as we walked down, our car following us down. This town is on the very frontier and, while it is one of the great tourist attractions of Luxembourg, it has a very German look, both as to village, castle and inhabitants. Everyone seemed afraid of us. There were no troops here of any description. Finally, from a window, we saw a little home-made American flag with only a few stripes on it, and three or four metal stars sewed on it. This got a salute from us, you can bet.

A crowd of the curious had gathered down the street. News of our coming had gotten them out. But there was no real enthusiasm, till finally an old man came running out of a hardware store, and in good French, asked if we were English, and welcome to their town. When he learned we were Americans, his joy knew no bounds. He was a decidedly Yankee type of a man, with a thin, keen face, and a brush of whiskers. His name was Schumaker, and the store was his.

Soon another friendly man arrived, and I talked with them. A number of the crowd came nearer to hear the conversation. We were the first American uniforms they had ever seen. The Germans had left last Saturday, and they had gotten busy and decorated their town to await the entry of their deliverers, which they understood was to be at once. And here we were the first, absolutely the first, of the Allies to arrive, and while the two men were so glad to see us, the others didn't know quite how to act. They may have been told by the Germans that we were to be feared when we did come. While the boys went back up the street to see an American Army water tank that the men said had been captured and brought there by the Germans, I talked with the men. They took me down to show me the view up at the ruin from the bridge and then I left.

Stopping to buy some postcards, a woman came rushing in to talk to the American that she heard was here and couldn't she bring her daughter in to talk to me; she had lived in Brooklyn. She brought her, a very bashful girl who spoke good English, but who seemed too shy to talk. Then we left.

How strange it all seemed, and there was something pathetic, too, about it all; their long wait for their deliverers with their decorations up, and no one arriving till they must have wondered why. They were anxious to know, then, when they might expect them. If it had been the Americans who were to come, we could have told them, but as for the French, we didn't know, but I told them I thought tomorrow, or the day after, at the latest; that we had seen them on their way here. What else could we say?

Had a great Thanksgiving dinner in Luxembourg tonight at the Press. They had hoped to buy some chickens in the market yesterday morning, but found they were bringing thirty francs apiece. So we had roast young pork instead, with so many good things added that we never missed the fowl. There was wine and champagne, and fine peach pie, and then Dunn and Major Bulger played the violin, and Major James was song leader, and succeeded in getting out of their systems about all the army songs ever sung. And Grantland Rice dashed off a fine parody of "Darling I Am Coming Home," and then we broke up. There was no dancing, as we had hoped, tho, at the Casino. But it had been a great day.

At Grevenmacher, on the way home, we saw a general who was driving around among the troops calling down many of the boys, and giving them pointed lectures on military bearing. There are so many replacements in these veteran divisions that make up the 3d Army, that they are concerned to get them into a class with the others as to their appearance.

Had a long talk after the dinner with Major James, at the office, as to our plans for the winter. It ended in his ordering us back tomorrow to go to Paris to look into the studio situation and to make a report. So back we will go, as there must be some action soon. We are to come back up here to go into Coblenz with the Army when it goes in around the 12th, and as there is nothing more . . . to keep us here now, it seemed to him, as to us, the proper time to investigate. The only difficulty is that we are not to close for anything, as they must take the matter up with General Nolan.

November 29, 1918

Go back to Neufchâteau. Stop for dinner at Metz at noon. I find the camera is back in the window. Wasn't paid for or something, so I get it, after all. Am happy, tho there is no case for it, and this will mean a hunt, as will the getting of films, unless I get German ones here at fancy prices.

December 1–8, 1918
❧

𝒲e arrive in Paris on a Sunday night at 8 o'clock. Eat first, then spend all the time till 11:45 finding a place to sleep. Everything is crowded. I finally take them over to the old Latin Quarter, thinking we can surely find room there. But it's the same there. Finally, one hotel suggests that they try the Lutetia for us on the phone, and they say they can give us an emergency accommodation. So we take it. This means beds made up on the floor, three of them in the billiard room. They have one fine apartment at thirty-five francs. Dunn takes this, and he keeps it all thro our stay in Paris. We are forced to keep ours for two nights, thro inability to find anything else. I finally do get a room at the Hotel du Tibre, where I always stay, and Harding and Aylward get a room for two in the Lutetia. I introduce the boys to Juven's for food. . . . And soon the boys are part of the Quarter and delighted with it.

We get a lot of information about studios . . . after having spent a more or less fruitless day. It's a serious proposition on account of the moratorium that lets all the mobilized artists keep their studios without having to pay any rent for them. They don't dare try to sublet them, for obvious reasons, and the landlords' hands are similarly tied. And there is now a great demand for studios by all sorts of civilians who are coming into the city. Here we are searching them out without any power to nail one down when we find it. We spend our entire time looking them up, tho getting a line on the situation in the various quarters.

I take up also the matter of the delay of our pictures in reaching Paris, and in getting away from there. Also the matter of the photos that were to be made of them for us that have never been delivered. Get a case for my new camera and films, after all sorts of exasperating red tape.

We see the King and Queen of Belgium on their arrival. And what a city it is this day, and night, too. The town is veritably wild.

I go to Mayol's one night. Good music hall stuff and much classier than anything at home would be.

Jo Davidson . . . has arrived in Paris to do portraits of the Army, we hear.[151]

Then back to Neufchâteau, coming down in the compartment with a general of the 27th Division. Had a very interesting talk with him. He had lots of questions to ask us, as they naturally had gotten little news of the happenings down in this part of the field, for they have spent their entire time since arrival in Belgium and in the north with the British, where they have distinguished themselves.

Home at last! And no one happy to be back here, either. No one is longer content here; have been here too long.

December 9, 1918
ૐ

Picking up loose ends of correspondence. Tomorrow to Coblenz!

December 10, 1918
ૐ

We leave for Coblenz this morning, going by way of Nancy, where at the Bank Alsace-Lorraine we purchase Marks at seventy-five *centimes*. Then on into Metz, where we have our lunch at the Stadt Lyon. We drove in thro the Rue Serpenoise, and were surprised to find that window after window had been smashed in the shops that we passed, and there were French soldiers guarding the stores that were closed, so it was easy to guess that the Lorrainers had been settling old scores with these Hun merchants who they probably knew well.

At the hotel, we asked some Frenchmen there about it, and they said that the soldiers had done it after the big celebration on Sunday, when the President and Clemenceau and Pershing and Foch . . . were there.[152] We found, on looking the place over after lunch, that shops all over town had been wrecked so, and this included all the big and very excellent department stores as well. It seems too bad to see the French doing this very thing that they have always condemned the Germans for. Yet I remember that in Paris, at the outbreak of the war, the same thing happened there with the German shops, and, in particular, the Maggi milk shops. But it does seem too bad. We found too, that at last they have gotten down the statue of the German soldier on the Esplanade, but it took dynamite to do it. It's pretty well wrecked now. The statue of the Emperor William as a saint, that graces the niche on the front of the cathedral high above the world, is still there, but they have hung a motto on him for all the world to read: "*Sic transit gloria mundi.*"

Then we go on thro Diedenhofen (now Thionville), up the Moselle to Remich, making a slight detour thro Mondorf, which brings us suddenly out on top of a great divide high above Remich, where we look across and down on one of the most startling and glorious views I have ever seen. The others in the crowd felt as I did. It was a sight that one will never forget. The divide, on which we were poised, dropped down so suddenly on either side of us, that it was as tho we were on some tall tower from which one looked in all directions at the wonderful hills that were so high ... that they were only separated from the sky by the delicate patches of vineyards and terraces in a wonderful sort of mother-of-pearl scheme. Below and under us was the river, and here and there the lovely little towns that hugged the river banks and nestled at the bottom of the hills. And above it all the glorious arch of Heaven! Too beautiful to be true. And we leave it, and dip down into the road below and up the road, but down the river, to Grevenmacher. Then on in the dusk, crossing the river at Wasserbillig, and entering Germany to the music of Dunn's harmonica, which he plays bravely, going thro the list of patriotic airs, and not forgetting the one which our boys have now adopted, "*Die Wacht am Rhein.*"

We arrive at Trier [Treves] in the dark at the hour of 4:30. Find rooms at the Reichshof, and have a very good dinner at a very reasonable price, all things considered. Soup seventy-five Pfennigs and meat four Marks and fifty Pfennigs to six Marks, including two vegetables. For the dessert, there was confiture, if one wished, at two Marks, and there was coffee, made from we couldn't decide what, unless it was the acorn coffee one reads about, at seventy-five Pfennigs. Bread we were supposed to furnish, as they had none, save a little, and, at that, the same old black bread that the military used. So we go to the Red Cross at the R.R. station across the street, and they give us enough for our supper and breakfast.

We are in Germany at last, and eating in a real German restaurant, with our hated enemy around us at the other tables, looking at us, most of the time, in strange ways, it seemed to us, tho not too unfriendly. But it is a queer feeling that I have — the realization that I am here with the Army of Occupation in an enemy country, an enemy that has been judged the most brutal and treacherous that has ever fought. . . . And now we were entering her country, not to plunder, pillage and burn as she had been doing, but to see merely that she lived up to her new contract, and to hold, as it were, as a guarantee, to control, and if necessary, to take, should she fail. A bitter pill, surely, for them to swallow. What wonder if they might a bit resent it all.

It has commenced to rain again, so I decide to sleep, while the others go to a movie.

December 11, 1918
❧

We look the town over a bit this morning before we start for Coblenz. The old Porta Nigra is a very impressive ruin — very Roman in character. Also the ruined Emperor's palace. We look thro a few of the shops, buying some books of war photographs.

Then we hit the trail that leads us down the Moselle and thro the vineyard-covered hills that roll along so close and high beside it. There are ruined castles everywhere, it seems, and they are wonderously strange and fine to look upon. How like a tapestry is the texture . . . of the hills. The vineyards showing the little rows of vines on their poles and all arranged in little patches that vary in color or tint, but not in tone, and following the modelling of the hills, are, for all the world, like delicate needlework. Or if not that, then, it's a painting by the most wonderful landscape man that the world has ever seen, perfect in every detail. And how clever he was in varying what might have been a monotony, in the little grey and pink stone terraces that spot the sides, to build them up here and there with little arches. Just the touch needed to give them a mysterious and haunting charm. And it's a long, endless panorama that never tires, but grows more beautiful instead. How one wants to get back to many of the places and Beilstein, in particular. And there's Cobern and Dieblich.

How strange it seems to have seen American troops passing along on serious business at the riverside, or patrolling the banks. We stopped at Cochem for lunch. This is 4th Corps HQ, so we assume that it will be easy to find food at an officers' mess. Alas — no. There have been so many casual officers passing thro for Coblenz that they have had to issue an order to their messes to feed no more of them. This sounds strange — that officers ordered to the zone of occupation have no food provided for them same as the others. An oversight on someone's part, that no special provision is made at such a point, which is about the middle of the trip up, and hence a logical point. It is 1 o'clock French time now, or 2 by German time — too late then to get anything at the German hotels, which are none too anxious, apparently, to serve us anyway. Finally, we prevail on a junior officers' mess to give us some coffee and bread, and they add butter and a piece of pie, so we make out well enough till supper.

We reach Coblenz at 4, just as it is getting dark. As yet, there are only a few troops in the town. The 2d Battalion was asked to come in to help police the town, so they are scattered over the place, and they are doing their work well, if the zeal with which they hold up all American cars for their travel orders or special passes can be taken as a criterion.[153] We have to run the gauntlet of four of them as we approach. They have never seen passes like ours, blanket passes that were issued us when we first came over, with an identical one in French issued by the French. They are not the kind they have been instructed to honor solely — but they either stare blankly at their strangeness and the impressiveness of the French document — or they catch the paragraph in the American one which says that it is the wish of the Commanding General that all commanding officers show us every courtesy and render us every assistance in the performance of our duties. This finishes whatever objection they might otherwise make, and we leave them with puzzled looks on their face, tho a satisfaction, no doubt, that they have done their duty well.

We pick our way thro the crowds of natives in the street, hunting the Fürsten Hof which is Press HQ. All rooming accommodations in the city have been requisitioned for our army, and there are rooms there, which look good to us. Plenty of heat and fine linen. But Major Bulger tells us we will find even better accommodations at the Coblenzer Hof, which is the finest hotel in town, and has been reserved for casuals with a fine mess there, so we go and get fine, large, double suites overlooking the Rhine, and right at the *Schiffbrücke,* or pontoon bridge, where our troops will cross later. The hotel is really elegant in the extreme, and one thinks at once of the crowds and the class of people who have frequented it in peace times. Even now, one knows that *Überoffiziers* have only just left it with the retreat of their forces, for there are still a number of them in the hotel, left behind to cooperate with the Americans in control. In coming up to our room, Captain Harding, mistaking our floor, kicks at a corresponding door, hears voices and bursts into the room to find it full of German officers.

Well content, we stow our things, clean up and walk the streets to see the town. It looks good too, tho how helpless I feel without being able to speak their tongue. I know now how the others feel in France with no knowledge of French, tho occasionally we find a shopkeeper here who talks excellent English and many of them French also. We explore the bookshops that we find, looking ever for war photographs. But their stock is low, and, as they say, there is no chance to get that sort of merchandise thro on the R.R.s. There are only a few officers in Coblenz as yet, and we seem to be quite a curiosity to most of the people, who look at us and pass remarks that don't seem to be in any way against us, as a rule, tho there are many sullen glances at us, too. We hadn't known quite what to expect. There were more or less orders or instructions that we were all to bring sidearms with us for emergency, and this had given us all a sort of an anxious, expectant feeling, which so far did not in any way seem justified.

We have a wonderfully good dinner at the mess at the hotel, showing what can be done with Army rations in the hands of real cooks. And with good service. Two Marks is the price . . . for the meals here, tho one has to deduct on his pay voucher the cost of the rations, fifty-seven cents per day.

Officers are arriving every minute tonight. I meet General Mitchell of our Air Force there. . . . Brigadier General Francis C. Marshall of the 2d Brigade, and Brigadier General Frank Parker of the 1st Brigade, 1st Division, are also there. General Mitchell introduces me to Colonel Rhea, Chief of the Bridgehead Commission, who has control of all affairs that have to do with the actual civil and military control of the bridgehead area. It is arranged that I am to do a portrait of the Colonel who, while he demurs, does seem to be keen for it, for he is a good-looking man, and knows it, and dresses it, too. Time to be set later, tho.

Everyone is going to the opera tonight, *Carmen,* by a good stock company, they tell us, so we decide to go. It will be interesting to see the people at this time at such a place, even tho the show should not be good. Every officer of ours in town must have been there, and they all seemed to be generals and colonels with a few majors and captains mixed in.

It was a thoroughly enjoyable performance, too. The voices would put to shame most of the voices in most of our good companies at home in the large cities. Good acting and good settings. And an orchestra that was all that one would expect in Germany, the home of orchestras. The people seem able to enjoy it all thoroughly. One would never imagine them to be a defeated people with peace terms threatening to crush them, and in the midst . . . of a humiliating armistice. There was nothing of this in the air. They seemed to take our presence as a matter of course. They could even smile naturally at us, or speak to us at times, as tho we might have been casual visitors in their town. Nor, I might add, was the attitude of the Americans there that of conquerors grinding a vanquished people under their heel. Perhaps the Germans sense this too, for it's no secret that they like the Americans, even as victors, and despise the French and the English. At times, when one hears it, it smacks of propaganda, as in Metz, but it often comes strait from the heart, I find. There is no doubt about it in my mind.

There was a hurried walk around the streets after the opera before we went to bed. The streets were well lighted. Opera begins at 7 German time, or 6 French, and is over tonight a little after 9:30. . . . So night life is just beginning. We drop into a cafe to have a glass of beer but take Moselle instead. Very good, but quite expensive here. While here, a German, nice looking, comes up and tries to explain to us that he has been thro the war, wounded four times, but that he wants us to know that now that we have won, and are here in their town, they want to help us to have a pleasant stay and mean to do it. He is a bit under the influence of his glass, and those of our crowd who understand German, Peixotto and Smith, pretend not to understand and hold aloof, till he grows excited at not being able to put over what he wanted to convey to us, and finally a waiter comes and leads him away. We had suddenly become the centre of all eyes and ears in the place. Our men might have treated him a little kindlier, but they pretended not to like, or to want to encourage, a remark he made about everyone being glad it was the Americans and not the French (whom they despised), who were coming to their town. We were the only Americans in the cafe. Numbers of the people nodded smilingly to us on entering and also on leaving. Others pretended to ignore us.

The town is filled with demobilized soldiers. One of our conditions or regulations was that no military uniforms were to be worn in the occupied territory, save by those duly authorized by us, and where it is necessary on the part of those officers who are assisting in the control or in aiding us to control the district. So that it is safe to assume that about every able-bodied man one meets wore a uniform only yesterday. He may have taken it off only today, for that matter, before he came home. By December 15, they must all be put away, and all firearms are being run down and collected from the civilians too.

The streets are gay. There are apparently no prostitutes on the street, tho, as one would expect in a town of that size. But our authorities will keep a close watch that they don't appear. . . . By this time, there are a few of our troops on the street. Where they came from at this hour, we don't know, probably an extra detail sent in to aid in policing, as the first of our troops are really to enter tomorrow.

Back to the hotel where we run thro our book purchases. Then to our very comfortable beds, after a fine bath in the biggest and finest tub I have ever set to sea in.

Having been misdirected in hunting the Adjutant tonight before dinner, three men — a Captain Smith, English; Lieutenant McCarty, Irish; and a Lieutenant Mooney, American — came to Dunn's and Aylward's room. They have been prisoners, wounded and in a hospital here in Coblenz for some time. Hearing the Americans had arrived, they had ventured over to see what the chances were for being sent back to their freedom. Captain Smith and McCarty both were in need of operations which they had elected to wait for till their ultimate freedom. They were fairly well otherwise. They all said they had been very well treated ever since their capture, and particularly well since the armistice. They have been quartered for their recuperation in some Brothers House, a religious institution, where they had been given considerable freedom, they said. Lieutenant Mooney was an aviator who was shot down, wounded, a couple of weeks after his squadron was put in with the British and set to work bombing in the north. He had only been in France the two weeks, and had seen nothing at all of our Army. So he knew absolutely nothing of anything that happened over here since his arrival, other than that we had won the war for the Allies. It was quite pathetic. He was fairly well recovered from his wounds now. He wore a Russian uniform, black with broad ochre stripe on the leg, and a band of same on the cap. We exchanged stories with them, or rather Dunn did. They promised to see us again before they got away. We saw Captain Smith at the opera with another wounded Englishman he had told us of having had in his charge ever since his capture — a man who had lost the use of both of his legs and whom gas and shell shock had made a physical wreck of. He had stuck by him thro it all, and meant to till he got him back to his people, he said. He told us of who the man was, someone of importance in England, but I forget — but I saw them at the opera and talked with them, and held the poor fellow for a time while Smith went back to the box for something. He surely was in bad shape, and shook and trembled and nodded his head all the while. He is bright and talks, but with a voice that breaks, and is so weak that one hears with difficulty. To think that he has been like this with good treatment for months, since last March, at least, when Smith went to the hospital.

December 12, 1918

We decide to stick around town today as the first of our troops are to enter. The 1st Brigade, 1st Division (General Parker) were to have the honor, and also they were to be the first to cross the Rhine on Friday the 13th.

We go down to a big *caserne* to 2d Battalion HQ to get a special pass for our area, which Colonel Rhea suggested we might do well to have, and while there, saw in the enclosure 384 of the trucks that Germany is getting ready to turn over to the Allies. German officers were inspecting them and making a list of the numbers. What a lot of them there were. Most of them were camouflaged. The covers on many of them were in unusual patterns that must have been decorated so, as much to please the fancy of some appreciative officer or man entrusted to do it, as for any real camouflage value it might have had.

Lieutenant McGrath, who was Adjutant and who made out our passes, told us something of things as they had happened there since his arrival on Sunday with the first troops for police work. How they had found the *casernes* all cleaned out thoroughly for our men, scrubbed and all the beds made up with sheets on them, fresh and clean. A large casino, that had been an officers' club, was all ready for their officers, beer on tap and stocked with food. The canteen for the men was in fine shape, with supplies left for them. And they had left a large supply of potatoes for the troops back of the *caserne*; as McGrath said, there were enough to feed a small army alone there. They had left an officer there to report each day, and see what there was that could be done for them, and the merest wish was carried out at once. This he took great delight in telling us, contrasting the conditions in which the French always left things for the Americans. For their jealousy keeps them from ever considering any such thoughtfulness as that, when they could well and easily do it.

He told us also of the great number of AWOLs, American, who had been drifting into town ever since they came; in fact, they had found numbers of them there when they arrived. They had already sent back 180, and had as many more under arrest and guard to go back soon. Many of these were officers. Told of one of our boys who, in an altercation, had been rightly shot in the head and badly wounded by a German policeman, which investigation had justified. It was over a matter of loot, which some German soldiers had hidden and feared to get, but which, making friends with the American, he, on his assumed right as a conqueror to get away with it, was attempting to get and deliver to his new friends. . . . He was caught and started a scrap, with result as stated.

As we were leaving, the first of our troops arrived, colors flying and band playing. There were no great crowds to see them come in, tho there was much interest on the part of many of those who did see them. Many frowns, of course, mixed in. But it sure was a great sight, and there was much enthusiasm on the part of all the Americans there. They kept coming all day . . . and were soon scattered all over town in all the little squares and open spaces, tho the greater part of them seemed to be in front

"Our Troops Entering Coblenz, Jesuit Place." *Courtesy of the National Archives. 111-SC-158652.*

of the Schloss or Emperor's Palace. The real show of interest was manifested by the poorer classes when our boys got their kitchens to working, and there were soon great crowds around these, tho there was no great show of begging, as in Luxembourg. In fact, in the streets here the children are always putting out their hands to shake yours, but they are never asking for Pfennigs, as have the children always, in France and Luxembourg. Once in a while, one demanded chocolate!

It had been raining all day and, save for the enthusiasm in seeing the troops, it was quite cold and cheerless. Now as evening approached, the glow of the fires and the smoke from the kitchen, and the merry voices of our men as they went about their work cutting up big quarters of meat and getting the suppers ready, seemed to warm the whole town. They were very interesting . . . to look upon in the little nooks and corners they had gotten into, or sometimes in the squares with their big tarpaulins over everything, ruddy in the glow from the fires. And then, the crowds of people and children around them. And the ceaseless tramp of the troops still coming into town. Troops and supply trains and batteries of 75s, which always seem to interest the natives, and awed them a bit, I think. By night, the town had become Olive Drab (OD), and the boys owned the place. They were as numerous, it seemed, as in Neufchâteau or any of our centres in France. They were everywhere buying out the postcard shops, and what they could find in the sweetmeat shops. And they are always to be found in the jewelry shops, buying whatever souvenirs the limited purses will afford.

So very many of our boys speak German, and they seemed to be talking to everyone, in a friendly fashion, as were the Germans in return, tho there is always a certain air about our men that is very business-like and much to the point, that commands respect. So that there is no danger of the Germans taking any liberty or assuming to — however much the French may fear this, as we hear they do. Perhaps there is design on the part of some of them, but, on the whole, I am sure that their smiles are sincere. One can readily tell when they are not. One can't help being struck by and admiring a bit, too, the philosophic way in which they take our occupation, which must, or might easily be, a bitter pill for them. But not so. They seem determined to take it as necessary now, and a matter of course. I shouldn't be surprised if there were very many who truly welcome it all, who welcome their defeat even, and see better times and a government more to their liking ahead of them, tho they must one and all dread . . . the realization of the ultimate and inevitable peace terms, for they all know that in spite of President Wilson, Marshal Foch has the whip hand.

This fact is even now dawning on many of our officers observing and hearing the French, as they have had such opportunity to. They are an embittered and unrelenting victor . . . and in spite of us, and they will insist to the end, and use the iron heel even as Germany would. This the Germans know, and they know that it is not our spirit nor our ideal to think or act so, hence their dread of the French occupation, and their relief at knowing that we are to occupy and control Coblenz, and not the French, as they had begun to suspect, because of the presence now of a large force at the newly established French Mission.

To the opera again tonight. *Der Vogelhändler.* Fine voices, pretty girls, good acting and fine music. The same Americans as the night before. Everyone enjoying it all. On serious thought, rather an unusual situation. Being entertained so easily by a conquered people, and they taking their pleasure, apparently, as easily as we.

December 13, 1918
Friday!
ᴈ⊀

The crossing of the Rhine! We are up betimes and it is scheduled for 8, to continue for two hours, when there is to be a break, and the pontoon bridge is to be opened for the river traffic, which our engineer in charge has insisted on, owing to the dependence of the country, and I even think he said our army (tho I am not sure as to this), on the regular flow of barges of supplies. Over they go at 8 sharp, and we are all out to see them as best we can, tho on account of the rain and the fog, it is not very light, and impossible to take photos. The band makes merry and the colors fly and the boys are in a happy mood. Historic event this! And on Friday the 13th!

All day they pass. Over go the guns. And machine gun battalion after battalion, it seems. There are a number of German officers who watch it all from the front of the hotel. They seem to be interested in studying and in favorable comment on our equipment, the details of our trucks and our water carts, and our various up-to-date supply wagons. How strange our old covered Westward Ho wagons seem, and pulled by great mules, six and eight to a wagon. They are very picturesque, and I am told, they are very efficient.

Strange to say, and to me unexplainably, there is a line of French officers and a *poilu* or two directly behind General Parker and his staff, but at the head of our boys in the crossing of the Rhine. Even this honor actually taken away from them as it has been on a number of other occasions. . . .

At 10, it all stopped on schedule and great strings of barges, pulled by long, flat sidewheel tugs, go streaming thro. There are many Holland barges among them. At 12, this stops and our troops begin again their forward march.

Had an appointment to do a portrait of Colonel Rhea at 3 today. But when I showed up for the sitting, found that he had gone out early, and they didn't expect him back till late. So asked them to tell him I had kept the appointment, and gave my room number so if he cares to make another, he may.

Had a leather case made for my camera today. Fine leather beautifully made to order and delivered in a half day. The carrying case that was furnished me by the Signal Corps I found much too heavy to carry about. This one is a joy to have and a joy to look at besides. Everyone thinks the price very reasonable, as leather is very scarce in Germany as it is in France. Fifty-five Marks, and inasmuch as we bought Marks at a bank here today — 140 Marks for 100 francs, that makes it cost me only about eight dollars. The same case in New York made to order would have been twice that. It would cost eighty to 100 francs in France today.

It has been a very interesting day. Meals at the mess continue good. A fine breakfast with wheat cakes and bacon and toast and good coffee — price one Mark.

December 14, 1918

ᕯ

We go across the river today following our troops. Have dinner and spend the afternoon at Montabaur, which is to be the HQ for the 1st Division. This is a good and typical old German town with fine half-timbered houses of an early date. It surrounds a high hill on which is the Schloss. Harding and I went up to this where we met the Governor or High Commissioner of this district, a Herr Berthold, of forty years of age perhaps, a thorough German of the upper class, and his wife, both of whom spoke English. It seems he was in difficulties with our MPs, who refused to let him in and out of the town in his auto on his necessary business with the neighboring towns. Harding goes down with him to straiten this out if possible, while I wait there for their return and talk to Frau Berthold and her sister, who also spoke excellent English, having lived for some time in England.

While we were talking, some of our boys came up with twenty-five mules to put in their barn. This seemed to get the women quite excited, for they had been expecting it. They rushed out to yell to the boys that they didn't think it a practical place because of the necessity of carrying up or leading the mules out for water, as there was none there; that the Germans had never used it for the same reasons. I suppose they were sincere, tho the boys doubted it. But one look at the barn seemed to convince them that there might be a better place as far as they were concerned, for there was easily two days' hard work for a number of men clearing out all sorts of rubbish and logs and implements that filled the stalls and shed.

I had a long talk with Madame. Soon all her children were around her and the sister. We talked of many things, the war and how terrible it had been. How they were glad it was over, and they seemed to be reconciled to the way it was settled, and said that perhaps it was best so, tho they really did fear that the Reds would get the upper hand — that they were truly afraid of a revolution. Being of the rich upper class, I imagine they well might, for they were, as they said, of the military party in the past, and her husband was what he was by grace of them. I imagine he may have been a high officer in the army, for he was of very military appearance. They said they had no doubt but that they would all be happy under the new regime if Wilson and his ideas had sufficient weight in the Peace Conference, tho they doubted that the French would ever relinquish any of the supreme authority that they seem determined to exercise. And what did I think? I said I thought that they would have to wait, and that there surely was no doubt but that with a democratic form of government, they were bound to be happy as we were. They said perhaps! But they were happy before — and having been brought up under a military system, they saw no evils in it, and that a military was always necessary, as we were discovering, and would always be. But they did hope that things worked out for the good of all. They had confidence in us, but they didn't like the French. They were glad we were in their immediate vicinity, and they didn't fear our boys, nor look forward to any license on their part. I assured them that well treated, our boys, I am sure, would behave well.

She apologized for the looks of her garden which we walked in. Said she had had the care of it herself but had had no time, as she had worked in the fields all the time, and had only just finished with the harvesting of the potatoes. It had certainly agreed with her, as she looked hale and strong and ruddy-cheeked, as were all the children. She was much concerned as to whether we would be able to rely on our own food supplies, as she said potatoes were the only thing of which there was really enough for their own peoples there. She apologized for the appearance of their town of which she was justly proud. The mud, she said, had come with the army transport, and that there was little hope of cleaning till our men were in and they could get at it. She said that practically all their men had now been demobilized, and were home and ready for work. How many of our men were to come? And would there, by any chance, be any French near? She said that some officers were to be quartered with them, and would I like to if I came back, for I assured her I was only there for the afternoon, tho I might return. The General, she said, had intended at first to take it, but decided against it, because of the possible trouble getting up the steep road with his car when the ice came in the winter, and that they had put at his disposal a fine house in the town that was in fine condition.

Our dinner at the Kaiserhof cost us four Marks — with wine two Marks extra per glass. No bread. But the dinner was very good, good meat and as we always find, heaps of vegetables, particularly potatoes.

When we get back to the hotel, we find that the 3d Army have definitely taken over the Coblenzer Hof for their higher officers, majors and over; also the mess. So all casuals must go to the billeting officer for new billets. Goodbye to our elegant quarters, which are to be taken by our former chief, Colonel McCabe. Finally, we are located in the Hansa Hotel. Good rooms in another part of town — Bahnhof Platz. We don't have to get out this night but must move in the morning. . . .

December 15, 1918

There had been rumors in the air for several days that the French were taking a part of our sector from us and no one knew why. A subtle feeling of dissatisfaction has been growing in our army among the officers for some time against the attitude of the French, and their treatment of us, and particularly from the time that we had really won the war for them, and they need not be beholden to us longer. It began to be expressed in words, perhaps at the time of the St. Mihiel drive, when, after taking the town for them, they entered as deliverers. Then the very pointed case at Sedan, where we were allowed to advance just to the river after fighting the Boche out. Then a few days later, they enter . . . as the saviours and deliverers of the enslaved peoples there. And now with the new coup here, by which they take almost half of the sector or bridgehead area that was formally assigned to us to occupy — all of it south of the Lahn River, swinging around on an arc (with Coblenz as the center) from a point midway between Diez and Limburg to the Rhine. No one seems to know just why, but French *poilus* have been mysteriously filtering thro the town for a couple of days, and now the French have taken the bridge above the pontoon for theirs, and they are going over in streams, colonials all, so that the Coblenz people have an idea that we are going on, and that the French are coming into Coblenz, and they are truly frightened, for stories are reaching them of the high-handed way in which they are controlling affairs around Mayence [Mainz] and in the German districts in Lorraine. Also tales of the bitterness with which the Belgians are handling their occupation in the north, and the British too, so that they appreciate much the poise and fairness with which we are treating them. It's this very fairness, many of us suspect, that is the real reason that the French insist on a certain contact with their troops and their methods, counting on its putting more iron in our grip on them, and our punishments, when they are needed. But we hear, too, that there is going to be a real and potent protest made at the proper time, and in the proper place, after all we have done for the French.

I must confess that there has been growing in my heart a hatred for the French officer and his supercilious aloofness from the world about him. If the German ever had a superman idea, it has a real counterpart in the mind of the average French officer. The very spick-spanness of their uniform has gotten to express their spirit to me. A fleck of dust on it becomes an humiliation. And they are jealous as can be of the Americans. This idea is often expressed by the French people themselves, and deprecated and apologized for. As they say themselves, it's a poor return for our aid. They lay much of it to the fact that we have, as officers, so much more money to dispense, and this, and our freedom in spending, and the interest in their women, so many of whom are becoming engaged to and marrying American men, is one of the main causes for their jealousy. This criticism applies to them as a class and not as individuals, for some of them are the finest on the earth, and they must sort of feel the stigma that, if they are not careful, the others are going to cast over all of them in the eyes of the Americans. Too much of this. It may not be true, and I hope it isn't. But they have taken much of our bridgehead away from us, to be explained later.

We drive out along the Lahn to Ems and Nassau where the French General has his . . . HQ. I had a long talk with him, and he showed me on his maps where his colonials were, and the point of liaison with our troops at Goergeshausen to the north, even of the river some seven kilometres, and out as far as Diez. Showed me the safest route for a heavy car as ours to get there, and said what difficulty he was having getting his camions around. For unlike us, he has only the main road along the river that is a good road. The others are little, narrow earth ones, and all mud now with all the rains, and on the sides of steep hills, so that heavy trucks are continually going over the edge. We are having great trouble in this way, even on our better roads.

His HQ were in a fine old beautifully furnished house in Nassau. This and Ems, a couple of kilos down the road, are famous bath towns, evidently very prosperous ones, and filled with fine hotels. Outside of Coblenz and Montabaur, they were the only large and prosperous towns in our sector, and now we have them not.

We go back by way of Ems to cut up across to Montabaur and then down from there to the liaison point. Have dinner at Ems at the Löwen Hof, the best meal, we voted, that we have had in Europe. Seven Marks. Soup, a tremendous portion of roast veal, fine fried potatoes in quantity, creamed Brussels sprouts, chocolate pudding and afterwards, two fine apples each. And good bread. For coffee, we decided on mocha, real mocha, for which they said they paid fifty-five Marks the pound. For this we had to pay two Marks each. But it was certainly good. There was good Munich beer here, as in so many of the places still, and fifty Pfennigs the stein.

Finding us looking over the papers here, the waitress brought, what she said were some English papers that we might like to read: the *English-American News*, "An Independent Non-Political Journal." This was #11, published in Berlin every Tuesday, Thursday and Saturday, and dated December 12, so that it had commenced its career after the armistice. "Independent" was right, for it turned out to be a propaganda sheet of the darkest color. We asked if we might keep the copies, and tried to get others, but they hadn't them. One smiles to think what the French will do to them if they catch them passing them out.

Then on to Montabaur where we find our boys in real possession. Then on to Goergeshausen, but we find nothing of interest here, so back to Montabaur where we pick up what we can of interest there. On inquiry, I learn that the mules were picketed in the barnyard at the Schloss, in spite of the water difficulty, and that a suspicion has crept into the minds of our men that the rubbish was put in the barn by design, and that notice is about to be served to clear it out at once, or take the consequences. So I didn't go near the place today for fear that Frau Berthold would take it out on me.

Back to Coblenz, where we enter just in time to see the glorious entry of the HQ troop with a band of many, many pieces mounted on fine horses that came blaring and beating its way into town in the grandest style imaginable. One thought of the gold and glitter and pomp of the old Ringling Brothers band. For here was a great drum on a white horse, and up in the lead, too, was a pair of large kettle drums slung astride of another white horse, and there was a drummer swinging his sticks and using hands turning and stopping with all the art of the drummer in the Philharmonic or the Boston Symphony. I wouldn't have missed this for anything. But Fate seems kind to me these days, for she has let me see many things which call forth the same remark. This band . . . resulted in great applause from the crowds that saw and heard it, for it was distinctly a thing to see, hear and remember.

There is an orchestral program at the Opera House tonight but I am too tired to go. We find madame at the new hotel kindness itself. Has just lost a son in the last few days of the war, and is still in great grief.

December 16, 1918

❧

*D*o the town this morning. More troops pass thro today. In the afternoon, the fellows go down the Moselle to Dieblich, but I stay to do a portrait of the Colonel, but find he has again gone out. My last attempt. So, driven in by the rain, I do a sketch of the Bahnhof from my window. Then as dark approaches, go up to the Press where I find a telegram saying credentials have been arranged for me for the Peace Conference, and to come to Paris at once. This has taken several days to be relayed up to me from Neufchâteau, but as we are starting back tomorrow, it will be alright, and I can learn when the Conference is to start there, for I know it has not yet begun.

As I walk up the street, I notice great crowds hurrying to the crossing and the square ahead where a long line of our 155 split-tail guns are crossing the town to the other side of the Moselle. These make a decided impression on the crowd. They are a formidable weapon, and would command anyone's respect. They are pulled by fine, large horses and these, too, are the cause of much interest. We certainly have been careful in picking the best we have for this occupation, and its effect is worth all it will cost us, too, in increased respect for our power or potentiality.

As I was standing here, I felt the gaze of a little woman who was standing near me, and she turns suddenly, and in good English, asks me where the guns were going, did I know? And what fine horses, and didn't the boys look well, and she was so glad to see them all again after four years there in Coblenz. Then she told me her story of visiting Coblenz, her husband's birthplace, with him before the outbreak of the war, and how they hadn't been able to leave, and of how her husband, being a construction engineer, had been impressed into this kind of service at factory construction. She told of her keenness to get home; of her discussions with the German people there over the war and its conduct. German as she was, she was born in America and was American to the core, she said. She spoke of the surprise of the people there at our military strength as they found it on the Western Front, and they could not believe it possible that so many of our men could be gotten to France, and where did they all come from, with the submarines operating as they were? I told her just how many, or rather how few, we had lost from such cause, and this was a revelation to her, for she said that this, of course, had been kept from them. . . . That the submarines were always held up as a great success, and that this was necessary, as the German people as a whole have always been opposed to the submarine campaign, and insisted that it was the straw that broke the camel's back and brought us into the war, which they had always regretted. And that this was one count that the people had against the powers there that they would never forget. She said that the feeling of the German people for the Americans was not one of hatred, as it was against the British and the French, and would never, and could never, be, on account of the blood ties, tho they did regret our coming into the war, for without our entry, they would have won. She spoke of how glad they were, too, that we were coming to Coblenz and not the British or the French. I spoke of the apparent plentifulness of food. She said this appeared so because the restaurants and the hotels could afford to buy it as a matter of business. And that the rich had the money to buy it, but that the middle class and poor lived on vegetables and their bread allowances as best they could. And that they had suffered. Also she spoke of the lack of fats for soap, so that they could not wash their clothes, and hadn't I noticed that their clothes were not clean? This I confessed I hadn't noticed. She gave me her address and asked me to call, and I promised, and I mean to, if I get there again. I should like to get a lot of details from her. She is sincere and American I know, and she has much to tell. She told of the many arguments she had with the Germans, and I would like to get her to recount some of them. I did call later, but their place was all dark. Mrs. Condear was her name, at #31 Schlosstrasse. She was from New York City. Formerly of New Haven, she said.

Had dinner at the Press mess tonight.

December 17, 1918

Leave for Neufchâteau this morning, reaching Trier at 4:30, stopping on the way to Beilstein. This we find quite up to our dreams. Simply wonderful in its age and its quaintness. Evidently prosperous from its vineyards, every house with as much individuality and character as the family within, and all the houses fraternizing and leaning on each other's shoulders as tho they were the inhabitants themselves. I long to get back here someday — that day when we are all here, my family and I.

We find rooms in Trier at the Hotel Christophel opposite the old ruined Porta Nigra. Our windows look out on it. We mess at the GHQ mess at the Hotel Porta Nigra. Five francs. Pretty high for an officers' mess, but good. Afterwards, we vote to go to a light opera. Interesting because it is built up on the life of Schubert, with many of his songs in it. Well costumed and staged, with fine light effects. Orchestra not in a class with the one at Coblenz; voices musical but a bit amateurish. But glad to have gone.

Rooms four Marks each. Good and clean.

December 18, 1918

As we leave Trier, I think it was at Euren, we find a ruin of quite a remarkable, old Roman tower. But we don't stop to examine it, as the drive down to Neufchâteau now is a long one. Guards try to stop us as we approach Metz, hoping to swing us on past and around the town to our objective. We must have dinner, we protest. Very well, we must have a pass to enter. So out comes our old reliable and, as usual, it works, tho, as usual, it leaves a sort of blank stare at us as we go. The French are trying to make a closed town out of it, apparently.

As we came down thro Diedenhofen, we notice that there are green signs in all the shop windows, "Maison Français." And they have cancelled all the Diedenhofen signs and made them to read, beyond all mistaking, "THIONVILLE."

In Metz, we find the broken shop fronts still in ruin, and the shops closed. Our little bookstore, where I had expected to get a little book I knew there on old German villages, with fine photos in it, had a sign in the window which I had failed to notice in my hurry in getting in. But an MP came in after me, and showed it to me: "Closed to soldiers of the Allied Armies." I could not get the real reason from him; it had to do with some altercation there between the patron and some French soldiers. I don't understand. He is undoubtedly Boche, tho he must have appealed to the police, and they came back at him in this way, along with their protection. It's a fine little shop, and it means loss of much trade to him, but by the appearance of the other Boche shops in town, he has gotten off lightly to date.

We slip out of the town and on our way home.

We have had a wonderful week with the Germans and our troops in their Moselle and Rhine country. We have accumulated mixed feelings as to the people and their sincerity now. But we are getting home now. In a few minutes we reach Corny; we are still along the Moselle banks and nearing Pont-à-Mousson. Suddenly, like a sharp rebuke, a ruined farmhouse, and then a little ruined village along the road, wake us from our dream, and we realize that not since we left this very spot the week before, have we seen a ruin, save the ones that reminded us now of that other Caesar back in the old days. Now we are in the midst of ruin, the work of the Kaiser's guns, and we begin to think and to wonder about this question of retribution. We ponder the problem of turning the other cheek! Not a mark had we seen in Germany that was the work of the Allied guns. Air bombs may have made their scars, but we saw them not, so that now the contrast was complete and startling. We saw again wounded men in numbers. Scarcely a one had we seen there, so that we feel, now, that there must have been a design in keeping them in other areas out of the sight of Allied eyes. We saw livestock in Germany, a thing we didn't see all the way up, nor do we see it now. We ponder again the food problem there and here, and the scale of prices. And we are in a quandary, and the old feeling of mistrust creeps in again. And the words "guile," "craft" and "cunning" creep into our thoughts, and we wonder if, after all, the French have a truer perspective than we have as to this old, old neighbor of theirs. But I still insist that the people and the militarists in Germany are two distinct things, much as they overlap, thro the Army being made up from the people. For, after all, they surely prefer peace to war, this mass of common clay. For they must have interests and hearts that are human, same as we.

CHAPTER 8

THE PEACE CONFERENCE

The Paris Peace Conference, which began informally on January 13, first focused on the creation of the League of Nations. In late March, attention turned to Germany itself.[154] The German delegation, however, did not arrive until April 29, and was not allowed to participate in the deliberations.[155] On May 7, the Germans received a draft of the treaty, and though they protested vigorously at the harshness of the terms, they accepted it after a government crisis. The Allies did grant a few concessions, but these were minor. The formal signing of the treaty occurred on June 28 in the Hall of Mirrors at the Versailles Palace, outside Paris, an act that gave the document its name: the Treaty of Versailles. Although the United States signed the document, the U.S. Senate failed to ratify it, and it was only in 1921 that U.S. involvement in World War I was ended by a separate peace with the Germans. Meanwhile, the treaties with the other Central Powers were drafted and signed, the last one with Turkey on August 20, 1920.

Like several of the other artists, Townsend took up residence in Paris to continue his work for the winter, renting a studio and quarters at No. 4, rue Belloni. He planned to accomplish two things: to attend the Paris Peace Conference, which opened officially on January 18, 1919, and to return to the battlefields to create some permanent artwork, covering at leisure areas where earlier he had had to move in haste.

Although Townsend was present in Paris only during the early phases of the drafting of the Treaty of Versailles, his impressions of the events of the day and the personalities assembled at Paris provide interesting commentary on the period.

December 18, 1918

Home at last. And I find the Bathos [family] in the midst of packing. He has had sudden orders to move to Lunéville from his Chief. Of course, they had counted on a move between Christmas and New Year's. I had gotten reconciled to this, and was trying to formulate plans that would fit in with this for my move. But this is sudden and disconcerting, and it will be difficult for me to arrange things well.

I find, oh joy! a bunch of letters from Cory and Barbara, and I see a Christmas package has showed up for someone at the Press. Christmas just one week away. Everything spoke of Christmas in Germany, too. Shops full of toys and everyone shopping. Men carrying sleds and skates home for, I take it, deserving boys. A promise, too, of snow and ice for all our fellows there this winter.

No word from our Chief in answer to our memorandums and questions regarding our plans for the winter. This was a decided disappointment, as it seems we must have a decision soon.

December 19–24, 1918

The days pass with the same monotony that we have grown to feel now in Neufchâteau when we work and wait. We have the anxiety of an awaited decision as to our future plans from GHQ, and in my case this is augmented by my necessity to find a new place, to pack and to move soon. One tries to work, but one finds it hard. This is not peculiar to my own case either, for it's the same with the others, I learn. Neufchâteau is as dead as a place could well be. There is talk of a Christmas affair with Margaret Wilson here but there seem to be no definite plans to build a hope on.[156]

Harding and Dunn have a talk at GHQ with Captain Stone who has already taken up our case with General Nolan, it seems. The general understands our situation and is favorable to the plan of going to Paris for the rest of the winter for better working conditions. Also, there seems to be a feeling on Captain Stone's part that if we send in individual memos covering our situation and our beliefs as to the plan under which we can best carry on our work, even should this be a desire to be ordered to the States, that that wish would be honored. So that a light does seem to break.

But what an excitement it has thrown into our camp of a sudden, and there are mixed feelings on the part of all, for, while the desire to get back to our folk and our immediate families is strong in all of us, there is the feeling too that, after all, this is in many ways a selfish feeling. For my part, much as I want to get back to my family, I do realize that there is much here that I would be leaving undone that ought to be done, and that unless a desire is expressed from Washington that we be returned, I would be untrue to a certain trust that must have been placed in me in sending me over here. I have left untouched as yet numbers of portraits that I can and feel I must do, that occasion has prevented the doing of. Then there is the interest in the life of the boys in the 3d Army that will furnish a chance for many pictures that I am sure will prove of interest at home. Then there is still the collection of a certain amount of detailed sketches on the battle-fields that there has never been time for, and that I feel I must do, without which a return home would feel to me like the end of a more or less unsuccessful expedition here in France. I would feel unequipped, either for further work for the War Staff College or for myself, when I am allowed to get at my own work once again. And now there is the immediate need of the covering of the Peace Conference and the preliminary parleys here in Paris and at Versailles. This is to fall to Morgan and me.[157]

Peixotto and Smith are off to Paris for keeps with the demands in their memos that they be returned home soon. So the exodus has begun. I am planning a trip up to look for a studio on the 26th, finding that should the Bathos [family] leave, I can feel secure in my rooms and the cache of my things here till as late as January 15th, as they have a lease till then. Captain Stone, in an interview, has approved my plan, or even suggested that to facilitate matters, I go up and find a suitable studio, taking it on my own lease, after which they will arrange with me, either as to taking it over, or as to a monthly refund for its cost. They understand the price problem and also the matter of necessity for a lease, tho he asked that I do all I can to get a six-month lease only.

Progress! How I want to get settled. And to serious work too.

There is to be real American Christmas weather, it seems, for our boys. Today on the 24th it snows. The ground is white, and the view of the distant hills against the sky is so unlike France as I have known it that I am transported to the States, if only I can blot out the lovely and typical roofline and the church that cut the foreground of my picture. This will undoubtedly mean a good frosty day, too, for the boys around Coblenz. How I would like to be up there with them for the holidays. I somehow have an idea that the Christmas spirit there will be a bit nearer to their hearts' desire than it will for the boys here in France, for, after all, Christmas is a real German institution. What preparations, too, they were making there.

December 25, 1918

𐡀

*W*hite Christmas! Peace on Earth! Good Will toward Men! Was there ever a Christmas that found a more ready and joyous welcome in the hearts of people than this one that comes on the eve of battle, and heralds the New Order, when the spirit of him whose day it is, can be said to have conquered truly throughout the world and the world stands ready for his guidance in all its seats of power? For spirit has triumphed over matter, Right has triumphed over Might, and while the price that has been paid in the great struggle figured in terms of matter has been great (and after all, the bodies of our brave who have fallen are only matter and the imperishable spirit that threw these bodies into the seething and consuming maelstrom of battle shall forever populate the real world about us, the world of mind), and while this price seems terrific, we know that we have purchased a freedom beyond price. And we know that this spirit will override the littlenesses of political and commercial interests that may still live in the corners of the Allied council chambers. But there is the hope and the certain knowledge that their corridors will be swept clean. And this Christmas will long stand memorable in the annals of Time for its true significance. . . . And what a spokesman President Wilson has become for that invisible God who has ruled over battles at last and who stands triumphant. Sometimes there are tiny doubts that cry for hearing, that would say that pride and selfishness and the feeling of revenge that we see manifested in little ways here and there by the Allies here who have suffered so long, are going to fight for breath in the Peace Conference, and in their death agonies strike out menace; that President Wilson is the John the Baptist of the new era — the Voice crying in the Wilderness, perhaps. But one, of course, has to believe in the inevitable. So we rest assured and know that the Christmas spirit, which bursts upon this snow-white, purified morning, shall reign now in the hearts of men. And the dead, and the marks of the struggle, even, are hidden this morning in this Christmas mantle of snow. What a symbol and a sign. . . .

And as Christmas goes in the material sense, it seems to be a merry one for all. Our boys are happy, and everything seems to have been done for them by the various welfare forces here at work that it was possible to do. And the poor and the stricken here in the devastated areas, the refugees and the orphaned children, have been looked after with a lavish hand. There are Christmas entertainments on every hand, till the sound of their merrymaking fills the land. And the French have caught the spirit of it all, so that this day has taken on an equal interest with their New Year, which has always been their real Fête.

This afternoon it snows again. I have a good day there at home with the Bathos [family], in spite of my being obliged to pack for my trip to Paris tomorrow. I forego the entertainment at the Transport Park for the French children (Miss Wilson singing there), also the dance in the evening, for meditation seemed to appeal most to me tonight. No Christmas box from home yet. But there are all sorts of thoughts that seem like true spirit messages from Cory and Barbara, and I enjoy a peace and a happiness that seem unreal.

December 26–31, 1918
※

*P*aris! At last I am on the way. The ride to Chaumont for the train was much like traveling over an extended Christmas card, the old familiar frosted one of boyhood days. For everywhere there was a white mantle, snow just wet enough to stick to everything and to clothe the trees like gloves, in white. And a struggling sun was reflected from all around till it hurt the eyes with its brilliance. Beautiful might express it to some, tho to me it was, as I say, a real reminder of the old frosted token that passed for art with the average soul and does still, for that matter. I arrive late in Paris and find that Mme. has saved me a room at the Hotel du Tibre in answer to my wire.

I hit the trail thro the jungles of the Latin Quarter hunting haven and Heaven but I find it not. What was difficult when we came on the same mission earlier, is doubly difficult now. It seems impossible to run them down, and all because "*ils n'existent pas.*" The peculiar relationship which exists between landlord and tenant owing to the war has left thousands of studios locked by the tenant and guarded for him with no rent to the landlord. And much as he would like to get them in his hands and rented, he cannot. . . .[158]

January 13, 1919
꙰

*C_A*t last I get things fixed up so that I may attend or at least enter to see as much as is possible of what is going on at the Peace Palace, the Palace d'Orsay. I go over with Lieutenant Wanger who takes me in and vouches for me as to my right to be there. And we stand near the head of the stairs and right near the *vestiaire* where the delegates are to check their coats and hats so that we can get a good look at them as they come in. Of course, this is not a general conference but is one of the so-called "secret" or closed ones at which only the big five are represented.[159] Today there are to be some special advisers there with them in their side room.

I am sort of lost in silent wonder and fancy of it all, and the fact that I am really here, able to look on and see and possibly hear some of this momentous affair that is possibly to consume so much time and so much of the world's interest ere it is finished, when, like a breeze, tho a slightly chilly one, there comes almost rushing up the stairs and down the long way thro salon after salon to the council chamber, a little old bear of a man who never even stops to take off his hat nor to check his overcoat with the men who wait so patiently for him, or someone else, to come. And he wears the famous grey gloves. It's Clemenceau, with that terribly serious, almost savage, look that seems to be a habit . . . with him, so occupied as he ever is in fighting and snarling at the world about him. He strides, almost runs, down the rooms with an air as tho it were his show, and the ringmaster also, with a whip in his hand.

Some little time elapses when there is an audible silence thrust suddenly on the place: I don't think anyone said "Sh—!" but you felt it, and there came striding, oh so solemnly and so majestically up the stairs, face strait ahead, tho his eyes moving from side-to-side in a slow "I see you" sort of a way, our own President Wilson. What a large man he seemed, too, and how large his head seemed and how very sober and serious he was, as tho he were bent on an overwhelming task — which, of course, he is. But he had today quite all the air of one of those old sedate and solemn Baptist ministers that used to pall on me so. He walks strait up to the counter, lays his silk hat on the table, inverted, slowly takes off his gloves, runs them thro his fingers and folds them and puts them in his hat, unbuttons his coat, turning slowly to the obsequious Frenchman, who waits this moment, and with all the air of one who is so used to it, lets his coat be taken from him. Then he takes his check, looks carefully at it, puts it in his pocket and walks slowly and solemnly down in the same direction as Clemenceau had gone.

One wonders at their meeting there, for somehow one gets the impression, from the little or big differences between them that seem to crop up at all times, that there are going to be clashes between them ere this thing is over.

In a moment, comes [Robert] Lansing almost as sober as Wilson.[160] There is his suave, smooth secretary with him. They seem inseparable and somehow one doesn't like his taste in secretaries either.

And now, like another breeze, tho of a pleasant sort, there comes up . . . a little man who one would swear was whistling, tho one did somehow miss the sound of it. He wears a wonderful smile and an air of assurance and the right to be there, and, anyway, content with the world, as tho now, at last, it rested easy on his shoulders. And gracious me! He looks over at us and actually gives us a decided smile. Taking off his coat in an easy operation, for he assists at it, turns and walks smiling around, and disappears down the rooms also. What a wonderful little man he seemed, and I must confess he made a great hit with me. I had expected to see a little man with a head out of all proportion to his size, and covered with great, shaggy grey locks, for somehow his photographs give that look to him. But they were wrong, for I find him a perfectly proportioned little man, neat and dapper. He wears today a cutaway frock and the striped grey trousers.[161]

Then there comes General [Tasker Howard] Bliss, and one wonders how we ever picked so sober and almost sad looking lot of men, tho one must confess that they do look wise and shrewd, which we know them to be, and we have every confidence in them as fighters and able to look after the interests, even of the rest of the world, which is what they are here for, in the main part anyway, now.[162] But they are sober, sedate men all of them. General Bliss has a bit the look of a quite old man, approaching the time when his vigor would go. He looks a bit fierce as Clemenceau does. I can picture how they could appear to be scowling across the conference table at each other, when in fact they might really be in jest with each other. There is a colonel as aide with him. I think it is Colonel U. S. Grant III.

Then there comes [Vittorio Emanuele] Orlando and [Giorgio Sidney, Baron] Sonnino.[163] Polished, pointed Italians. Then our own Barney Baruch with a secretary and a portfolio, for he is called in today for counsel.[164] Then the silent, mysterious Japs. Like dark horses they are, and one wonders what surprises they are to spring on the really suspecting world. They are very small men and impress one as being very young men to stand so high in the rule of so powerful a people as the Japs have become.

And now comes [Herbert] Hoover, with Captain Gilbert White for a secretary.[165] I wonder how and why. Hoover is a very fine and capable-looking man. Like [David] Lloyd George, he made a real hit with me. He is very well dressed too, and wears one of those same smiles of supreme confidence and content that Lloyd George had. No wonder, tho, that the whole world of Europe treats him with the respect that they do, for he holds their Fate and their food in his hands, as it were, and he lets them have it as he thinks best. Well, today they need his advice, and also they need his promises.

After him, saunter in, in a most casual way, bland and pink-cheeked, and very dapper as to uniform, two English officers, who I don't know. Things do not rest outwardly heavy on their minds, one would say.

The last one to come, and he is really ten minutes late, is Arthur James Balfour.[166] Great, tall man he is, too. He has an immense fur collar on a long, black overcoat. He seems like a very well-preserved man, too. There is a slight smile on his face, tho he wears a faraway look in his eyes as tho they were seeing things at a great distance. Not at all out of keeping with his present occupation. He, too, is to the manner born in the matter of having himself groomed by the trusty there at the desk. He turns slowly on his heel, in an absentminded manner, without so much as looking down for or taking his coat check, which had been thrust at him, and yes sir, as I suspected, he is going off and down to the rooms without it. This seems to be all of them, and the cameramen on the outside have fired their parting salutes of flashes out there in the poor daylight.

The stage had all been set for the entry of all these great men — these perhaps most precious men in all the world today. Outside in the streets, and peering thro the grill for a sight of them as they drove up and alighted at the entrance, were what seemed a goodly part of Paris. One would have liked to hear the comment that was passed there. And inside, lined up in a great semicircle in front of the door where they were alighting and beside the steps up which they must go, were all the cameramen. This was as far as they were allowed to get, and they took all the advantage of it they could. They seemed to snap everybody at every opportunity, till one doesn't wonder that the great men will have none of it inside the council chamber. Weather is surely against them tho, and they are getting poor negatives and that is one reason they are so earnest in their endeavors to get as many exposures as they can, hoping that out of all of them, there will be some good ones. They began using flashes outside for some of the late arrivals, and these were distinctly audible and visible inside, and they did seem just a bit out of keeping with the dignity of the occasion.

We stay around a bit after walking thro the rooms and taking a good look at the large Salon l'Horloge where the big conferences are held. Also at the smaller salons, where the advisers and others wait till they are called. Then we left amid the curious interest and respect, too, of the immense crowd outside.

January 18, 1919

Full conference and I missed it thro finding that I had no adequate pass arranged for it, and I was unable to find Lieutenant Wanger, either yesterday or today, to fix it up for me. The Press finally won out, and have been granted limited privileges in attending and viewing and hearing these sessions from the antirooms aside. This is the opening formally of the Conference today, and I should have liked so much to have been there, inside. I try a few sketches outside to content myself.

So I get a car and go out to the Depot Quartermaster at Port St. Denis to look for some Army furniture for the studio, thro a part of Paris that I didn't know at all. A glorious day, too, tho cold, and as it settles into late afternoon, there are wonderful banks of real Brangwyn clouds on all sides, lit with a wonderful sunset glow, and I see around the edges of the town, cut out against this marvelous background of clouds, aeroplanes here and there.[167] What a sight! And then I see the big Farman aeroplane that is to inaugurate the passenger airline between Paris and London, for it flies at a low altitude directly over my head. Five other ships of the same type are nearing completion and they expect soon to have a daily service between the two points. They figure three hours for the trip at a charge of 400 francs each way. It sounds like a real service this time. There seems to be no bluff about this venture.

Paris-London air service has been delayed owing to Great Britain's objection to civilian foreigners, or some such, landing from aeroplanes on her soil. Rumor has it that it is her idea to assume control thus of the air route, but France can easily come back at her in like wise.

January 21, 1919

The Big Five had another conference at Palace d'Orsay today. They are deep in the Russian question, and today had in the Danish Minister to

Russia for information. I go over and look the place over thoroughly again for possible situations and stay to see them break up and come out.

While waiting, I meet Sir George Riddell who is in charge of the British press representatives. He is a very interesting man. He seemed interested in my mission there, and informed me that he expected to see Augustus John and [William] Orpen there tomorrow.[168] We talked of all sorts of things, including interior decoration, particularly modern English. From his talk, I gather that he is in some way connected with the English publication, *Country Life*. There was a Lieutenant Harmsworth there, too, who seemed to be a sort of watchdog for the English Mission or members and, as were the duties of our own Mr. Sommer in keeping out those who had no right in, his were much the same for the British. He is a son, I believe, of Alfred Harmsworth, the editor and publisher.[169] Mr. Sommer, our man there in plain clothes, is from G-2, Military Intelligence. He seems to take quite an interest in helping me out, and has promised to look after me and see that I get into the big general conference.

A little later, Megan George, Lloyd George's daughter, about fourteen or fifteen years of age I should guess, comes in and has a long visit with Sir George whom she seems to know intimately. They have a great old visit, then she sets out to look over the big conference room.

In the meantime, the meeting breaks up and the men come out in groups. Wilson and Lloyd George are together. They go over near the mantle and enter into earnest but pleasant discussion which ends with a funny story by Wilson at which they both laugh heartily. Balfour and the Italians are having a discussion on the other side of the room, then as the Italians withdraw, Balfour's aides appear from the chamber and talk with him, and Balfour is heard to remark, as he shakes his head vigorously, "Well just who is one to believe anyway after hearing all these different stories?"

The cameramen are all waiting for them as they leave. And so is the populace, without the gates as usual. It seems that all of Paris is always there. And at last I walk out, resplendent in my best boots and spurs, and I bask in the sunshine of the great, of which the crowd seems to think I am a part, for they pay as much attention to me as to the rest. What Ho! Oh well, they will never know, so it's all right. And I get a little reflected glory.

January 22, 1919
꙳

*C*onference still at the Russian question and today Wilson leaves alone and with a long, serious face. His private guard falls cautiously and casually in behind at a disarming distance and follows him out. There is a sudden call for the English shipping experts who have been waiting in the ante-room with the rest of us. An English major, who is ever in attendance at the meetings as a secretary, I think, brings them information and a demand that they at once put certain shipping into the hands of the Allies for some sort of shipping at once for Russia. They nod in approval and vanish quickly.

Clemenceau and one of the Japanese come out now. Clemenceau is joking and laughing (something I didn't suspect him capable of), and he is pounding the poor uncomfortable little Jap on the back with resounding thumps and saying that he has hopes yet of seeing Japan before he dies, and please won't he fix that up for him, meaning, I suppose, some arrangements for a trip there. It struck me as very droll. Click go the cameras like so many machine guns. Buzz go the gossiping crowds there at the gates, then it's all over for this day.

Harding and Dunn leave suddenly today for Brest to board a battle-ship there for Washington.[170] Some change was made in their plans for them at Tours, and they had no warning nor any time to see any of us, so they left me a note asking me to see that their crates followed them on. Also they left a promise to write me fully as to the developments there as to our future.

January 24, 1919
꙳

*T*oday Parisians are surprised to find that there is a strike (*grève*) in all the subways in town. It was called very suddenly, and demands are presented by the workers for an increase in pay of two francs per day, a war bonus for the past year, three weeks annual holiday with pay, annual pensions after twenty years' service and an eight-hour day. Strait away the companies have demanded the right to increase their fares, which so far the city had refused them. So taxicabs are at a premium and it is impossible to get one, tho some clever boy hit on a scheme which has caught on rapidly, so that tonight there are boys at all important centres who hunt out persons who are going more-or-less in the same direction, then for his fee he hunts a taxi and bundles them all in, and they go on their way rejoicing, . . . where in the old way only one or two persons would have had it and the others gone begging. Fine idea.

Things seem to be still exciting at the Conference at the Palace d'Orsay, tho they seem to be making progress, from the reports we get at the Crillon.[171] I must go around again, for tomorrow there is to be a plenary session, and it is likely that Wilson will read the draft of the articles drawn up and agreed to by the delegates for the League of Nations.

January 25, 1919

The League of Nations Principles were adopted today by all the delegates at the Peace Conference. What a memorable meeting. I arrived late owing to the strike and the impossibility of finding a taxi until the very last minute, and I arrived at such a late hour that I was unable to get a place from which I could see well enough, or really be free enough of movement, to make sketches which I went prepared to do. However, I was able to see over the heads of the correspondents in front of me and to hear perfectly. It was really an impressive lot of men who sat in at that meeting there. And what a serious one, too, but why shouldn't they be, with the purpose for which they were gathered from the four corners of the globe?

The delegates of the smaller nations were the first to arrive and take their places at once, then came leisurely and so complacently the others. Wilson arrived one of the very last, numbers of the delegates greeting him cordially and shaking his hand. Lloyd George was most friendly, and even Clemenceau was profuse in his greeting. Grey gloves as usual, Clemenceau wore. And how serious he looked today, tho he always does, for that matter. He settled back in his great chair at the head of the table, waited for them to take their places and, promptly on the hour, rose and called the meeting to order, turned to President Wilson, mentioned his name, bowed to him, and Wilson rose slowly, a slight smile on his face, and the thing that the world has waited for at least since the Armistice, yes, even for a much longer time, was done, or at least the evidence that it was actually in the throes of being born was presented with the reading, and then the adoption of the preliminary resolutions for the actual creation of a League of Nations. The five preliminary resolutions had been printed and distributed to all the delegates and, as well, to all the representatives of the press in the chamber adjoining.

Wilson's speech in presenting them was most forceful and most simple; there was no effect of oratory; in fact, it had all the simpleness and the seriousness of a sermon, tho I ought to make no such (undignified) comparisons. One noted somehow a sense of great satisfaction spread over his features when he came to the phrase that will be memorable henceforth, "Gentlemen, the select classes of mankind are no longer the governors of mankind. The fortunes of mankind are now in the hands of the plain peoples of the whole world. Satisfy them and you have not only justified their confidence . . . but established peace. Fail to satisfy them, and no arrangement that you can make will either set up, or steady, the peace of the world."

He spoke feelingly of our boys who had come into the war; had come to fight not so much to settle a war, he said, as to win a cause, after our Government had voiced its purposes in pursuit of a principle. So he felt it necessary on his part to labor, at whatever cost, now, to accomplish the object for which they had fought.

He was listened to most attentively, even breathlessly at times, by everybody, Clemenceau and Lloyd George often keeping their eyes fixed on him, leaning forward in their chairs and nodding their heads in silent but emphatic approval.

Everyone seemed to feel the bigness, the import of the occasion, and there was no applause, save that of a reverent silence. Lloyd George, at a nod from the Tiger, was on his feet in an instant, and in a manner as simple and eloquent thro its very simplicity and earnestness. I was much impressed with a certain thing he said after telling of a recent visit of his to the devastated regions of France. "I drove for hours thro a country which did not appear like the habitation of living men and women and children, but like the excavation of a buried province—shattered, torn, rent. I went to one city where I witnessed a scene of devastation that no indemnity can ever repair — one of the beautiful things of the world, disfigured and defaced beyond repair. And one of the cruellest features, to my mind, was what I could see had happened — that Frenchmen — who loved their land almost beyond any nation — in order to establish the justice of their cause, had to assist a cruel enemy in demolishing their own homes, and I felt these are the results — only part of the results — of the only method, the only organized method, that civilized nations have ever attempted or established, to settle disputes between them. And my feeling was surely it is time, surely it is time that a saner plan for settling disputes between peoples be established than this organized savagery."

It was most interesting to watch Wilson as he uttered these words. He sat there with face upturned to Lloyd George, utterly wrapped in what he was saying, his head nodding in an approval that seemed to say, "What an argument." It was as tho a new light broke in his own argumentative mind for this supreme idea of his, the utter abolition of war from the face of the earth. And it surely was a telling arraignment of modern warfare and a powerful argument for the new League. And yet he used no argument really. Only a few plain words to make that simple statement. A powerful second it was to a powerful proposal.

What a contrast these were to the argument then made for the League by Leon Bourgeois for France.[172] Equally sincere beyond a shadow of a doubt, for there can be no nation more vitally interested in a world peace for all time than France, with her frontiers otherwise a continual menace to her, necessitating the continuation of her burden of a perpetual military force and life. But here came polished oratory, a great music of the voice that ran the gamut of the vocal scale, with the accompanying and expressive physical discourse as well.

And then Signor Orlando, with his great mop of snow-white hair, rises on behalf of Italy.[173] And Bourgeois was outdone at once, for here was the full fire of the Latin temperament with a grand opportunity, and he rose to it in all his might. One would have thought that he must have been making some most impassioned plea — it was as tho it were the reading of some grand drama by one of his Italian idols perhaps, and what a voice and what a deluge of movement. Arms that were waving with the fury of a windmill in a gale; Delsarte to the full.[174] And when we got the translation (what a trial it is to have to sit thro all the interpreters' second readings too), all he had said was that Italy acquiesced in the adoption or adherence to the principles of the League or for the founding of it.

I think tho, that it was Orlando who preceded Bourgeois. Either of them might have been conducting an orchestra if one were to take their actions only for a clue to their intentions. And as I say, it was such a contrast to the more-or-less suppressed emotion of our northern speakers. Wilson dropped his voice almost to a whisper at times. Lloyd George was conducting a conversation as to an intimate friend on a serious matter. It was a striking revelation of the difference of temperament of the Latin races. A glance at the press room showed much the same contrast. Black, firey fellows were all southern representatives, France, of course, included in this category, practically all of them bearded, and practically all of them aesthetic or super-aesthetic types, in marked contrast, too, to the more or less beefiness of the American or British correspondents. Yet there was as marked a difference between the English and the Americans too, in spite of their similarity. And this same difference was noticeable to a degree in the Conference room.

Up till now, things had gone quietly and smoothly. Clemenceau seemed to beam with his satisfaction. But now there was a new note heard. [William Morris] Hughes of Australia rose.[175] Approval for his country, to a degree, but at the proper moment he wanted to discuss the scheme. His manner was most brisk. "I should like an opportunity of discussing the scheme when it is finished." This Clemenceau promised.

Then came a Chinese delegate who said merely, and in only a few words, that his country wished to help the Western nations in abolishing war.

Then there was a Polish delegate who said that the Polish people blessed the idea and hoped for its fulfillment.

And then, with flashing eyes, and a storm of protest after the Conference had voted its adoption of the preliminary resolutions and Clemenceau had named the committees to consider them, [Paul] Hymans of Belgium was on his feet and in conflict with the easy acquiescence of the meeting.[176] For he felt that Belgium, who had suffered so much and whose geographical position was exposed, was inadequately represented on the committees. Also he felt that she should be included in the membership of the greater powers on the committee for the League of Nations. He was most dramatic in his plea.

There was a veritable duel, for a time, between him and Clemenceau, whose great desire for smooth sailing and a desire to get ahead with things, made him a steamroller, as it were, and his retorts were one syllable almost and finally Hymans, and the support he had elicited from the other more-or-less suspicious small nations, Serbia, [Eleutherios] Venizelos for Greece with a very interesting speech (what an interesting man he seemed), Portugal, Romania and Poland, were squelched.[177] They all felt, too, that they were not sufficiently represented on the proposed committees. But Clemenceau started the steamroller, demanding adherence to the scheme of the five great powers, assuring them in no uncertain words that it was only thro their grace and because of their conception of this League of Nations that the little powers were to be saved and have their peace arranged for them, and that since they had merely been asked to come into the thing thro a feeling of interest for their peace, they might well let the five settle a few of the preliminary things, since it was undoubtedly true that the larger the committees the smaller the amount of work done and the longer in the doing. This insight came from his long experience in serving on committees. And as work was what was now demanded with all speed, he challenged anyone to vote "No" to the program as adopted, or laid out for the commencement of the League. Hymans protested that he had no desire to hinder progress. And gave in.

All this was most interesting, and, in a way, a pleasant change from the quietness that had preceded. One knew too well that this was to come eventually, and it seemed the better to break at once. And in spite of Clemenceau's apparent mastery, one felt that the air was much purer and that the smaller powers had been well represented and that, too, they would gain much thro this taking the bit in their teeth at once.

The Arabians sat so quietly thro it all. With their interesting costumes, the only strange note in the assembly, their heads in their hands all the time it seemed, they lent rather an air of mystery to the meeting.

The Japanese had nothing to say as usual — there were enigmatic smiles from time-to-time and one knows that it's a sleeping volcano there — that Fujiyama will burst into eruption again in the not distant future. For these men, in spite of their approval to date, are biding their time to open the discussion, and that they will have much to say in a few words later on. One feels that there will be no oratory ever with them, either. Clemenceau, most of the time, lay back in his great chair, eyes turned to the ceiling, his grey gloves always on his hands and, because of their more-or-less unusualness, always in evidence. He makes short shrift of all the seeming difficulties, and with a word, short or curt as occasion demands, and with a wave of his hand, things proceed, and this getting ahead with things is now a hobby of his.

The press delegates were all ears and eyes. Spread out like a great fan from the open doorways to the Conference room, women mingled with the men, and straining forward, everyone trying to get a better glimpse or hearing of the one speaking. Low questions as to who was the speaker were asked. Sometimes there were disconcerting discussions on the part of thoughtless ones too, for there was too much talking at times on the part of those who couldn't see, and there were many who could not. It bothered at times the delegates who were nearest in the Conference, and they threw anxious and wondering glances sometimes toward the noise. It did strike me as most disrespectful. If it continues, no doubt there will be trouble, for, after all, the press is there under protest.

A most interesting day. I could make no sketches, tho I mean another time to get there earlier and up to the fore as did Dorville, the Frenchman who was in the front row. There was an older Frenchman there, too, who seemed to be making sketches in a very tiny book.

Tremendous crowds waited outside today.

January 26, 1919
❧

The strike on the subways promises to end today thro a threat of the Government to take them over. Soldiers have been on guard since the beginning. Limited service was resumed yesterday on some lines. Thro Clemenceau a decree was issued insisting on the resumption of an indispensable service with the threat to take the lines. It was demanded also that the two parties to the quarrel get together at once to settle the difficulty. But the lines must run. And they are running again.

February 14, 1919
❧

And what a Valentine was presented to the world today. For there was a plenary session of the Peace Conference and the result of the deliberation of the last two weeks by the committee to draft the articles to the League of Nations was presented to the world by him who, after all, must be given the greatest credit for the birth, both of the idea and the League itself, which one can truly say was born today, in that it sees the full light of the world, and even as I write this, practically the whole world has seen the infant and admires or condemns its appearance and promise. Surely this was Wilson's day. How he has labored for this, and at last he has achieved it, and one wonders at what actual conflict in those secret meetings, for we know it has been will against will, argument against argument, yes and unselfishness against selfishness, openmindedness against bias. Someday one will get, perhaps, the inside story of those meetings between these strong men of the earth.

Having arranged thro Ray Stannard Baker for entrance to the press gallery or room, I arrived early and after considerable argument, and the discovery that Dorville, the French artist, was already inside at work on details, I was allowed to get in ahead of the press, which was being kept out till a quarter of an hour before the opening of the session.[178] To get in ahead of them seemed imperative if one wished to make sketches. I got into the opening in which was the table for the Jap secretaries, with a chair, thinking that I would be protected there, for at the preceding open session there had been no crowding into these spaces other than the chairs that were in them.

Soon the delegates began to arrive, and in most cases they kept their own counsel and took their places at once. A few who were now friends, talked and passed remarks that brought smiles. Others were serious as could be. The Arabians came in and sat down head in hands as usual. Clemenceau arrives and the English, minus Lloyd George who was forced to go to his duties for a time in London. Balfour looks unusually tall, weary and almost blasé today as he takes his seat, settles back, and, in an abstract way, gazes into the beyond. Soon Wilson arrives, greeted quietly here and there with an outstretched hand and a word. He seems as matter-of-fact as a businessman entering his office for a day's work. Clemenceau tries to force him to take the seat at the head of the table where today there is a marvelous, old, high-backed chair in red. But he refuses to the last, so when Wilson isn't looking, Clemenceau has his chair exchanged for this big one, and he is forced so to take it, which he does, appreciating the joke.

Before one realizes it, Clemenceau has opened the meeting and the President is on his feet and launched at once into the reading of the twenty-seven articles of the draft for the League of Nations, making at times slight explanations of certain clauses therein. The reading of the articles occupied most of an hour, after which he made remarks that one might call a speech were it not delivered in such a matter-of-fact, un-dramatic way. So casual, unemotional even, on such a momentous occasion and one that was truly his, for it was his day, for which he has thought and laboured so long. The consummation of one will of all that our army fought for, after all; the big idea that is today put before the world with an assurance of being now an established fact; this desire and determination on the part of the nations of the world to live in unity and peace and cooperation. There was no sense of drama on such a dramatic occasion. Simplicity was the note, and he established that note to the limit. There was scarcely a gesture even, tho there was at times a slight stress in his voice or a suggestion of a suppressed emotion as he uttered some telling point. One felt that he would like to have hit hard when he said that, "We are done with annexations of helpless peoples, meant in some instances by some powers, to be used merely for exploitation," and, too, when he referred to the impossibility henceforth of secret treaties.

About midway of his speech, Mrs. Wilson entered quietly and unno-ticed at the rear, and took a seat in the group of women secretaries or stenographers there. Even the President gave no sign of having seen her, and she seemed determined to give no evidence of the pride she must have felt in her now distinguished husband. She was as casual as he, tho on both their parts, I imagine, it was a studied casualness, to a degree.

Lord Robert Cecil followed Wilson with a short talk on the unanimity of feeling and opinion and the good feeling that had existed throughout in the drawing up of the articles in committee.[179] Bourgeois followed, making it known, as did Cecil, that later there were points to discuss and things to be incorporated in the constitution. For the limitation of armament and definite guarantees of armed protection at all times are worrying France, who still has her frontiers to watch in case of sudden emergency.

Orlando followed. Then Baron [Nobuaki] Makino for Japan with the simple statement also that when the time came for discussion, Japan would be prepared to present certain principles. Of course, all knew what these meant, for the immigration question lies close to her heart. And it's a question that I imagine worries our delegates a bit, for no matter how they may feel about the question and the justice of the point of view of Japan under the new ideals for which the League stands, and knowing, too, that we are *the idealists* of the nations and that our troops and our President have fought for this very League, they still have that large sectional bias, and it is large, that fills our western coast facing Japan. This will be one of the knotty points in the adoption of, and signing of, final acceptance of the League's principles, making us members of it.

[George N.] Barnes, the British Labor leader, followed Bourgeois in a plea for an armed international force, then Venizelos in much the same tenor.[180]

Then the Arabian rose to ask in regard to the mandatories over peoples not yet considered as being able to govern themselves and as to what was to become of existing treaties they might have.[181] He was told that this would all come up for discussion later.

Then Hughes of Australia was back at Clemenceau again with a demand to know when and where, then, the discussions on these mandatories was to take place. All the answer he got was that the document was to lie on the table now (presumably till Wilson has returned from the States where he is to go at once), and that it would be discussed at a future date. And before he could rise and come back with further questions, he found, to his evident chagrin and embarrassment, that Clemenceau had dismissed the session. There is to be fire later one knows, for the same difficulty came up between them at the previous meeting.

As before, the translation made a full half of the meeting, a tiresome affair packed in . . . as we were there. Alas my plans to sketch. How little I had counted on these actual conditions to exist there. For impatient as the press was at their forced delay in entering till the tables were practically all set and the show about to begin, when they were finally admitted, they were like a ravenous lot at sight of food, and came crashing down on the three openings that were to provide them sight of the Conference room. They rushed over the tops of the table guarding the openings and the secretaries in front, and jumped down into the little wells there and took the secretaries' chairs, for they had not yet arrived. My protests were of no avail, for . . . they seemed to imply, who was I, even if I did want to draw, that should have any more right to see than they, who, after all, were really there to listen? I was pinned in so tight that there was no room to move my arms. Pushed forward against, and half under, a curtain that crackled at every move, and on the other side of which was a Jap secretary standing, leaning against it and taking advantage of every move I made, the situation was hopeless, and the few slight sketches that I made were futile, it seemed to me. But what could one do? And the crowd today was so highhanded and caused so much annoyance at times with their noise to the delegates at the Conference, that I am sure there will be some restrictions made that will clear conditions at these open sessions. Certainly, there were numbers of people there today whose only interest was selfish curiosity, with no relations to any press, hence under the original grant of liberty to the press, with no right there at all.

But it was a great day in spite of my disappointment.

And tonight the President takes the train for Brest to rush back to Washington. The Gare is decorated in his honor, and is as gay as can be. A distinguished assembly is to see them off, and he promises to be back, they say, as early as the 5th or 6th of March, tho how he is to do it one can't quite see. However, if he has determined on a certain date for his return, it will be accomplished, one can rest assured of that.[182]

CHAPTER 9

LAST WEEKS

Townsend hoped to get back to the battlefields and do some serious artwork, but cold, inclement weather kept him from accomplishing much of substance there. He did observe the massive cleanup operations, which often proceeded with the help of German prisoners. And he had only sympathy for the graves registration personnel engaged in their gruesome but necessary jobs. The battlefields also now drew junketing U.S. congressmen and officials, seeking their first glimpses of the war zone, and Townsend observed some of these.

In addition, he struggled with his own mixed emotions as to whether he should stay in France or go home. His hesitancy in resolving the conflict resulted in some tensions with his wife, Cory, which ended only when he set sail for the United States. To be sure, his contacts with an old friend, a certain Mlle. Lissagaray, might have contributed to Cory's concerns. So, too, might have the rumors rampant in the States that the men who stayed in France were suffering from venereal diseases and could only sail home following a cure.

Back in Paris from the battle zone, Townsend noted the deteriorating relations among the former Allies as the peace negotiations continued, as well as some internal pressures within France, that surfaced as May Day approached.

Meanwhile, he journeyed to Chaumont, where, if nothing else, he observed General Pershing dancing. A livelier event was his own first flight — at last — in an aircraft, a D.H. 4. The experience was all that he expected, and he wrote lyrically of it.

In May of 1919, Townsend turned his steps belatedly homeward. His war experiences rapidly receded as he launched his peacetime career.

February 22, 1919
⁂

*W*ashington's birthday and there are celebrations here today and Pershing's own band has been sent up from Chaumont to furnish the music, staying on for a week to play for the Parisians and the Americans in Paris. Tomorrow there is to be a concert in the Luxembourg Gardens. Will go and hear them then, as I didn't feel like getting out today in the pouring rain.

Afterwards, when it cleared up, went up to the office and from there on up to see if I might find Mlle. Lissagaray in at last, for I've tried a number of times without success. And a letter from Cory asking about her put the notion in my head of trying again today. Successful this time, for I did find her. Greeted me in a working blouse, and what a surprise I had to find her a hard-working artist and what wonderful things she showed me after we had visited for a time and asked innumerable questions of each other — I getting all the news that we had wanted for so long of our Montreuil friends. . . .

Then as she casually remarked that maybe I would be interested in seeing some of the drawings she made in India, I awoke to the fact that hadn't been at all clear; that she was really an artist. . . . She also stated that she was a friend of [Bernard] Naudin.[183] And it developed, too, one . . . of Anatole France, and before I left, she showed me a book by Naudin, text by France.[184] He had written an inscription in it for her, and Naudin had made a fine large pencil drawing in it for her.

She had begun by asking all sorts of questions about us, particularly Cory and Barbara, who she remembered . . . so well, even down to tiny details, and of the days there in Montreuil. So that I was very pleased to find that she was quite so glad to learn of us all. Now I am writing to Cory of my visit, telling her how happy I am to have found her, and how I wish I had looked her up sooner, for she will mean a lot to my existence here in Paris henceforth, for, lacking Cory and her fine appreciation, and really knowing no women of truly artistic sensibilities here now, she will help fill a void that is very noticeable in my life here. So that if she seems willing, I will be happy, for I have always liked her besides. This sounds like a confession, but since I am writing frankly to Cory about it, and will of my visits there in the future, I feel free to write this here, and to indulge my feelings to the extent of feeling not quite so alone in a great city.

Afterwards, I went to dinner at the Châteaudun with the boys.

February 23, 1919

Church and then to the concert in the Luxembourg. Not having been over thro the Gardens for some time, I was surprised and transported to the old times by finding apparently all of Paris out as in those old days. For the weather was mild and spring-like, and children seemed more numerous than ever (probably true, too), and the merry-go-rounds were all running and the Punch and Judy shows were playing to the same delighted crowds of children. . . .

Quite spring-like today, and everyone seemed to sense it and enjoy what they must feel is a relief from a hard winter with all its coal and wood famine. And the spring now will fortify them better to bear the high cost of living that helps to oppress them as it does.

February 24, 1919

Still spring-like and it surely feels good after the winter. Everyone seems out in the sunshine, tho they do have to put up their umbrellas every little while, for showers tumble down out of nothing, it seems.

Go up to Lissagaray's tonight. . . . It was quite a pleasant evening. We talked much of Montreuil. . . .

March 10, 1919

My birthday today. Forty years — think of it, but I know I am not that old, and yet I know I am far older. And the war has added a lot mentally, I am sure, tho physically I believe it has taken years off me, and I feel that I could equal all my endurance of the past, even in a game of tennis, tho I might be disillusioned should I try. But I am determined to continue to believe that one is only as old as he feels, and so at that rate, I am still the youth of twenty years ago. Tonight I shall celebrate by dancing at the Aero Club. Will take Mlle. Lissagaray and know that Cory will not mind, for they have written that they hope I will celebrate. Oh, if she will only understand, yet I am sure she will. And if she only knew how much I do think of her here, and how I wish she were here tonight to take.

In a way, I am glad I am here in Paris today instead of somewhere down on the old front as I had expected to be by now. But I despair of getting that car that they have promised me. After all, things don't look too promising as to our being properly looked after as to getting around.

March 11, 1919

*H*ad a fine time at the dance, a nice dinner there first. Floor not at all crowded, and a number of fine dancers were there. We danced pretty well together, tho I find I still am unable to waltz well; the French waltz baffles me, and anyway I much prefer the old-fashioned one that Cory and I know so well. But I am somehow going to learn this one.

Things seem none too smooth at the Conference, tho one is assured that progress is being made all the time in the small committees.

Politics at home is showing itself up in rather a bad light over here. What a fool [Henry Cabot] Lodge has made of himself.[185]

March 12, 1919

*I*t seems impossible to keep this old diary going here in Paris where, after all, in spite of its being the hub of the universe, there seems so little to write, and I have such difficulty making myself write. For it's the same humdrum existence; night after night it's the same old dinner with Jack and Wallace, fine as they are, tho it gets down to a monotony. And dinners seem much the same, tho we do sort of vary them a bit. And day succeeds day with the same dull look, trying to get ahead here, and waiting vainly, it seems, for some action in regard to the car which doesn't arrive. Always some excuse. Still the weather is none too good for outdoor work, and I do have doubts if one could really accomplish anything painting down there in the Vosges.

In the meantime, I work away at the charcoals and try to finish up the oils. And worry till I am most sick as to future plans. How I do want Cory and Barbara over here, and I write her time after time to that effect; still come the letters from her from time-to-time, discouraged and blue and mistrusting me, and I think down in her heart she has the feeling that I don't want to come home or that I don't really miss them. How little she knows of how much I think of them and of the nights I lay here in bed in tears over it all. To be sure, I don't somehow look forward to going back to the States, and I would be so happy if I could get them over. But it seems nothing can be done at this end on account of that Army restriction. But she, as I write her, might be able to get passports there, and on the ground most likely of our having had residence here for a protracted time when the war broke out. But she doesn't answer on this phase of it, and seems to hold it against me that I don't get some action here at this end. And she has to wait such spells, too, for my letters there, which seem to get held up somewhere. But someday it will all be over, and she will forget all the sacrifice she has made so lovingly, and I do know trustingly, and I must try to get some outdoor studies made, for it is for that that I am staying, as she knows, when once I find there is no hope of her arranging there to come over.

But as to further diary, I will resort as I did after I came up here, I think, to now and then a retrospective affair, marking from time-to-time the high spots, perhaps.

Morgan and Smith are scheduled to go home soon. Aylward is sure he will be able to get Ida and the boy over, and is taking it up with a letter to Washington. In any case, he will stay six months or more to work up a set of drawings covering the ports.

Dropped in to see the [Lucian] Jonas exhibit.[186] What a lot of junk it is, too, and my worst fears were justified. Yet he is the man who is being hailed as the one artist that has come out of the war, and as having had . . . such a spiritual uplift by his dreadful participation. Spiritual fiddlesticks! And it makes one want to actually quit the whole game when one hears how critics, and public as well, fall for this sort of commonplace illustration. Why don't they rave about [Charles] Hoffbauer if they want to see some really nice things done by a real artist who has seen as much of the war as Jonas and gotten more true inspiration?[187] I am sickened at times, and think that I will be glad when people will forget that I have tried to make them think I was in any sense a recorder of the war as they thought it ought to be done. Oh, that bunch of knockers there in New York too, and will they ever forget and will we always be looked on as failures? Tho the reports from the show in Pittsburgh did sound as tho they were really prejudiced in New York, for we are supposed to have more than held our own in Pittsburgh as looking authentic. After all, we do know something of how lots of the English stuff was done, and if they ever had a chance to accuse us of loitering in the back areas and doing peaceful stuff (and gracious knows we were near enough the front all the time), how much more they can accuse some of the big hits of the British show, and how does it come that we hear nothing of the peace and quiet of the Orpen things?[188] Masterly I am sure they are, and I know I would like them, but why are the critics silenced when their show comes, yet they still keep up the grudge against us?

And so to bed, Pepys fashion. . . .[189]

Why keep a diary any longer anyway? And it would be sordid reading if I write as I feel and do each day. There is a bright spot from time-to-time when I go up to the Lissagarays' to eat and talk things over with them, and art with Mlle. Sometimes we go to a different restaurant, we fellows, and once we dropped in, I remember, at the Casino de Paris . . . after we had dined at Boivins. And we saw little to amuse there. Once in a while, we see Mrs. Mackenzie, and one night we went to help her arrange her card files on our "lost and found" boys.[190] What an interesting, yet a sad, sort of job this is. A pretty important one too, and fraught with so much joy or sadness for so many fathers and mothers and wives at home. Yes, and lovers too. She is a pretty capable woman, it seems to me, and is certainly making good at the job. She took us back to the hotel and we had champagne and a visit there. Cameron Mackenzie is now in Warsaw close to [Charles] Paderewski, sending back interesting stuff to the *Herald* on the situation there.[191]

No word comes from Harding till I am beginning to mistrust him. He seemed so eager to present my situation, along with his own, there in Washington, that I was sure he would write at once as he promised he would. Can his letter be lost? Soon Dunn will write, I am sure. Peixotto still wants me to take a teaching job at the art school on the Seine but I can't see it now. . . .[192]

Soon there's to be a [Edgar] Degas exhibit and sale, and I hope I may be here to see it.

March 30, 1919

🦋

*W*ill make a milestone out of this date anyway. Went to a tea dance at Mme. Zo's the other afternoon at 5, and had a rather nice time. . . .

Then to Aero Club with Lissagaray for their Mi-Careme dance, which was the last chance to dance there, as they are breaking up the club today.

Along about 11, when they ordinarily stop there, they brought out all the paraphernalia that goes with a Fête, rattles and noise makers and little battledores and ping-pong balls to bat around and colored streamers to throw till the dancers were wrapped in them. Then they hung a curtain over the face of the clock, and danced on. It was one o'clock when they stopped. Had to walk home. Wrote Cory all about it. Know she will understand. And now my dancing is over. Didn't last long, after all. And it really was a good change for me, for the days are getting pretty dull here. I never seem to get to any shows anymore owing to a desire to guard my cash so that I may keep up the extra forty home each month. I find I am always letting the fellows spend their money on me when it comes to a matter of buying an aperitif or a liqueur. I think they understand tho, and don't mind. Still, I have a conscience, and it worries me at times.

And Wallace Morgan and André Smith are gone. It's a week now, and Wallace gave me *The Tree of Heaven* as a parting gift.[193] I have wept over it. What delightful pages those are about the children. . . .

Will only touch on things from time-to-time in this book of mine, for will write in detail to Cory. And that will save rewriting. And it will be less work for me. And now there is all the excitement over the reports that the *Lorraine,* in which Wallace and André sailed, has been in a collision at sea, and they are unable to get any verifications or denials as yet from the steamship company.

Paper reports that *Lorraine* arrived in New York on the 29th. Good, quick trip that, and we will be interested to hear how their experiment of going home on a commercial liner worked out; how much army red tape they actually dodged so. And as to comfort, looks like a good bet to me. Think I will try it when I go, as go I feel I certainly shall, for something tells me that we are not to be together over here after all. I fear to write this to Cory tho, yet I am sure she will not make the effort there to get passports, and I am recording this belief here. And I really think she would rather not come over, for somehow they have a belief in the States that there is a very unstable feeling here, and that there is great likelihood of another war, and she has expressed her fears that I might be drawn into another war. Not I. I've had enough.

Begins to look as tho I might really get away at last on my trip. Car promised again, tho I do hope if I do, I can split up the trip, so that on coming back from a trip out to the Marne, I can get a peek at the Degas show on the 5th before going on down to Chaumont.

April 5, 1919
ᘒ

Car broke down on way up for me. Am to depend now on District of Paris, who will try to arrange for me in time.[194] So saw the show after all. Managed to run down a fine illustrated catalogue like the one for the first show that Mr. Destree of Durand Ruel gave me last summer. Also I got one of the second sale that I had missed also. Am promised a couple more of this sale. Will send one to Cory and give one to Lissagaray who is a Degas fan also. How Cory will like the little drawings in the catalogue. In a way, they are more satisfactory than the original, for I am sure he never really meant these drawings to see the light of day, for they are merest studies, tho strong ones, done over and over for his important pictures. But they are lovely after all, mussy as some of them may seem.

Went to the show with Mlle. Lissagaray, meeting there Mrs. Mackenzie . . . and also Duncan by arrangement. Afterwards Lissagaray and I go to Francis Jourdan's to look over his very interesting shop. It's near the gallery on the Rue de Seze. Writing Cory full particulars of their stock there. How much better she could do. I have been much interested in her letters in which she talks of getting into the interior decoration game, and have answered her enthusiastically on it, I am sure, tho there are many difficulties in the way of breaking into that game successfully. How many have taken a fling at it. But it does seem to me that the two of us ought to be able to somehow collaborate on it. And make a go of it. . . .

Car is scheduled for me for April 7, Monday. Will take Duncan out on a two-day trip to Château-Thierry region.

Cory's long, sad letter arrived and I am writing her fully how I feel today.

Am off!

April 7, 1919
ᘒ

Now that I have returned, will go back and cover lightly the points touched in my trip. My travel orders called for Chaumont, Toul, Baccarat, St. Mihiel and Montfaucon. To this was added the Marne, and I went there and spent the first two days. Took Duncan with me and we had fairly decent weather, tho it was cold in spite of the sun. Weren't we proud, too, of the car they assigned me for the trip: a brand-new Winton Six touring car, and Sergeant Boyle for driver, a fellow who was in the Argonne fight.

It was a beautiful trip out to Château-Thierry by way of Meaux which I was glad to see again. Had lunch at a good hotel in Château-Thierry, then out to Belleau Wood and the points around there. A bus of officers brought out to Belleau a couple of old Marine officers, Majors Larsen and Kingman. We found them out in the fields looking over the old ground they had fought so fiercely over. Took them in our car, and had an interesting afternoon going over the ground and listening to their stories of the awful fight our men had there to reach and gain the woods. Larsen said that his losses were actually 71 and 1/4 percent. Which is pretty heavy. His men were on the left side of the attack and had the greater difficulty. Major Kingman was on the right, and while they had bitter fighting, they had an easier proposition, for the attack of the left end was across deadly open spaces that, as one looked at them now, seemed impossible, raked as they were by such concentrated machine gun fire as the Boche had so well hidden in the woods on the side of the hill commanding the fields.

At night, we found a little Hotel des Cignes where they had a double room for us that they apologized for, because it had been bombarded, but one could see that they were carefully guarding it for the capital they could make out of it now that the rush of visitors is beginning. And it had surely been bombarded, and the night was cold and rainy and there was no way of keeping the weather out. But we enjoyed it all and, after a quick trip down thro Gland and Mt. Saint Père, we shot back to Lucy to make some sketches there. Left about 5, getting back to Paris in good season.

Lay over one day here letting the driver get the car in shape and get away on the morning of the 10th for Chaumont, going via Fontainebleau, as I had never seen this route before, and it is only a matter of a half-hour longer. We had fine weather as we started; stopped at Moret, famous old haunt of the artists of the past, and had a nice lunch there at an old restaurant that the *artistes* did and still do frequent, we were told. It was amusing to us to watch the great excitement our car seemed to cause to all the French officers who saw it, and on account of its size and its very modernity, self-starter and all, they would look it over most carefully, missing nothing even to the inside of it. We found the same curiosity at Château-Thierry. And they would always watch us off with envious eyes, it seemed. We were only leaving Moret when it began what proved to be a perpetual rain. And I was glad that I had had nice sunshine in which to come down thro the Barbizon fields and thro the forest of Fontainebleau.

Had a good look at the town of Fontainebleau and the Palace there. Beautiful.

At Sens we saw a detachment of the American-Polish troops marching to the train on their way at last to Poland to help . . . in the great war that they came over to take part in.[195] And what have been their vicissitudes after giving up their jobs and their homes there in the States, only to find when they get here, that they are to be kept in the back areas in France waiting till arrangements can be made, or decisions, rather, on the part of the Allies, that they are to be allowed to go to Poland. . . . Then means have to be found to get them there, and now, after months have passed and the Armistice has about worn itself out, Germany finally consents to let them thro (think of it) her country. And now they are off, for they are badly needed there, as even the Allies can see, so at last they arrange to get them there. What a powerful-looking lot of fellows they were, too. They seemed happy to be away, and they were singing continually a lusty and stirring song . . . save when some of them stopped and smiled and shouted to us in good English. It was quite stirring, this leaving of theirs, and I was glad to have seen it.

We got into Chaumont late, having stopped for food and gas at Bar-sur-Aube, 1st Army HQ at Chaumont, found a room at the old Hotel de France that I knew, sharing it . . . with a Lieutenant Baylis, a Marine officer just out of the hospital, having been wounded and gassed in the early Argonne fighting. Quite a siege of it, but out at last, and now on his way home, but, as he said, taking a week off here in Chaumont to spend with the nurse who looked after him so long in the hospital, and to whom he is now engaged. She had been transferred to a hospital in Chaumont so was taking advantage of the opportunity. . . .

I seem to be running into Marines everywhere these days, and they surely are a fine, simple lot of fellows. My sympathy goes to them always, for they sure do get it hard from the Army, and they are not to blame, either, for the making good they have showed at all times or for the publicity they have gotten. There is simply something about both their spirit and the jobs they have always been given to do, and the way in which they have done them, that has been irresistible from the point of view both of the newspapermen and the public who have read of it. It's a shame that there should be any jealousy on the part of the Army. And it's not to their credit, either.

April 11, 1919
❧

*H*ad intended to get out of Chaumont on the 11th, stopping either at Toul or at least at Neufchâteau for the night, but waited instead till the following morning to make a clean break. Had the weather been good, would have stayed longer at Chaumont, as they arranged at Air HQ to give me some flying there at the field nearby. But it was raining hard and cold, so it was left that I was to get in some flying at Toul by presenting myself at the field there. . . . Got in touch with the ordnance also in regard to some hand grenades for my collection which they were to send me and did. Then off. Stopped at Marthemont to have lunch. . . .

Then we went on thro Nancy to Lunéville, where I stopped to give notice to the Bathos [family] and incidentally surprise them greatly by my appearance. Yes, I was to come back there for the night. This was about three that we were there.

So we drove on out to Baccarat and to Domèvre to look over the old front there. It was interesting to see it again, but it has all fallen into decay somehow, the trenches and the gun positions, and it was very depressing. And in Domèvre we found them putting up, with the aid of great crowds of German prisoners working away in the rain, numbers of the new government huts being furnished in the devastated regions. It looks like a very comfortable and fairly pleasing-looking temporary home.

Decided that this one look over was all I would give down there. Had a nice supper and a visit with the Bathos [family]. They have a nice place and a garden, tho not in a class with their place in Neufchâteau. What a lot of questions they asked of me and of Cory and Barbara, and they tried to make me stay longer and were quite disappointed that I wouldn't. And when we were all here, we must surely come out and visit them. They had recovered all the choice pieces of furniture from their home at Cirey and, marvel of marvels, the Boche had in no way abused any of it. Upholstered chairs, taken into other homes there to be used, scattered about generally, were still in good condition. No broken mirrors nor anything of the sort, so that it set one wondering a bit about the vandalism. To be sure, the Germans have practiced it generally enough elsewhere, but one wonders why not throughout.

We had had some tire trouble already. Going back to Toul, via Pont-à-Mousson to glance over the fields on the way thro the St. Mihiel section, our troubles came on us in an endless line of blowouts, till poor Boyle was thoroughly discouraged, and we had to pick our way along so slowly that it was 7:45 when we reached Toul, having left Lunéville, fifty miles away, at 8:30 in the morning. It had been raining hard all day, and it was bitter cold and windy, and one felt sorry for the poor driver having to tug and tussle with those heavy tires in the mud and the rain and the cold. And, too, one got to cursing the luck that gave him such a heavy car for such a trip as I was out on, and not yet hitting the worst roads we were to have. Whatever would we do was our constant thought, I am afraid. Before we got anywhere near Toul, all our reserve tires were gone, and our tubes too, and it was a case of trying to patch old tubes and make them hold with shoes on tires already blown out till we could get into Toul and try to get a new set of tires, either from the garage there, or from Paris. We were pretty discouraged when we arrived late there. Had difficulty finding a room, and then food, and didn't it taste good! Our situation was complicated by the fact that the next day was Sunday, and we might have difficulty in finding either the Chief of Transport there, or our Chief in Paris, if necessary to wire or phone there. . . .

What weather. Pouring in the morning. We go to the Transportation Office and, lo and behold, they have the very tires we want. And what was most unusual, they were glad to let us have them, too. The driver assured me that it had been his experience that one could never get tires from any but your own garage, for he had tried it many times. At best, we were hoping here to get them on a promise of others being sent at once to them from Paris. But we found the 2d Army in the process of breaking up, so they were glad enough to get them off their hands.[196] We were delighted. Boyle asked for time till 11 o'clock to get them all on and in shape.

It was still raining furiously, but in spite of it, I decided to walk out to the aviation field to see Captain Robertson in command of the 141st Pursuit, an old friend of mine. . . . We all stayed to dinner with the squadron there, then I rode back to Toul with them, . . . getting away early the next morning.

Stopped at a salvage dump on the way in and got a number of pieces of equipment that I need for my collection. Then out to Flirey and Limey to see if it were possible to work there. It's still raining, but I do attempt to work, when we have another blowout, but it is so cold and windy that my fingers freeze. And it seems mighty good to get back to Toul again.

Get my dinner at the YMCA officers' club. There's a southern woman, a Mrs. Ackerman who runs it, and has real southern food and all one wants of it — five francs for dinner. It surely was good; real American food. Had my breakfast there too, three francs, hot waffles and a fried egg, and hot rolls and coffee, and oatmeal and fruit.

Out to the St. Mihiel section again where, while I try to work at Limey — Boyle drives up to Thiaucourt to get the Graves Registration man, a Lieutenant Keating, either to give him the exact location of Captain Moore's brother's grave, or else to send someone down with the car to find it for us, as I promised Captain Moore I would look it up and make a photo of it.[197] It seemed hopeless on account of the weather, but will try it, says I, and while I am waiting around in the cold and rain for him to come back, Boyle is having his own troubles with two more blowouts on the bad roads up there. Finally, he comes back with neither information nor a guide, but with the invitation to come up there for dinner first. We had counted on dinner there, the only likely place, so up we go, and after looking over the big cemetery there, and getting our stomachs full of all the terrible and gruesome details of their work transferring the poor boys' bodies from where they are now buried on the battlefields to this final resting place, we go back with Keating.

After a long search in the rain, we find it. It proves an interesting search tho, for the path snakes around over the top of the hill there in what was the worst-fought-over and most shell-torn place in the whole St. Mihiel drive. Saw many Boche dugouts and artillery positions that were of interest, particularly one elaborate underground heavy ammunition dump with the windlass and railroad track as tho it were still of use. What a terrible place it must have been in the shelled trenches there on the top of the ridge in sight of Flirey. Everywhere among the blownup trenches and in the shellholes are pieces of what were once men. Here and there, a whole or a piece of a bone; here and there, a shoe with a foot still in it. Here and there, a piece of a garment that has rotted, blood still on it. And what countless shells and air bombs and trench mortar projectiles sticking around everywhere in the ground unexploded. And grenades by the thousands and potato mashers.[198] And the strange freaks of shell fragments everywhere. . . .

We had no sooner than located the grave — and apparently he fell in the thick of it — when there is a furious storm scurrying along over the hills and valleys toward us. We look out over Flirey and I notice the lovely old ruin there of the church and had just remarked to Keating as to how remarkable it was that it had stood, that delicate lacework of a tower all these years of the war, when at that very moment the storm struck it, and in a cloud of dust that we could scarce believe, it fell before our eyes. One of the landmarks and one of the lovely ruins of this section gone!

We had difficulty in getting our side curtains on before it hit us and it surely did blow. As soon as practicable, we turned . . . back to Thiaucourt where . . . the storm had blown down a number of the barracks there, doing considerable damage. It was a regular hurricane. Then we came back and, the rain letting up for a moment, I took a few photos, without much hope of anything decent coming of them. Then on back to Toul.

Fine supper and then I go to an Army show — 20th Machine Gun Folies. A pretty funny show, too, with a couple of made-up girls that were peaches.[199] Try to run down some more salvage and hunt for a German machine gun. But no luck, tho I learn where they are, and get travel orders to get there.

We go out again to Seicheprey, and I start a large sketch of Seicheprey and Montsec in the rain. But find I can scarcely hold the brushes.

Make one more try at it the following day, as we head for the Verdun section, where we are going to make Moraine Farm for the night. This is the château run by the Visitor's Bureau. Work a bit more at it, but am by now so thoroughly disgusted that I have little hope of accomplishing anything.

We go thro Pannes and Béney, then take the upper road that wasn't so much shot up, this taking us thro St. Benoît, Woël, Doncourt to Fresnes. Then on to Étain, to Amel, to Billy and Moraine Farm which is just outside of this. Here we found that they would be glad to take us in. . . . Madame Matigny and Josephine, who used to run the guest house at Neufchâteau, were here, so it was like being at home. Two parties were there, one of two congressmen and other a Mr. and Mrs. Honnald, or some such name, a director in the Guarantee Trust Company here on some financial commission negotiating the Belgian loan, I understood. They were very nice and friendly, and asked me to come to the Hotel Mirabeau to see them.

This was very interesting country around here and very German, thro the four and a half years occupation perhaps, tho it had a very different look to the rest of France. Still it rains constantly.

I made a few little side trips around here, and, incidentally, go on up the line toward Arlon, stopping at Longwy at a salvage dump. From here, I go on to Aubange, which is in Belgium. Here I get a machine gun and am happy. Happy also to have gotten into Belgium. Come back thro Longuyon. Also saw the old forts at Longwy, very much demolished by the terrific shelling the Boche gave them when they broke thro into France in '14.

Two nights at the château. The second night, there were two more parties there. One with Mr. and Mrs. Thomas Howard Birch; he is our minister to Portugal. A fine, jolly type of a man. They are from New Jersey. Have been five years in Portugal.

The other party included Congressmen [W. Frank] James of Michigan and M. Clyde Kelly of Pittsburgh. They are over on the Military Investigations Committee. The talk was very interesting between them and Mr. Birch, who knew many of their associates. They talked at great length on the liquor question, they all apparently being dry men, tho they all liked their drink, as they admitted. . . . [200]

On to Montfaucon in the Argonne. Go by way of Verdun. What an interesting ride to Verdun from Étain. One can see over those beautiful hills to his right the old forts of Vaux and Douamont, and over to his left and down below him, he can see the worst-pocked hills imaginable. How anyone could live in such a hell of shellfire is beyond belief. And perhaps they didn't! Verdun itself is a very interesting town.

Then we go on to Montfaucon, taking the short route up thro Dombasle, Montzeville, Esnes, Haucourt and Malancourt. This route had been recommended to me as being a better road than the longer one via Varennes. However, if there are any worse roads than we found this, I will certainly keep clear of them, for our trip was almost impossible in our large car. Yet in as bad mood as I was in, I wouldn't have missed this trip . . . in the bad weather in which we saw it, for it converted this probably most shot-up and fought-over of all our territory in the Argonne, or for that matter, in the whole American battle areas, into the most forlorn, miserable and silent testimony to the horrors and devastations of war imaginable.

One appreciated, first of all, the almost impossible situation in which our troops found themselves. Those awful stretches of open distance to be raked as they were by enemy machine gun fire from protected positions across there. One could take this in at a glance. And it made one realize that, after all, it was as some officers have said in answer to the charge of our having thrown green troops into the fight here that, while that fact was true, and there were men here who had not been away from the States two months, the situation called for fighters and not soldiers, and that the green man was as effective as the veteran.

Today as we passed up, there was actually the silence of death over the great countryside, and it is a vast one here, and one sees for miles to the hills beyond. Everything seems razed to the ground. The few towns which we passed thro were nothing but a few standing fragments of walls if even so much as that. There wasn't a sign of life anywhere, not a bird in the sky, nothing of living things save those terrible rats that one saw scurrying across the road here and there, or whisking out or into a trench. Here and there in some shell crater, one saw the inevitable fragment of a bone or a shred of clothing.

Esnes was a picture of war and desolation. As one approached thro the trenches, foxholes, and gun emplacements with camouflage beginning to shred and tatter in the winds and the incessant rains, one saw Esnes with a long, low range of hills close beyond it. This hillside bore the marks of all sorts of defense and protection of the boys there, entrances to dugouts, shelters, foxholes, gun positions, ammunition dugouts, first-aid stations, etc., pockmarked on its side, sharp little black holes, and all mixed . . . with shellholes here and there and old wrecked trench systems.

Malancourt we found absolutely razed to the ground; not a stone that didn't seem to be shattered into fragments till they lay like a pile of litter on the hill here; not a tree stump anywhere to be seen, but here and there a piece of iron balustrade, or a bit of twisted iron gate or the like sticking from the wreckage. Here we found at noon, sitting and taking their lunch rather matter-of-factly, a family in the midst of what must have been the ruins of their old home, from the manner in which they had hunted it out, their old, two-seated buggy and their old horse beside them. It was a pathetic picture, save that there was, as has become the habitude of the devastated French, little of pathos in their own attitude thro the long years of their suffering and loss. The only real evidence I have seen to the contrary was the more or less weepy family we passed at the wreck of their home on the road from Pont-à-Mousson to Metz, which they had gone back to see immediately after the armistice.

On into Montfaucon now. From this commanding height what a view in all directions. What a ruin, too. One easily realized the importance of Montfaucon as a point of observation and as a position commanding such easily swept miles of open country. Here I saw in the large cemetery the largest shellholes I have ever seen. And what a debris had been thrown up from them. Pieces of corpses and coffin, and tiny bones all over. Here, too, a large mausoleum that was partly shot away, and the vault beneath broken and open, which revealed the corpse still lying there in torn, weather-stained black, all at a tipped, sliding angle thro the sinking of the ground beneath. It all lay so still and mysterious there that it gave one a queer feeling, and one wondered at the frame of mind of the officers or men who had to climb and sit and watch from the observation post that the Americans had built in the top of the mausoleum, looking out to the Boche hills beyond, all the while this strange, black corpse, some fifteen feet below, looking up at one all the time. Strange thoughts I took away from Montfaucon.

Still raining, we beat on now to Varennes, hoping to find a place to get some food there with some of the labor organizations. Here at Varennes we find the remnants of an Engineer outfit that had been working the railhead there and the railroad, all thro the offensive. The officer in command was a Lieutenant Lister (?), an old passenger conductor on the Michigan Central, who had been one of the first R.R. Engineer troops over. He was kindness itself, glad to see me to have a talk, for it seems few visitors ever drop in on him, and he has never had a leave since he took over the job. Glad also to feed us, and it surely was a good feed. And I did enjoy it, only somehow I felt rather out of place a captain, and he, with all his ability and important position, still only a lieutenant. But the treatment of the R.R. men over here in the matter of commissions has been one of the crying shames of the AEF. He has a wife and two grown daughters at home, and I think he said he was thirty-nine. At one time, he had fifty-two locomotives working overtime here, he said. At present, he was down to two, and was getting out salvage at the rate of thirty cars a day, tho a short time before, it had been a hundred. They were now thro, and the rest of the salvage was to be left and sold on the field.

From here, we go back thro Verdun, taking the right bank of the river down to St. Mihiel, on our way home. For I decide to go home. And what's more, I had made up my mind that once in Paris I was decided to clean up and get back to the States, since it wasn't worth the game trying to stay over to collect the kind of material that I had wanted, in view of the weather, the transportation, and also the discontent at home on Cory's part, which I am sure, from her point of view, is really justified, and more so, if I waste more time here unable to accomplish what I want, as it seems I am unable to do.

Leaving Varennes, we saw some of our first prisoners wearing American doughboy uniforms. They look quite like our men in them. Later, as we got out of Verdun, we were surprised to see coming down the road what seemed to be a bunch of Americans, only to discover a French *poilu* bringing up the rear as guard, with bayonetted rifle.

We hurry thro St. Mihiel, and on thro Bar-le-Duc to Vitry-le-François, determined to get as near to Paris as we could that night, and finish the trip early the next morning.

We make Fère-Champenoise, where we get a couple of rooms at the Hotel de Paris, three francs each, run our car, with all its load of equipment we had collected, into their courtyard where it is safe under lock and key for the night, then we have a bully supper. It's a hotel to remember for later. A nice, refined couple run it, and the little son, Louis, about nine or ten years of age, waited on us, a peach of a youngster who enjoys it all thoroughly, taking the part of a waiter with professional talent almost.

Away at 8 the next morning, and into the studio at 11. It has been a pretty discouraging trip. There are things I have gotten out of this trip that I am glad I got, impressions and sights, I mean. I was unable to work at all, owing to cold and rain at all times, and was the more disgusted that it began to clear up as we start back, but I had kept the car longer than I was supposed to, and had wired Colonel Roach that I was keeping it several days longer and named a day for my return, which I kept gladly.

The things I saw and learned in the Montfaucon sector, the experience with the Graves Registration crowd and the stories I heard of their horrible work, and the awful stained hands of the boys from handling this raw, rotting flesh of their dead comrades. The dangers they undergo thro the vile habit our salvage men have had of burying hand grenades in little shallow pits in the fields and marking the place generally with a little cross, or often so, which the graves people, searching for the dead, find and dig into with their picks, only to be answered in their quest by an explosion and more wounded comrades. This I learned has happened numbers of times. Horrible thought! Also the thought of the poor farmers, and particularly the mere youths, who are going to so innocently guide their plows into unseen half-buried, clay-covered grenades and duds that will lie so long a menace to them, and already one hears of these accidents. . . .

The custom of dressing the German prisoners in American uniforms was a necessary one, we were told at the time, but I hear that thro their being exact counterparts of our boys, they have been escaping easily, so that we are taking steps to clothe them differently when their old German ones wear out. This had been the cause of their being furnished khaki now, because we had such an abundance of it, and not enough Boche clothing captured or on hand.

I find no mail from home on my return, strange to say. This was a great disappointment, for I had wanted much to hear more from Cory, and to hear at last that she had gotten the money sent her. She will be pleased to hear that I have made up my mind about returning.

April 24, 1919

Today the blow fell. Wilson has given to the press his appeal to the Italian people and to the world, that they stand by the Fourteen Points.[201] And the Italians are withdrawing from the Conference, leaving the world agasp at the possibilities lurking in a deadlock.[202] To me, it seems he has done well, for the Italians, selfish throughout the entire conflict, and trying now to hang to that secret Treaty of London, have played the dog in the manger, or worse.[203] And they merit the censure of all the Allies, which, tho this is felt deep in the Allied consciousness no doubt, they have not openly said anything for fearing to lose her as an Ally. France has decided she must stand by the *Pacte de Londres,* and standing so, England feels that she must too. This leaves Wilson and America in that splendid isolation that has always been their boast, but the more splendid now![204]

To Lissagaray's to dinner tonight. A letter just reached them from a friend who lives at Pau, saying that space there was at a premium owing to the hordes of rich refugees arriving from Paris fleeing that much-talked-of (underground) revolution of the Bolsheviks that is scheduled for the first of May, tho which everyone seems to shrug their shoulders at and put aside as nonsense. There are some, tho, who think that there is the germ of another French Revolution bursting into flower.

Letter from Captain Dunn, also from Major Banning, explaining a bit the lack of interest in Washington as to the official artists. Poor reading for me who am now about at the breaking point. How long I have waited for some sort of a peg to hang our feeble — no, ardent — hope on, but I can see now that it is useless, for Aylward has had a letter from Washington putting a snuffer on his hope to have his family over. Alas and alack. And it's out of the service, or at least home for me now, I am sure, and at as early a date as it is possible to pack up and to first clean up a few of the drawings begun here. How sad it will be to leave Paris and not to bring over Cory and Barbara, bless them, who have been so patient about it all. How happy they will be, tho. I know that at last we will be together again, tho I sort of feel, too, that it is best for them to stay there in the States for a time, for they would be a bit worried, perhaps, at all the currents in the air here. It's rumor and counter-rumor all the time, it seems.

April 25, 1919

*And today the "Flaming Onion" of the Peace Conference, Orlando, has come back at Wilson with a pompous note to the press.[205] And full of strange insinuations, as well as expressions of surprise, at the Western method of taking the great public into his confidence. And there is a half-veiled suggestion that our way of settling the war, and the Armistice and all, on the Fourteen Points was partly responsible for not carrying the war to a proper and definite conclusion. Does he dare, too, to insinuate or to suggest, that without the Pact of London, Italy would never have joined the Allies? Knowing on what terms America came into the war, and with what ideals for the future peace of the world and justice to the little peoples, as well as the big, does he dare to insist still that the Pact of London, a secret pact and one of the things that America has at all times insisted must not exist further, must still stand when he must realize only too well, as do the other Allies, that without our entry into the war, they would have lost all. The other Allies admit this. Why, then, must he still insist that America hasn't a slight right to insist on what seems only a fair disposition of the Eastern Adriatic question on the lines of the Fourteen Points . . . ? There are rumors that Wilson's note was not permitted printed in the Italian papers, or at least not till after the Italian delegation had had a chance to get there ahead of it, and prepare their peoples.

In accordance with the request of Major Banning, I ran down our delinquent drawings, and find that they have been held all this time at the Signal Corps laboratories here in Paris thro somebody's fault, of course, tho it is now someone who is out of the service.[206] Passing the buck! But I had the satisfaction, a slight one I admit, of seeing them all packed up and ready to go to Paris by courier after all these months hidden away on a shelf there among a lot of enlargements, tho they insist that photos went to Washington as regularly as they were delivered and photographed. This, however, is not in accord with the advice from Banning, for according to him, they have had no idea as to what or how many drawings we have been making. What a fiasco it has all been. And to suffer the cost of all this carelessness as we have had to do, for we are the ones who pay, after all.

Met the fellows at the Regence tonight. . . . We go . . . to dinner, climbing the Butte Montmartre, the Sacred Mont, the Hills of Hymettus, to a little old wooden house called Le Veille Châtel, where at Chez Ni-Ni we have a fine dinner ordered in advance and prepared while we walk around and overlook Paris in the sunset. From here we go to . . . Le Lapin Agile. Run by Freddie, a Walt Whitman type of a man, who knew veritably how to run a place of the sort, where there were poets to recite their poems and singers to sing their songs, and most of all, there was Freddie himself with his sabots and his long, grey locks and his finger-stained guitar, and his fine, sweet voice, despite his age. And he sang and he kept things moving and everyone smiling, and how they sang the refrain "*O près de ma blonde, qui fait bon, fait bon, fait bon — O près de ma blonde, qui fait bien dormir.*" And there was no bothering to demand would one have another drink, and at 11 everyone put on their things and left. And we voted we had had one of the most interesting evenings of our time in Paris.

At home tonight and there is a cable from Cory, poor dear old Cory, trusting yet worrying there, and I must send her a cable tomorrow telling her that I will come at the first opportunity now. And there was a letter enclosing one to her from Harding in which he takes a pessimistic attitude as to the whole situation there. And Cory, I am sure, is more discouraged than ever over my having stayed, for she seems to have the impression that it was to wait for his letter that I have stayed, when it was really to get out over the old fields that I was staying. But my heart is no longer in this, it seems, after the bad experience I have been thro the last two weeks. But things will right themselves soon, I know.

April 26, 1919

*F*ound Lieutenant Alling of the Visitor's Bureau at Vefours for dinner. He had just returned from his three weeks leave in Italy. After the trouble here in Paris, he says the Italians were very disagreeable to the American soldiers and officers there, hissing and insulting them in many ways. Overbearing, too, in their manners, even before there was definite word in the papers of the difficulty. In fact, he says at the commencement of his leave there the Italian officers were most unbearable. . . . On the way back, he was told by one who saw it that the American flag was torn down, or an attempt was made to tear it down, in front of an American hut of some kind at Turin; that there was a fight there between Americans and Italians. Also that the American MPs are being withdrawn all over, and that it will be closed to Americans as a leave centre, of course. Interesting!

April 27, 1919

*P*aper this morning tells of Orlando's speech in Rome in which he shouts from the housetops the astounding news that Italy is more ready than she ever was to maintain her position and her honor before even the whole world. More ready than in 1915, the year she came into the war. What a statement, and is it a threat? Certainly as a threat, it can mean little to America other than that Italy is already outside the pale.

I mean to run down the stories, old ones about so many Italian troops having been killed by English artillery. It seems to be history that the Italians were only sufficiently bolstered up in their last offensive and victory against the Austrians by the English army, and Lieutenant Alling found confirmation, or further evidence from English officers he met in Italy, that the English had to fire into the Italian rear to prevent their retreat at a crucial time, when it was absolutely necessary that they advance or hold. The white feather became a red feather, it seems.

What a state the Allied world is in; yet I still maintain that Wilson was justified, tho it looks rather fatal for the League of Nations unless there is a compromise, or England and France will make a peace without Italy, which they say they can't do in violation of the Pact of London, a secret pact, and the League, of which they were such stout champions, took a firm stand . . . against secret treaties. What a position, unless their ministers finally bow to a peoples' mandate, which may even in England eventually support Wilson.

And now the *Confédération Générale du Travail,* the great French union, has come out with a letter backing up Wilson in the Italian matter. And today I took lunch with Edward Charpentier, an old friend, who is in town on a few days *permission,* and he says that there is no doubt but that the mass of French people, and politicians even, are back of Wilson, however much they may be against him on the literal interpretation of the Fourteen Points or the practicability of the League of Nations. . . .

Oh yes, I sent Cory a cable yesterday telling her that I had decided to return, possibly the first of June. And I will surely get there for Barbara's birthday.

April 28, 1919
꙰

*R*ead this morning of heavy snow in the Eastern U.S., then look out of my window a little later and find that the increasing cold wave here has turned our incessant rains of the last week into a violent snowstorm also.

There has been much talk of late of the Revolution May 1st. The paper this morning seems to think there is little danger of it, and Edward yesterday, who says he is in touch with some of the leaders in the movement, says that it is not yet the time for a show of strength; that it would please the Government too much to crush at once an abortive effort as it would be sure to be. That they will wait till there has been a far greater demobilization, for they could not depend on the army or rather a sufficient number of the malcontents in the army yet. Also the new developments in the Conference need waiting on to see where the wind really blows.

May 1, 1919
✸

*E*ngaged passage tentatively for the 31st, and possibly for the 24th, if a certain man gives up his sailing. Arranged to go down to GHQ today to talk things over when, in asking for a car to take me to the station, since on account of the strike there was to be no transportation running this morning, I found that there were to be no movements whatever of American cars, and that no one was to travel today. That orders had been issued from GHQ that all officers and men were to keep to their quarters unless absolutely necessary in line of duty. For they are determined that there shall be the smallest possible chance of any trouble occurring in which Americans might be involved. Perhaps it is better so. Everything is closed today. There is no food to be had, so it is lucky that I had enough canned stuff in the house to make out. So it's up in the morning and down to Chaumont to settle my troubles. Have been sorting out a lot of my accumulation today that will be that much out of the way later. . . .

It is raining hard all day today. A poor day for a holiday for the workers, for this is their day. How quiet the city is. All day I have heard but two taxis. They had planned a great parade from Concorde to Republic, but I read that the City had given notice that no *manifestations* would be permitted, so am wondering what happened there and if there was any trouble. Only one will never know of any incidents that have arisen today, for the censor now is as bad as at his worst. It all seems inexplicable the things he has done of late.

May 2, 1919
✸

*O*ff to Chaumont this morning. It's cold still but there is a pale sun today and in the comfort of the coach, one has a vision of Spring and loveliness thro the windows.

Am surprised to read in the morning papers of the demonstration yesterday. In spite of the peace and quiet of my quarter of the city, there was considerable trouble over where they tried to pull off the announced demonstration. And now there is the usual complaint about the government at cross purposes with the will of the people, and about the awful situation the government put the police and the soldiers into yesterday by using them against their brothers to the extent that many on both sides

were injured and one poor demonstrator, or civilian, was killed by a stray
bullet. From the reports, it seems that the police say that 200 of their men
were injured and there were some 60 or more of the troublemakers hurt.
Rather an unfair proportion, it seems to me. In the arrests that were made,
practically all the ones in the demonstration carried revolvers, blackjacks
or brass knuckles; Americans, they call them in the papers. So that it
doesn't look as tho the demonstration was not looking for trouble and
ready to make it as they protest, tho peaceable were their intentions they
insist. But they are just like the strikers at home; no better. . . .

At Chaumont, on time for the first time during the war. Fine lunch on
the train. Go strait to the office and take up the matter of being sent home
and also of getting my things thro, both of which they assure me can be
done. They take the matter up with General Nolan, who adheres to his old
policy of allowing the official artists to make their own plans, and then
helps them to carry them out. The idea of mine to go on liner suits them,
and they assure me it will be safe to go ahead and engage the stateroom.
They, at the suggestion of one of the G-1 men whom I consulted, get
General Nolan to write a memorandum to Chief of G-1, SOS, in regard
to taking my things as excess baggage and to give some authority that
would get them thro customs free of duty.[207] Now all that remains is to
take up the routine of seeing the proper person in the Adjutant General's
office in Tours as to permit to go on liner, which privilege is accorded to
officers. So that May 24 suits everybody. And now it's a matter of paying
for the berth to be sure of it, then wiring Cory. I wonder will she be as
happy as she has tried to say when she really hears I am coming home? For
I am sure, from the cable that awaited me here when I returned, that she
won't be. And now who knows what my decision will be?

Spend the night at Chaumont at the YMCA; find that "*Stop Thief*"
with a professional cast is playing there, so go and enjoy myself immensely,
for it is a scream from start to finish. Then discover, when I get out, that
there is an officers' dance in progress at the YMCA hut in the dining room,
a regular Friday night institution, so I go in and dance till the end at
midnight. Generals Pershing, Bullard and McAndrew, who have been at
the show, are all there, and General Pershing dances all the dances as
young as the best of us.[208] Like all officers' dances seem to be in the AEF,
this one is a cut-in dance, and you have no sooner than stolen somebody's
partner, who you decide is a fine dancer, till someone takes her away from
you. But I noticed that no one seemed to dare take the General's girl away
from him once he started with her, and she was none too good a dancer at
that, tho she was mighty good-looking. . . .

Had intended to go home on the 2:18 Saturday, but the weather having tried to clear up with some wonderful clouds, I decided that here was my time to fly, since Major Walker at Air HQ . . . suggested that I go out to the field with him in the afternoon if the weather was good. I reported at 3 and we went out. He promised to send me up in a Salmson. This is the best of all the two-seaters, and the safest in every way, but when we got there, we found that the Salmson had been taken out a few minutes before we arrived, so he had to send me up in a Liberty-powered D.H. 4 that was all tuned up and ready.

Now every one of the pilots that one talks to has it in for the D.H. 4 that we have built and used in the war. They have undoubtedly been the end of countless of our aviators. But as a peacetime ship it certainly is reliable, and has an engine that no one ever really knocks. And in peacetime flying the engine is the main thing. The D.H. proved a poor ship for war, but I knew that many men were flying her safely now that the war is over, and outside of the landing difficulty, there was nothing to fear, and with a pilot that was used to her, she can be landed safely as any other. The new ones with her have had their troubles because of the weight of the engine which has made her very nose-heavy.

We watched Lieutenant Parks play around in a new Boche Fokker that they had there and that is supposed to be such a wonderful machine. It is able to climb almost strait into the air, and is said to be able to hang on her propeller for some time in the air.

At last, [the lieutenant] bundles me up in his Teddy Bears and I am up in the machine and we are off; off before I really knew it, so solid is the machine and so gentle the going.[209] I am strapped in for emergency giving me enough strap that I may stand up if I wish. But there is little need for this as I am sitting on the gunner's seat which, like a piano stool, whirls easily in a complete circle. With a caution to keep my feet off the rudder bar, I am free to do as I like in my little cabin there.

What a picture around, under and above me. I have often tried to imagine it all from photos I have seen and from what I have always known the color and the look of the landscape to be. But here was something so different, so unreal, and altogether beautiful, that it was another world, and granted an aviator had a real appreciation for the beautiful (and he must soon get it in such surroundings), I can see how he would become perfectly enamoured of it all there in the air. There are no words to describe it. I watched my altimeter as we shot up, and we tipped up too, strange to say, into that world above without ever seeming to be off the level, or to feel that one was in any way leaning backward or making an effort to keep his equilibrium.

At 2,500 feet, we reached the first little fleecy clouds and passed them.

From the ground, the clouds had seemed to be almost a solid floor, with here and there a hole thro which one could see the sky beyond. We found them really a great flock of all sizes piled up close together, yet there was plenty of room to play around in them as we did, swinging along beside them, till one could put out his hand and slap their great white flanks, so solid they seemed. And then we would coast up and over and down them on the other side and then plunge into one, its dense, white mist striking one almost hard in the face as one entered its cool, wet midst.

Higher and higher we went. What a cubist painting below, and cubist paintings would appeal, if only they could catch some of the beauty of color and design of all those lovely patches on the canvas beneath us. I have glanced thro in the past some great classic book on *Design in Nature.*[210] Yet the author missed one of the greatest evidences of all in that he had never seen the earth from the air. Perfect in every way; not a jarring note as to form or balance, and not a jarring color note, it seemed. If in painting, one could only find an atmosphere to bathe his picture in, such as the light and the moisture in the air with which nature plays her great mastery of the art. It was beautiful beyond wild dreams. Here and there one caught the earth way down there between the clouds, struck now by the sunlight and thrown into a wondrous high key of light, citrons and greens and lavender. And here and there thrown into shadow by the clouds, one saw it in rich, low tones like music, close and melodious, purples and low greens and earth that were like bass to the high tenor of the sun. Soon we had passed thro the mass of clouds and had only the blue sky. . . .

Around and below us now was a carpet or plain of clouds that, looking toward the sun, glistened with the sun's glory. Looking away from it, yellowed by the sun's rays, with here and there a little cloud dome rising up . . . and bathed golden in the sunlight. It had hunted the sun, too, and found it.

It was altogether pleasant there in this new world. No wonder old Henri loved it with all that artist's heart and sympathy that he had. And I couldn't but think of him this day away there on that high patrol of his, at that rendezvous beyond the stars. Who can doubt but that he flies happy there as he did here when he left. I thought of Cory, and wondered if she would like it there by my side. I wasn't sure of her, but oh I was sure that Barbara would, and I wished them both there, tho I didn't tell them so in the letter I sent, lest they might think me too enthusiastic and apt to fly again.

We reached 7,000 feet, flew around at a level for some time, then I gave the pilot signal to descend. And the ride down thro and around the clouds was as lovely as the ride up. I never thought to ask just what towns we flew over; we must have been down over Langres and beyond, but there is no recognizing the landscape with my limited experience in the air, for what a flattener the height is. And I was sure that Chaumont looked from the air much more extensive than it really is. And how the rivers do wind and how they throw back at us the sun or the sky. And every little water lays there like a jewel, either a turquoise, an amethyst or a diamond as one views it.

At last, we pass what seem like the same little, fleecy clouds that we first met on the way up. Larger and larger grow the objects on the ground beneath as we get lower and lower and circle around to find our field. And at last we circle it and land, and a perfect landing, as gentle as a French train, which is the quintessence of gentleness in arrested motion, I am sure. This was equally as gentle. And we rolled up to the hangars.

Not a thing marred my time in the air, tho here I must, as a matter of record, record the miserable fact that as gently and as peacefully as we landed, came up my dinner. No distress, no warning! And it all happened in my cabin there so that I was spared the curiosity of the people who saw me climb out, thank my pilot, and beat it for the barracks to get out of my Teddy Bear which now seemed to be fairly roasting me. I was convinced when I left the ground that I was too warmly dressed; was conscious of it in the air a bit, for my hands were perspiring in my fur gloves, and now I was sure that I was too warm. So off they came, and down I lay on a bunk there, and let things settle and repictured all I had seen.

A few minutes after I was down, it all seemed so unreal to me that it might have been a dream almost, a dream I shall never forget, and I thank the God that was so good to me as to at last have led me to this field before I go back, and let me have this very flight I had longed for among the very kind of clouds that I longed to be among, oh, if only once. So that I was wildly happy, and the little sickness was nothing, for after all, don't even the *chasse* pilots get sick in the air as they go about their daily business of fighting the Hun, yes and lose their dinners there in their fight too? And go madly sick sometimes, they tell one, when they go into a sudden or a dizzy *vrillé?* So I wasn't discouraged. And worse accidents than sickness have happened to civilians on their first flights when malevolent pilots have given them long, quick drops in the air and brought them up with a jerk. I can say this now that there is another world, a veritable heaven for beauty, and it isn't far from this earth either, and one can go there easily, if one wishes. And I wished hard enough and I have been. . . .

Back Sunday night, last night. No letters, but strange and disturbing, there was a cable from Cory that, coming on the end of my arrangements made in Chaumont for going home and saying that she had passports pending there and to stay unless my coming back meant that we would return later together, threw me into a strange state. I thought I would faint for a minute, for where I was so sure I was doing the right thing for us all . . . in deciding to return, I was now not certain. Of course, I don't understand the passport proposition, for she has at all times seemed to be opposed to trying to get it there, and has said so. And this cable doesn't necessarily say that they are certain. So I don't know what to do now.

I got me a bite of supper, decided not to build my fire, and went to a restaurant; walked the streets for a time, then decided to go up to Lissagaray's and talk about the Salon, which she had intended to see Saturday. I had counted on telling them at once about my decision to return to the States, but with this new complication, decided to wait till it was absolutely settled. . . .

May 5, 1919
❧

*T*wo letters came this morning from Cory. They are in the old vein, so that they only serve to make the cable more inexplicable. She brings up the very interesting question of the YMCA girl in the AEF and her observations on, and relations with, the American officers. It seems Mae Cameron, who is coming home soon, has said some very pertinent or impertinent things on the officers' treatment of the American girl and his price for favor or opportunity. It doesn't sound quite right to me, and too, I've seen many YMCA and Red Cross girls, so that from their appearance and from the stories one hears, particularly in the leave centres, it is all a bit discounted with me.

There is no doubt there are a lot of officers who are brutal and masterful, perhaps, in their conduct with them. But it certainly is not true of all. Nor is it true that all the officers prefer the French girls, as is so often said, implying certain moral laxity thereby, as tho there couldn't be a clean, decent French girl for them to associate with, and losing sight of the fact that many of the officers have had the added excuse for associating with French families and French women in order to learn the language.

Many men's friendships were formed in the old days when only the old and certainly unattractive YMCA girls and nurses were sent over. Later this type has given place to the more attractive, as one can easily testify to by looking in the streets for them now. And I am sure these girls can't complain as to not having men friends. As to the other side of it, perhaps the free and easy ones among them have led the officers to suspect they are all alike, and who knows but that the American girl, incensed as they used to be at the companionship existing between the French girl and the American soldier — doughboy or officer — and the many marriages that were taking place, may have thrown herself into their society here much as they imagine the French girl has. Undoubtedly, many of the marriages of our boys have been forced ones, forced, that is, by their commanding officer, but it can only apply to a small lot of them as compared to the great number in which the boys are really terribly in love with the girls. For the doughboy does see the very human side of these families in the small towns in which they are billeted, and it is here that most of the courtships take place. And, as I have heard many of them say, they do see at once and appreciate the thrift and the homelife of the French girl, or rather the French woman which each French girl is going to be. And I have heard many times their simple nature compared to what the boys consider the sophistication and the ambition of the regular American girl. So that there is undoubtedly a lot of jealousy on the part of the girls at home.

There is pathetic reading here, and it would make better argument to the girls there if they could only hear of the very great number of cases in which their girls — thro that awful campaign that has been going on at home about the prevalence of venereal disease here among our boys, and thro the issuing of that, at the time, innocent warning here to the boys that if, in going home, it was found that any of them had venereal disease, they would be kept behind, and put in labor battalions or later, it was said, in concentrations camps — wrote them terrible letters, letting them know it was all over between them, or worse yet, not writing at all, or else having a friend write, because their boy hadn't come home with his outfit. And without ever understanding that there are thousands upon thousands of men and officers who, right at the port, are suddenly, to their great sorrow, detached and kept here for some need of men.

So that it is strange commentary on the sexual situation, for as the whole world knows now, the divorce courts in Canada and England are full of cases where, on returning home, a man has found himself supplanted by another. This has proved true in France too, of course, and is proving true at home, they say. Of course, the French soldiers or officers like to blame the Americans for their troubles, for they are very jealous of them, but it seems to be more common at home where there is no foreign military with more money to spend, so that the Frenchman is not really correct when he lays the blame where he does, for they know that their situation was just the same before the Americans came. So in spite of all

Miss Cameron says, she isn't fair in making the American officer out as bad as she does.

Met Lissagaray at the Salon. A pretty stupid show all round. The only bright spots in it are [Frederick Carl] Frieseke with only one thing, and the large [Gaston Oliver] Desvalliers decoration, for they have opened their doors this season to artists of all schools who were mobilized, and the old Automne Salon crowd show up to the disadvantage of the others. Then there are two fine things by a pal of Lissagaray's, a Mlle. Cormier.[211] The war pictures are horrible examples, and I wish some of the folk at home, who have set [François] Flameng, [Lucien] Jonas and [Georges] Scott on pedestals, could see the stuff here.[212] Hoffbauer had watercolors one had seen, and a couple of small oils, repainted, and not better nor so good as the watercolors. Sculpture, too, on a low level. It all made art seem rather hopeless.

Tried to find Duncan afterwards for dinner but failed, so ate at Jouvens and home to bed.

May 7, 1919
ᕭ

Today is the great day at Versailles and tomorrow we will know what the peace is to be. For sign it the Germans must, whether they want to or not, tho they will undoubtedly do a lot of whining about it. It will be a bitter pill.

Have decided I must go home, but will go down to Tours tomorrow and discuss the commercial liner proposition with the Adjutant General, so I will know whether I may take the berth that is being held for me till the 10th.

Spring is certainly in the air, and it's all sunshine now that I want to go home, and why couldn't I have had some weather like this earlier, so that I could go back with a better grace, in my own eyes, at any rate?

May 8, 1919
ᕭ

Took 8:00 train for Tours.[213] They were gracious as could be there when I explained my case and asked, why pay my own passage, and only 2d class at that, when perhaps if I went down to the steamship reservation officer there in another office, they might be able to send me on the Government on the same boat, if I would tell them the one I would like to go on. So you bet I hurried down to see him, and he was nice as could be, and called up to see if there would be an extra first-class berth for me and found there would, so wired the officer at the port of Havre to reserve me a first-class accommodation. I am to present myself there twenty-four hours in advance, that's the only difference. I can take my excess baggage just the same, and won't have to pay the excess either, unless possibly from Paris to Havre.

Took the 3:30 train back to Paris but it is behind time. It has been a hot, lovely ride down thro the blossoms today, and how different a look the country in that direction wears. When I get home tonight, there is a letter from Cory, and also a letter from Chief of the SOS for me to present to the customs officer at port of New York to let me get my things thro there without duty or trouble. Things will move quickly now, and I will have a lot to do at that. Something tells me I won't get up to see dear old Henri after all.[214]

RETROSPECT

What a chance the group of official American artists had to see the World War! And how lucky I counted myself to have been chosen one of the eight men sent over, with a captain's commission and orders and a free hand to go wherever we would and to gather material and make pictures for historical records for the War College in Washington. I shall never forget those hectic days that launched me into this new world of warfare, and a new warfare as we found, so unlike any that the world had ever seen before, so different from anything that one even imagined from war as it had been pictured in the past. What a life to go back over in memory, from that day when I left New York in a blinding snow, into the submarine zone with its constant alarms, and thro it. My trip thro London with a few days stay there with an air raid thrown in, and almost nightly alerts beside. The interest I found in the life in the shelters there during the raids and the nervous excitement of finding myself suddenly in the war zone, for, while one realized at all times the danger on the sea, one really felt he had arrived when he found himself in the midst of the bursting of enemy bombs and the sight of enemy planes.

Then there was the trip across the Channel, then the ride thro the France that I knew and loved so much, which we had seen, my family and I, as it passed thro those never-to-be-forgotten days of mobilization at the outbreak in 1914. I met air raids, too, in Paris, on my way down to our General Headquarters where I was to report for duty. How strange it seemed to be back in the old quarters again. But how different it all was now. Lightless and in a state of siege.

Then the arrival at GHQ, where I found three of the other artists who had preceded me, and who had gone over tentative plans for the best carrying on of our activities with our chief there, and had made the necessary arrangements, or rather the best that could be made under all the circumstances, with the more-or-less limited transportation which the AEF at that time had.

Now my life as a war artist was begun. The others had already been getting familiar with what our army consisted of, what it was doing, which, up to that time — the first of May — was practically nothing, save an occasional trench raid, but for me, everything that I saw was absolutely a new world. And what an interesting one. Save for an occasional boom of artillery from unexpected places, and a stray rifle shot, and now and then, out of what seemed a long, treacherous silence, the put-put-put of some restless machine gun, the hum of the motors of our aeroplanes that were constantly on the wing, and the sound occasionally of a bursting shell somewhere back of our lines, the Western Front, as held by our army, was a quiet rest sector, with our men training and waiting for the hour when it was up to them. And everyone knew that hour was to come soon. I say everyone. There was an amazing secretiveness in the AEF, and a wonderful lack of knowledge of Staff plans on the part of the units that made up the AEF, but things were sensed, and everyone felt the tenseness of the times.

The air was filled with expectancy for the moment, which arrived even earlier than was expected, in the frantic appeal to us from the French on the Marne at Château-Thierry at the beginning of June. By that time, I had gotten around pretty well over our sector, had slipped and nosed around into all sorts of strange places, filling my poor, bewildered brain with all sorts of new and strange impressions, and drunk, as it were, with the future pictorial possibilities in what I saw, and what my imagination saw, in the warfare that was so soon to come.

I shall never forget my first visit to the first-line trenches in a certain area that had been quiet for a long time, tho watched constantly by German balloons. Our trip over a shell-torn road under observation by them, tho on this particular day, under poor observation on account of the weather. Of our standing up on the firing step on a glorious moment when full sunlight burst, and we could look across "No-Man's Land" and had our first sight of the enemy. We could see their men walking about back of a little ruined village thro which their forest-line trench ran. We could see two of them on watch in the belfry of the ruined church. Undoubtedly, they could see us as well, there in the sun. I shall never forget my sensations as I realized that we were, after all, a fair target for a sniper, rifle or machine gun, and I was conscious of the beauty of the wealth of wild poppies that covered the trenches and the strip of wire-entangled ground that lay between them and the enemy. To me, this visit was memorable, marking as it did my first actual sight of the foe, peaceful tho it was. I remember, too, on our way back from this spot, and very near it, our watching, for a time, our boys playing ball in their gas masks, and what a droll sight it was.

Then came my trip up on the call from Château-Thierry for our men. And my first experience under shellfire. For this was real warfare, tho of a much different sort than our men went thro later. My first sight, too, of refugees fleeing a sudden storm-tossed area, with all the sorrow and misery and pathos that went with it, and how grateful and hopeful they all seemed as they met us on the way to defend their homes and to stop what seemed a sure gain for the Huns.

Here, too, during these days, I saw my first enemy aeroplanes closely, and saw my first balloon shot into flames. It was one of our balloons, and the observer took his leap to safety. This was one of the most thrilling things I ever saw, I think, this first burning balloon, and the successful escape of the two Boche planes that got it as they picked their way thro and out of the maze of shrapnel that burst around them, and then their chase by our planes.

Now I seemed well into things, but how hard a task it was, to do my work. For conditions made it almost impossible to do more than make the very most fragmentary or stenographic notes that one could only hope to later find time to put into permanent form. And, alas, that time seemed never to come, with all the feverish activity that was now about us, and that continued till the end came, and while we did make a certain number of things regularly, which were shown each month to General Pershing and his Staff, then turned into the machine for delivery at Washington to serve a sudden propaganda need, we naturally and rightly spent most of our time seeing every move that our forces made, storing up facts and impressions for later development when there should be a lull, and we could get back calmly to our billets and concentrate.

There came soon the stirring 14th of July in Paris, with the wonderful ovation given the troops in the parade there, and especially to our men. Captain Morgan and I were sent up to see this; in fact, were driven up by our chief, and as we neared Paris, I remember we were told casually by him that things of great moment were expected to break within the next day or two at the latest. That an attack by the Germans was sure to be made, and a drive toward Paris, and for us to be ready to go on out to headquarters there near the point of the attack.

Big Bertha began again her firing on Paris while we were there, after a long silence. How strange a sensation it was to hear the burst of a shell, first here on one side, even to see one burst just across the Seine and the mass of dust and smoke thrown into the air as it demolished the building where it lands. Then, after an interval, to hear another in another quarter. And to see the French people meet it all with a little shrug and a laugh as tho it were nothing after all they had gone thro, and as tho they were determined that the Hun should in no way break their morale with it as he had hoped to do.

Then, suddenly in the night, we hear and we feel the booming of great guns and actually feel a trembling of the whole world you are in. The attack has begun as expected. The real test for our men has arrived. And how we had planned suddenly and almost superhumanly to meet it and to defend, and as it proved, to save the life of Paris. One little knew, nor could he realize it quite, till he saw the packing of division after division into those few miles only, that by now separated Paris from the Hun.

Morgan went back to get equipment and our car. I had come to Paris for a celebration and parade, not for this, so I had to hunt up a helmet and gas mask and go out into a headquarters town that was being shelled at the moment, I heard, and air-raided at night. And I went nervously, I remember. But on the way out, I saw our troops, what masses of them there were, backing up and ready to relieve the ones that had been thrown into the teeth of the German drive that had simply hurled back the French in front of them. What happened is now history.

Later St. Mihiel, and our first use of the tanks, and the added picturesqueness they gave to it all. The interest, too, I found in our aviation from now on. There seemed to be work for a lifetime for me in tanks, aviation and artillery, for pictorially they appealed to me with their decorative forms, if ever things quieted down so I might really think and make pictures.

Then the Meuse-Argonne so soon after, with that terrible struggle and blight of death for our men, an offensive in which the losses were actually the heaviest of the whole war for the number of men involved. What terrible things I saw here, and how sick of war I had become. And yet how fascinated, too. What subject for pictures when we really got the opportunity later to really do what we felt we could do.

Then came the end so suddenly, just as we were getting the hang of things, beginning to be able to really pick and choose, just learning how to gather material in the most advantageous way and finding, each one of us, his field of work, what suited him best to do. Finished! And how happy we were! And that first night of relief from the tension of the whole four years of the war, when shutters could be left open, lights lit, and the French people could dare to believe that at last the menace was over. How all of France changed on the stroke of the hour: the eleventh hour of the eleventh day of the eleventh month.

Yet while the fighting was over, there was yet much traveling for us, for there was the advance to the frontier, and then into Germany, and then the crossing of the Rhine. There was the following up first of the retreating German army thro the liberated regions, and in all this, thro a sudden idea that came to me, and a realization of the possibility of carrying it out, an entry into Metz, to which city all American eyes had been so long set, with the hope of capturing soon, in that new and what was to have been terrible and amazing offensive on the part of our new 2d Army, that was to have been launched on the twelfth of November, but which the Boche prevented by his sudden armistice.

Well, the French decided to occupy Metz, and this sentimentally was a great disappointment to the Americans. But I thought I saw a way to get my car there, picked up three more of our fellows and we set out. Balked by the last American sentry, and turned back, we crossed the Moselle, into French territory, used our old French pass on their sentries as we encountered them, were on the point of losing them several times, passed countless French troops on the way camped by the wayside, got by what proved to be the last French sentry after a very nervous moment, and by what was a fluke, and drove into Metz to the wonderment of the people packing the streets there. Found that they didn't know we were Americans at first; found that there were no French yet in the town, tho they had rumors that they were to enter at 5 o'clock in the afternoon, and thought we were leading them in, hence their great excitement in seeing us. Those we encountered first were the real Lorrainers, the French, and this was the very first minute of their freedom after all the years of suppression of the French language, and this the first day they had been able to use it openly without fear.... Those were great days there while we waited for the entry of the French and the greater review by General Pétain.

Then on to Luxembourg. Then into Germany with the crossing of the Rhine and the interesting observation of life and conditions among the Germans. And as we pushed out into our bridgehead across the Rhine, being in many cases the first Americans, hence victors, to talk to them or eat among them, tho I don't think they ever looked on us as victors, tho they frankly told us that it was the Americans that caused them to quit.

Then suddenly a telegram to me to come back and go to Paris where credentials were being arranged for me to attend the Peace Conference. And my attendance there at all the open meetings week after week, and my working around in the anterooms getting glimpses and sketches of the great men as they came into and out of their closed meetings. How memorable it all seemed to me, the dignity and solemnity of it all, and the respect, almost reverence, paid to Wilson those days there in a tribute that showered on him, which was meant as well for the American people, as for him its representative. And one felt proud those days to be an American, and a member of the army of the people, who had, at last, stood behind, and finally had been the means of saving France, it seemed, let alone all the other things for which the Fourteen Points stood. And it shall always be a red-letter day for me after I heard Wilson read to the Conference his Covenant. And then the touching words of Lloyd George in seconding it.

By now, the artists were all getting quarters in which they would be able to settle down and work properly, a thing that till now had been out of the question, tho there was still much traveling around in our old sectors to be done collecting material that one had never had time for till now. Weather permitting, this is still to be done. Then the realization that it is, after all, impossible, for it is all water that has passed the mill. The Western Front of actual fighting days is over, gone never to be seen by eyes other than those who went through the Hell there while the fight was on. To have seen the battlefields, other than during those tense days, is never to have really seen them at all. One was struck by this, even a few days after the Armistice, for at once the work of reconstruction had begun, for the leaders knew wisely that the best way was to employ the soldiers' time, and the soldiers became laborers in many cases, and salvage began, trenches were torn up and filled, barbwire removed, shell-torn roads remade in the devastated regions, ruined villages that hadn't been further demolished by our labor units even while the battle raged, in order to get stone to fill shellholes, were now completely leveled in many cases to carry on the good work. Nothing was left untouched, it seemed. Great gangs of prisoners helped. And the cold, sweeping rains did all they could to wipe out and change the face of the entire zone.

The artists began to pack up, come home and be demobilized. I took one last farewell trip over our entire front. How different it all was. Tragic and moving, to be sure, for what things had happened since we came, let alone the things of the earlier days of the war. But I knew that not to have seen it during the conflict was not to have seen it as it really was, even for pictorial reference. And I realized, too, that not to have seen and experienced something of the Battles of the Marne, and of St. Mihiel and the Meuse-Argonne, was really not to have seen the war, either. And I am thankful I was there, and I am conscious of the opportunity I had to see and gather material and, better than the actual material, the impressions, spiritual and material, that alone can furnish the inspiration for a convincing pictorial record of what the great struggle was like. I marvel at the morale and the physical strength of the American doughboy who rose to his job and who, of all the soldiers there, really endured and suffered. And only those near to it all can know what endurance and suffering that was. Superhuman at times.

I had seen something of every activity in the front areas, had been thro the four offensives, had gotten in considerable time with our aviation, had done considerable flying, and had realized my desire to get among and above the clouds in that other world there into which my brother — God bless him — had flown, never to return. And now I felt ready to achieve something of my ambitions, counting as of little, even of ephemeral value, the things we had been able or had had to do during the time we were so nervously, yet energetically, storing up for the future. Little did we do, measured by what the British and the French had achieved, and were showing as a result of their four years with occasional offensives, and long waits between, when their artists could calm themselves and work. Our few, short months were packed to the limits, and they brought the end. And now, whereas it had been understood that we would be possibly continued in the service if we wished, in order to do something permanent of what we had seen and felt and lived through, it was suddenly decided at Washington to release us, and as they said, for us to go ahead and produce on our own. We may, now or hereafter according to our circumstances, do as we would like to do in the matter of production. But we are thrown back into the economic struggle in the midst of a great unrest, while undoubtedly things ought to be done while their imprint is still fresh, while still that memory is so keen that it will take time to dim, and we can do our best and trust to the strength of our inspirations.

Perhaps the greatest pictures of the war can only come with time. Certainly out of it all, in time, will come some pictures that will merit some attention as expressing something of what took place over there. There is much I want to do to justify my selection as one of the official artists with the AEF. That we did please the Staff there and the War College in Washington does not entirely satisfy. For we have yet ourselves to please. May we be able to do this?

NOTES

1. Creel has discussed his activities in *How We Advertised America* (New York: Harper and Brothers, 1920) and in *The Creel Report* (Washington, D.C.: U.S. Government Printing Office, 1920). See also Stephen Vaughn, *Holding Fast the Inner Lines: Democracy, Nationalism and the Committee on Public Information* (Chapel Hill: University of North Carolina Press, 1980).

2. Letter, from Major General William M. Black to Harry Townsend, Washington, D.C., February 15, 1918, copy in collection "Portfolio of World War Sketches," 70.57.1–214 LIC, in the Sanford Low Memorial Collection of American Illustration, the New Britain Museum of American Art, New Britain, Connecticut. Material from this collection will be hereafter cited as: 70.57.1–214 LIC.

3. Monthly report for May 1918, from Captain Harry E. Townsend to Chief, G-2-D, June 1, 1918, in Record Group 120: "Records of the American Expeditionary Forces (World War I), 1917–23"; subseries, "Censorship and Press Division (G-2-D)"; Entry 224; "Artists With the AEF," Case 70, Drawer 3, Folder 2. Documents from this source will be hereafter cited as: Record Group 120, Entry 224, Case 70, Drawer 3, followed by the relevant folder number. See also officer's qualification card for Captain Harry E. Townsend, GHQ, AEF, February 25, 1919, and memorandum from GHQ, AEF, to Captain Harry E. Townsend, May 6, 1918, in ibid, Folder 2.

4. Conditions at Neufchâteau are described in detail in Emmet Crozier, *American Reporters on the Western Front, 1914–1918* (New York: Oxford University Press, 1959).

5. There are numerous documents in Record Group 120, Entry 224, Case 70, Drawer 3, Folder 2, pertaining to Townsend's service during these months, especially the monthly reports that Chaumont required. For details of his wartime service, see also Walt Reed, "Harry Townsend: On Assignment During World War I," *American Artist*, vol. 36, no. 358 (May 1972): 62–67, 86–87.

6. Initially, the War College was directly involved, but in early 1918, the War College Division was replaced by the War Plans Division.

7. See introduction to J. André Smith, *In France With the American Expeditionary Forces* (New York: Arthur H. Hahlo and Company, 1919); Ernest Clifford Peixotto, *The American Front* (New York: Charles Scribner's Sons, 1919); and two articles by George Harding: "Drawing the War," *The American Magazine of Art*, vol. 32, no. 10 (October 1939): 568–573, and "The American Artist at the Front," *The American Magazine of Art*, vol. 10, no. 12 (October 1919): 451–456. Parts of Townsend's diary have been published in Reed, "Harry Townsend: On Assignment During World War I," pp. 62–67, 86–87.

8. There are biographical sketches in articles in the *New Canaan* (Connecticut) *Advertiser*, August 23, 1934; the *Bridgeport* (Connecticut) *Sunday Post*, October 9, 1938; and the *Norwalk* (Connecticut) *Hour*, July 30, 1941.

9. "I have always been a lover of the Indian character," Townsend once asserted. He especially admired the way in which native Americans conducted themselves overseas in the AEF. They were particularly effective on reconnaissance work behind enemy lines where, "stolid and intrepid," they invariably returned with information and prisoners. Fourteen tribes were involved in combat operations. Back home, native Americans had pledged over $13 million in Liberty Loan drives and, in addition, generously responded to appeals for funds by the YMCA, the Red Cross, and the Knights of Columbus. Townsend hoped that as a result of their loyal service and help during the war their lot would improve afterward. His comments are in undated notes in 70.57.1–214 LIC.

10. Townsend's art was recognized long before he joined the army. In 1910, for example, the City Art Museum of St. Louis featured his illustrations, together with some by the illustrators John Scott Williams, Charles S. Chapman, Howard McCormick, and John Rutherford Boyd. See exhibition catalog published by the museum and entitled *A Collection of Works by Five American Illustrators.*

11. "Big Bertha" was the popular name of what is more properly referred to as the Paris Gun. This was a very long-range weapon developed by the Germans — firing about seventy-five miles, an unheard of distance at that time. On Easter Sunday, 1918, a shell from the gun struck a crowded church, killing and wounding numerous people.

12. See excerpt from the toiletries trade journal, *Toilet Requisites* (n.d., but circa 1918), p. 16, which has a brief account of the service of Lieutenant W. H. Townsend as a pilot in the Royal Flying Corps (soon designated the Royal Air Force) and his death over the western front, in 70.57.1–214 LIC. For letters to Harry Townsend from W. H. Townsend's squadron mate, Lieutenant Rex Willey, 57 Squadron, RAF, April 28, 1918; to Cory and Barbara Townsend from Harry Townsend, France, August 19, 1918; and to Dwight Townsend, W. H. Townsend's wife, from Harry Townsend, France, August 20, 1918, see 70.57.1–214 LIC.

13. In Record Group, 120, Entry 224, Case 70, Drawer 3, Folder 2, see Townsend's monthly reports for the early months of 1919, Special Orders No. 9, Paragraph 125, GHQ, AEF, January 9, 1919, Special Orders No. 60, Paragraph 127, GHQ, AEF, March 1, 1919, and Special Orders No. 137, Paragraph 72, GHQ, AEF, May 17, 1919, all to Captain Harry Townsend; and memorandum from Brigadier General Dennis E. Nolan to Personnel Bureau, GHQ, AEF, May 16, 1919. See also copy of Townsend's discharge in 70.57.1–214 LIC.

14. As one critic noted, Townsend's studio "in a mellow red barn which has been remodelled, is gratifying to the visitor because of its fine possessions. These include some of the artist's masterpieces; excellent antique furniture (a clavichord which sheds a glow of romance); a fine collection of Japanese prints; an ancient Buddha carved in wood. Here is an artist highly sensitive to the beauty of oriental art." See Virginia Brown, "Our Silver Mine Neighbors," *New Canaan* (Connecticut) *Advertiser,* August 23, 1934.

15. Ibid.

16. Ibid. Important studies of the New Deal art programs include Marlene Park and Gerald E. Markowitz, *Democratic Vistas* (Philadelphia: Temple University Press,

1985), and Karal Ann Marling, *Wall-to-Wall America: A Cultural History of Post-Office Murals in the Great Depression* (Minneapolis: University of Minnesota Press, 1982).

17. *Bridgeport* (Connecticut) *Sunday Post,* October 9, 1938; *Norwalk* (Connecticut) *Hour,* October 4, 1938.

18. Obituary, *Norwalk* (Connecticut) *Hour,* July 30, 1941.

19. Barbara later married A. W. Harrison of Nob Hill Road, Ridgefield, Connecticut. Both she and her mother, Cory, are now deceased.

20. Brown, "Our Silver Mine Neighbors."

21. "Brothers in Art," *The Art Student,* vol. I, no. 8 (Fall 1916): 243–245. This was a publication of the Art Institute of Chicago, and the article consisted of a letter from Harry to Lee Townsend, then a student at the institute.

22. See correspondence and catalog relating to Accession No. 64592 in file, "Accession No. 64592, Office of the Registrar," 1919, Smithsonian Institution, Washington, D.C.

23. For the U.S. involvement in World War I, see Laurence Stallings, *The Doughboys: The Story of the AEF, 1917–1918* (New York: Harper and Row, 1963); Edward M. Coffman, *The War to End All Wars: The American Military Experience in World War I* (New York: Oxford University Press, 1968); and Robert H. Ferrell, *Woodrow Wilson and World War I, 1917–1921* (New York: Harper and Row, 1985). The U.S. home front is best discussed by David M. Kennedy in his *Over Here: The First World War and American Society* (New York: Oxford University Press, 1980). Maps, together with other details of the U.S. involvement in Europe, can be located in American Battle Monuments Commission, *American Armies and Battlefields in Europe: A History, Guide and Reference Book* (Washington, D.C.: U.S. Government Printing Office, 1938), and Vincent J. Esposito, *The West Point Atlas of American Wars,* vol. 2 (New York: Frederick A. Praeger, 1959). A general survey of the history of the U.S. Army is found in Russell F. Weigley, *The History of the United States Army* (New York: Macmillan, 1967). A solid general account of the war is given in James L. Stokesbury, *A Short History of World War I* (New York: William Morrow and Company, 1981).

24. For Pershing's career in France, see the superb study by Donald Smythe, *Pershing: General of the Armies* (Bloomington: Indiana University Press, 1986); the useful study by Frank E. Vandiver, *Black Jack: The Life and Times of John J. Pershing,* 2 vols. (College Station: Texas A & M University Press, 1977); as well as the general's own fine account, *My Experiences in the World War,* 2 vols. (New York: Frederick A. Stokes Company, 1931).

25. Issoudun became the main site of Air Service training, where a huge complex of twelve flying fields was established. "Field Thirteen" became the designation of the base's cemetery.

26. Louis Raemaekers was the well-known Dutch artist who, basing his impressions of the war in the early months on accounts of refugees coming into Holland, depicted the German atrocities in graphic cartoons that gained wide circulation. The Germans were so incensed that they placed a 12,000 Mark price on his head.

27. Benjamin West (1738–1820) painted portraits of British royalty, enjoying the patronage of George III. He also served as president of the Royal Academy.

28. Howard Pyle was a renowned artist-teacher. Numerous U.S. illustrators were trained by Pyle, including Dunn, Aylward, and Townsend, all official AEF artists.

29. The French employed numerous natives from Annam (Vietnam), French Indochina, as laborers and truck drivers behind the lines during World War I.

30. He refers to the architect, Thomas Raymond Ball (1896–1943), who served overseas in 1918–1919 with the Camouflage Section, 40th U.S. Engineers. He was a member of the Connecticut House of Representatives from 1927–1937, before serving in the U.S. Congress from 1939 to 1941.

31. The RFC was the Royal Flying Corps, the British air service; in 1918, it became the Royal Air Force, a separate branch of Britain's armed forces. The U.S. Air Service hoped that it, too, might emerge as a separate branch, but this was accomplished only after World War II.

32. Antiaircraft fire was commonly referred to as "archie," so named by the British in reference to a popular music hall tune, "Archibald! Certainly not!!"

33. The reference here is to Townsend's brother who was killed on April 23, 1918, by German antiaircraft fire, his aircraft crashing near his home field. Harry's deep interest in aviation was intensified by his brother's service as a Royal Flying Corps pilot and his death as a combatant.

34. The 102d Infantry Regiment was part of the 51st Infantry Brigade of the 26th Division; the 103d was part of the 52d Brigade of the same division. These details are in U.S. Army, *Order of Battle of the United States Land Forces in the World War, Vol. 2: American Expeditionary Forces: Divisions* (Washington, D.C.: U.S. Government Printing Office, 1931), pp. 113–129.

35. Townsend, like most doughboys, soon adopted French expressions and terms, such as "camions," used in this sentence.

36. Elsie Janis, "The Sweetheart of the AEF," was a well-known vaudeville and musical comedy star in the United States before volunteering to entertain troops abroad. She was often accompanied by her mother. Her memoirs were published as *So Far, So Good!* (New York: E. P. Dutton and Company, 1932); pp. 182–235 are devoted to her stay in France.

37. The 101st Regiment was part of the 51st Infantry Brigade, the 26th Division.

38. The 166th Infantry Regiment was attached to the 83d Infantry Brigade of the 42d or "Rainbow" Division. The division occupied the Baccarat sector of Lorraine from March 31 to June 21, 1918.

39. Lincoln Eyre was an accredited correspondent with the U.S. Army, representing the *New York World*. Details of the activities of correspondents with the U.S. forces are in Crozier, *American Reporters on the Western Front*.

40. These squadrons were part of the U.S. Air Service's 1st Pursuit Group, which also included the 27th and 147th Pursuit Squadrons, the 185th Night Pursuit Squadron, and the 4th Park (maintenance) unit. Many of the top U.S. aces (including the leading scorer, Captain Eddie V. Rickenbacker of the 94th "Hat-in-the-Ring" Squadron) were in the 1st. This organization was commanded from August 21, 1918, to the end of the war by Lieutenant Colonel Harold E. Hartney, a Canadian who had flown combat in the Royal Flying Corps before transferring to the U.S. Air Service. His memoirs have been published as *Up and At 'Em* (Garden City, New York: Doubleday and Company, 1971), reprint edition.

41. Major Raoul Lufbery, while commander of the 94th Squadron, was killed on May 19, 1918, almost over his own airdrome. His aircraft was set on fire by an enemy bullet, and he jumped from his plane, falling to his death as he came down on a picket fence. No parachutes were used at the time by Allied pilots, except for balloon observers. Lufbery had earlier gained fame as a member of the Lafayette Escadrille, composed of U.S. pilots who flew for France before their nation's entry into the war.

42. Captain Franklin Pierce Adams, popularly referred to simply as F.P.A., was a U.S. newspaper columnist and reporter of note before the war; for a time, he was on the staff of the doughboy newspaper, the *Stars and Stripes,* in Paris.

43. Here, Townsend is referring to the battles along the Marne River in the autumn of 1914.

44. The 3d Division maintained its headquarters at Viels-Maisons from June 1–6, 1918.

45. The French 75-millimeter, rapid-fire, multipurpose light artillery piece was the best known gun of the war. It was used in large numbers by U.S. artillery units because few guns of U.S. manufacture appeared in France in time to participate in the conflict. The gun was greatly loved by its crews. Captain Harry Truman commanded a battery of four 75s and was greatly impressed with their efficiency. Other French guns used in great numbers by U.S. artillery outfits included the trench mortar and the 155-millimeter howitzer.

46. Montreuil-aux-Lions was the headquarters of the 2d Division from May 31–June 10, 1918.

47. Townsend is referring to a former student of the Art Students' League of New York City, where he was once an instructor.

48. Floyd Gibbons was a colorful war correspondent even before the U.S. entry into World War I. In France, he represented the *Chicago Tribune* as war correspondent accredited to the AEF. His wounds were not fatal, though he wore a black patch over his eye socket from then on. He soon returned to his duties.

49. Press headquarters had been shifted from Neufchâteau to Paris for a brief time and then to Meaux, on June 7, closer to the action. Meaux was about halfway between Paris and Château-Thierry, and the main battles fought at that time were less than an hour's drive away. Paris was easily accessible by frequent trains. The correspondents were comfortably lodged in the Hotel Sirene. The press headquarters were later located successively at Bar-le-Duc, Verdun, Trier, and eventually, Coblenz.

50. McCabe, at this time, was chief field officer of G-2-D.

51. Colonel (later Brigadier General) William (Billy) Mitchell was chief of the U.S. Air Service of the Zone of the Advance and as such was in direct command of all combat air operations of the AEF. He was later best known for his dramatic court-martial, stemming from his criticism of War and Navy Department policies; he resigned from the army on February 1, 1926. A tireless, outspoken champion of a separate U.S. air force and the development of strategic air power, he published his memoirs under the title *Memoirs of World War I,* which appeared serially in *Liberty Weekly* in 1928; it was published in book form by Random House in 1960.

52. Major Bozeman Bulger was the chief field press officer, G-2-D, having replaced Major A.L. James, Jr. Bulger had earlier been a sports writer for the *New York Evening World.*

53. The 27th and the 147th Squadrons were the first two to arrive at the front that had trained together as squadrons. Based at Epiez, near Toul, they were equipped with the Nieuport 28, a graceful, agile French pursuit aircraft that Townsend's artist's eye greatly appreciated. The French pilots, who preferred other aircraft types, were pleased to palm them off on the U.S. fliers. The plane did have disadvantages, notably a propensity to lose wing fabric in steep dives. But if care was used, the plane was a fine one, and the U.S. pilots later hated to give them up when all spares had been used. They were given Spads instead, which some of them preferred but others strongly disliked. There is a discussion of this in Hartney, *Up and At 'Em,* pp. 182–183.

54. Camp Borden was in Canada.

55. Major Bonnell's troubles and something of his character are discussed in Hartney, *Up and At 'Em,* pp. 102, 118–120, and 183. He was relieved of his command of the 147th Squadron on July 22, 1918, shortly after Townsend left Saints. He was replaced by First Lieutenant James A. Meissner, who was promoted to captain on October 11, 1918.

56. The Spad was a single-seat, single-engine fighter aircraft renowned for its ruggedness and high performance. The version known as the Spad XIII was built in greater numbers than any other Allied fighter aircraft type during the war. By the end of hostilities, it equipped eighty-one French squadrons and was the main type used by sixteen pursuit squadrons of the U.S. Air Service.

57. The Sopwith "Camel," a one-seat, single-engine plane, was Britain's most successful World War I fighter; its pilots scored 1,294 victories. Some 5,490 "Camels" were manufactured before the end of the war, praised for their maneuverability if not their speed.

58. The British De Havilland D.H. 4, a two-place observation and light bombing aircraft, was selected to be built under license in the United States (by the Dayton-Wright Aeroplane Company and the Fisher Body Company) and sent in great numbers to France. It was powered by a U.S.-designed and -built, 400-horsepower "Liberty" engine. Its selection was hotly debated, for many pilots did not like the "flaming coffin." Others felt that the plane was a solid choice. The Liberty engine, once the bugs were worked out, did perform well, but the aircraft — the only type built in the United States to see combat in World War I — did not arrive in the huge numbers anticipated. Therefore, the great majority of U.S. pilots who flew combat did so in aircraft produced by the other Allies. Another great controversy swirled around this fact as well, because the U.S. people had been led to believe, by official announcements and newspaper accounts, that the nation would almost immediately send "clouds of aircraft" to support the doughboys in Europe.

59. The engines that equipped the aircraft flown by the U.S. pilots could only be cut off entirely, not throttled back. This made formation flying extremely difficult, if not impossible.

60. World War I was certainly a "singing war," and the British airmen were among the most vocal. Numerous references appear in the literature of the era regarding this. See, for example, Arch Whitehouse, *The Fledgling: An Autobiography* (New York:

Duell, Sloan and Pearce, 1964), pp. 166–167; Guy Chapman, *A Passionate Prodigality* (New York: Holt, Rinehart and Winston, 1933), p. 120; and Arthur Gould Lee, *No Parachute: A Fighter Pilot in World War I* (New York: Harper and Row, 1968), pp. 65, 126, and *passim.*

61. Major General Clarence Edwards was controversial among his peers because he seemed to be too lenient with his men and lacked zeal, though he was beloved by his troops. General Pershing later relieved him of his command, turning the New Englanders over to Brigadier General Frank E. Bamford on October 25, 1918. This dismissal was one of the most controversial of the war, leading to a debate that lasted for years.

62. The headquarters of the 26th Division at this time was the Grand-Rû Ferme, located 1.25 kilometers southeast of Etrepilly. It had been established there on July 21 and would remain until July 30.

63. Frank P. Sibley was assigned to the 26th Division, keeping not only the *Globe* but other New England newspapers well informed of the doings of local boys in the war. See his book *With the Yankee Division in France* (Boston: Little, Brown, 1919).

64. The German counterpart to the much better known French 75 was the 77-millimeter light artillery piece. It, too, was an effective, efficient weapon.

65. The *New York Herald* published a Paris edition that circulated widely among the troops of the AEF.

66. Major General Joseph T. Dickman commanded the 3d Division from April 12 to August 18, 1918; he then commanded IV Corps from August 18 to October 12, 1918, and I Corps from October 12 to November 11, 1918. He was subsequently appointed commander-in-chief of the 3d Army, which was the occupation force stationed in the U.S. zone in Germany following the armistice.

67. Townsend is apparently referring to Ernest Jean Delahaye, a French genre and portrait painter most prominent in the 1880s and 1890s.

68. Townsend is speaking of the work of English artist George Morland (1763–1804), who specialized in painting picturesque rustic scenes.

69. There are details in Mitchell, *Memoirs of World War I*, p. 213. Avery, of the 95th Squadron of the 1st Pursuit Group, later shot down another German aircraft before he himself turned up missing.

70. Reference here is to 1st Lieutenant Ralph A. O'Neil, who scored six victories over German aircraft during the war.

71. Captain James A. Meissner did work out well as the squadron's new commanding officer. He ended the war with a bag of eight German aircraft.

72. Townsend apparently means 1st Lieutenant Joseph C. Raible, Jr., who, by war's end, had destroyed two enemy aircraft, and 2d Lieutenant Thomas J. Abernathy, who shot down three Germans.

73. Manfred Baron von Richthofen, the famed "Red Baron," was Germany's leading ace in World War I with eighty victories to his credit before he himself was shot down. He created the "Flying Circus," a formidable unit that plagued Allied counterparts.

74. *Arbi* is the French word for shelter and usually referred to air raid shelters in towns and villages or dugouts in the trenches.

75. The naming of aircraft in World War I was far less common than during World War II, but Townsend's brother clearly named his.

76. The Bréguet Br 14 observation and light bombing aircraft and the Salmson 2 observation plane, both two-seaters, were the most common types used late in the war by the French for artillery spotting and other observation duties, as well as light bombing raids.

77. The British Handley-Page Aircraft Company made heavy bombers, a twin-engined version, the 0/400 type being the largest British bomber used in the war. Powered by two Rolls Royce engines of 275 horsepower each, it had an endurance of eight hours and carried a 2,000-pound bomb load.

78. Details of this rather primitive field are found in Hartney, *Up and At 'Em*, p. 202.

79. Major Kendall Banning, before being commissioned in the army, was in charge of photographs and films for the Division of Films of George Creel's Committee on Public Information. He was commissioned a major in the Signal Corps Reserve and stationed at the War College, Washington, D.C. He also initially had a hand in appointing the official artists. In Washington, Banning was chief of the Pictorial Section of the Historical Branch, War Plans Division — formerly the War College Division — the General Staff, and received the artwork from France. Townsend is referring to a letter from Banning to Smith, dated August 13, 1918. A copy is available in Record Group 120, Entry 224, Case 70, Drawer 3, Folder 10; there are other relevant documents in Folder 4. Of particular interest is the report of Captain J. André Smith to Major A. L. James, Jr., Chief, G-2-D, October 21, 1918, on the official artists; it describes in detail how they were appointed, how they saw their mission, and how they performed it. Townsend also responded to Banning's complaints; see his memorandum to Chief, G-2-D, November 16, 1918, in Folder 2.

80. Casey was art editor of *Collier's Weekly;* Charles Dana Gibson, creator of the famed "Gibson Girl," was chairman of the Division of Pictorial Publicity of the Committee on Public Information, having been appointed on April 17, 1917. Casey was vice chairman and secretary of the division. "Keppel's" refers to the firm of Frederick Keppel and Company, dealers and importers of artworks.

81. There are several documents in Record Group 120, Entry 224, Case 70, Drawer 3, Folder 10 indicating procedures to be followed by the artists and how officials at GHQ, Chaumont, felt about them and their work. Generally, they were favorably disposed toward them, and the monthly exhibitions of art that the artists arranged at headquarters were successes.

82. As a colonel, James Guthrie Harbord sailed to Europe with Pershing, who selected him to become the AEF's first chief-of-staff, a position that he held for a year. His promotion to brigadier general came on October 8, 1917. On May 7, 1918, he became commanding general of the Marine Brigade of the 2d Division. Promoted to major general, he commanded the 2d Division from July 15 to July 27, 1918, then was abruptly appointed chief-of-staff, Services of Supply, on July 27, where he remained until the end of the war. In this post, he was in charge of the AEF's vast logistical network. See his memoirs, *The American Army in France, 1917–1919* (Boston: Little, Brown, 1936).

83. John Purroy Mitchel was mayor of New York City from 1914–1917.

84. This is a reference to the U.S. artist George Bellows (1882–1925) and those associated with him, best known for organizing the Armory Show held in 1913 at a

regimental armory in New York City that introduced modern art to the United States.

85. Lieutenant Paul-René Fonck, later a captain, emerged from the war as France's leading ace with seventy-five victories.

86. On August 29, 1918, the 1st Army headquarters were established at Ligny-en-Barrois, twenty-five miles southeast of St. Mihiel.

87. Townsend was no doubt alluding to an incident that occurred on May 25, 1918, involving Lieutenant Colonel Waldo, commander of the 126th Infantry Regiment of the 32d Division, commanded by Major General William G. Haan. Waldo strongly criticized the AEF's policy of employing official artists and vigorously opposed Captain Peixotto's painting pictures in his regimental area. The colonel was strongly reprimanded for his attitude and action. See relevant documents in Record Group 120, Entry 224, Case 70, Drawer 3, Folder 3.

88. The Renault tank was a six-ton, two-man vehicle, almost 3,000 of which were made during the war. They were armed with a variety of weapons up to the 75 light artillery piece. U.S. light tank units were equipped with Renaults.

89. Pioneers were construction and engineering troops in the U.S. Army.

90. Thomas Wood Stevens (1880–1942) was a U.S. author and playwright. He produced the pageant "Joan of Arc" while with U.S. troops at Domrémy, France, in September 1918. He was later head of the drama department and director of the Goodman Theater at the Art Institute of Chicago from 1924–1930. Subsequently, he was on the art faculty of the University of Wisconsin and the Carnegie Institute of Technology.

91. Georges Clemenceau (the "Tiger") became the French premier in November of 1917 and served past the end of the war.

92. Bailey was of the *London Daily Mail*, Johnson of the *New York Sun*, James of the *New York Times*, Parke served the International News Service, Ruhl represented *Collier's Weekly*, and Don Martin wrote for the *New York Herald*.

93. *Simplicissimus* was a German satirical review published in Munich that was somewhat reminiscent of the British publication *Punch*.

94. The Gotha was a large, twin-engine bomber used by the Germans to mount strategic bombing operations against London and other targets in Britain, as well as Paris and many sites behind the lines.

95. Luke, of the 27th Pursuit Squadron, was one of the U.S. Air Service's most famous aces, shooting down eighteen German airplanes and balloons. In a meteoric career, soon to be cut short by his death, he specialized in shooting down observation balloons. He was often accompanied in his "balloon-busting" operations by Lieutenant Joe Wehner of the same squadron. Before he was killed, Wehner shot down five German aircraft. There is a detailed account of their exploits in Hartney, *Up and At 'Em*, pp. 239–276.

96. For various reasons, including that of pride, combat fliers were not equipped with parachutes, though balloon observers were. Only late in the conflict did the Germans begin to equip their airplane crewmen with chutes, which caused considerable interest in Allied circles; hence, Townsend's comments. Many lives would have been saved had parachutes been in general use during the war. See a discussion of this in Hartney, *Up and At 'Em*, p. 336.

97. See memorandum to the official artists, from Major A. L. James, Jr., Chief, G-2-D, September 19, 1918, in Record Group 120, Entry 224, Case 70, Drawer 3, Folder 10.

98. Nolan had just been promoted to brigadier general. There are additional documents bearing on James's order and the reaction to it in Record Group 120, Entry 224, Case 70, Drawer 3, Folder 10.

99. Obviously, Townsend's contemplated trip back to the SOS was now scrapped, much to his chagrin.

100. Henri Farré was a French airman-artist who had produced striking aviation art depicting French air operations. Numerous examples of his work toured the United States to critical acclaim. His art is discussed by Kimberly Keefer in "The Art of Henry Farré," *American History Illustrated,* vol. 17, no. 5 (September 1982): 30–32.

101. Brigadier General Benjamin D. Foulois became the AEF's chief of the Air Service on November 27, 1917. On May 29, 1918, Pershing placed Brigadier General Mason M. Patrick in that position. Foulois ended the war as assistant chief of the Air Service under Patrick.

102. The press moved its headquarters from Neufchâteau to Paris, only remaining there for a short time before moving to Meaux for the Château-Thierry action, to Nancy for the St. Mihiel operation, and to Bar-le-Duc for the last weeks of the war.

103. Townsend was clearly taken in by U.S. ruses designed to convince the Germans that the United States planned to move into Germany through the Belfort Gap, near the Swiss border. Though undertaken mainly at the time of the St. Mihiel operation, U.S. activities in the area continued to stoke rumors. There is a discussion of this in Stallings, *The Doughboys,* pp. 207–208.

104. Townsend was still of the opinion that the main U.S. operations would be in the Alsace region.

105. Townsend was plainly too optimistic regarding U.S. successes early in the Meuse-Argonne operations. These were soon followed by disarray.

106. In fact, the U.S. tanks did not perform well. They lagged behind, and when they went forward, the doughboys refused to accompany them because they were such inviting targets for German artillery. In some instances, the tanks did capture towns, but, unsupported by infantry, they could not hold them, and they were systematically disabled by German forces. There is a discussion of this in Smythe, *Pershing,* p. 196.

107. Marshal Louis Félix Franchet d'Esperey, having failed on the western front as an army commander, was sent to the Balkans where he assumed command of Allied operations. His successes were notable, and he won his marshal's baton while carrying out victorious campaigns against the lesser Central Powers. His answer to Bulgaria's overtures were mentioned by Townsend in his diary entry of September 28.

108. The Bulgarian Armistice Convention was signed on September 29, 1918. The text is in Harry R. Rudin, *Armistice 1918* (New Haven: Yale University Press, 1944), pp. 404–405.

109. Andrée Spinelli was a French actress who appeared in light musicals and revues in various Paris theaters and cabarets, such as the Moulin Rouge and the Varietes, and

in the production "*Plus ça change*" at the Michel, the Gymnase, and Antoine theaters in 1917–1918.

110. In response to President Wilson's demands that before armistice negotiations could ensue the Germans had to reform their government to allow for genuine representation of the population, the Germans responded by initiating changes calculated to attain these ends and so informed Wilson. There is a lengthy discussion on this topic in Rudin, *Armistice 1918, passim.*

111. There is a similar letter from Banning to Townsend dated October 25, 1918, in "Portfolio of World War Sketches," 70.57.1–214 LIC.

112. Peixotto had maintained a residence at Samois-sur-Seine for many years before the outbreak of hostilities. Though he and his wife returned to the United States shortly after the beginning of the war, he kept his home in France. Townsend was apparently in error regarding the presence of Peixotto's wife in France at that time, however.

113. General Erich Ludendorff, with Field Marshal Paul von Hindenburg, headed the German forces. He was forced to resign on October 26, 1918, by the newly created government of Prince Max of Baden. This move was calculated to speed up the armistice talks.

114. On the eve of the outbreak of the war, Friedrich Adam Jules von Bernhardi, a German general and writer, published his book *Germany and the Next War* (London: E. Arnold, 1914), setting forth, in a provocative manner, Germany's avowed imperialistic aims in any future conflict.

115. Luke was shot down on September 29, 1918. Having crash-landed, he was killed by German troops while attempting to defend himself with his pistol. He was awarded the Congressional Medal of Honor for his exploits.

116. 2d Lieutenant Maxwell O. Parry, of the 147th Squadron, was listed as missing in action.

117. Stuart Walker was a U.S. theatrical producer and playwright who organized the Portmanteau Theater in Indianapolis and directed the Repertory Company of that city from 1917 to 1921. The Washington Square Players were a group who performed on stages in New York City from 1914–1918; they were a forerunner of the Theatre Guild, which was prominent on the New York theater scene in the 1920s and 1930s.

118. The terms of the armistice document signed with Turkey on October 31 are in Rudin, *Armistice 1918,* pp. 410–411.

119. Istvan Count Tisza de Boros-Jeno was the wartime prime minister of Austria-Hungary. He was assassinated on October 31, 1918, by Communist Red Guards in Budapest.

120. Captain Guy T. Viskniskki was the officer in charge of the *Stars and Stripes,* the doughboy newspaper published in Paris.

121. The terms of the Austro-Hungarian armistice are given in Rudin, *Armistice 1918,* pp. 406–409.

122. The heavy guns involved were those of a detachment of naval gunners under Rear Admiral Plunkett. With their five 14-inch naval guns, they greatly aided in breaking

up the traffic on the main railway line supplying the German armies opposite the U.S. forces at this time.

123. No doubt partially because of the actions of the Republicans at this time, Townsend later changed his party affiliation, becoming a Democrat.

124. There was indeed a premature announcement of the armistice, recounted in Crozier, *American Reporters on the Western Front,* pp. 257–267.

125. Among the numerous accounts of this controversy is Stallings, *The Doughboys,* pp. 356–365. In fact, at least three divisions were involved: the 1st, the 77th, and the 42d. In the event, the French were permitted the honor of officially taking Sedan.

126. The portraits that the Historical Section wanted were done later mainly by other artists, including Joseph Cummings Chase. See, for example, his book *Soldiers All: Portraits and Sketches of the Men of the A.E.F.* (New York: George H. Doran Company, 1920).

127. The text of the armistice with Germany is in Rudin, *Armistice 1918,* pp. 426–432; a discussion of the negotiations is given on pp. 285–391.

128. The kaiser entered Holland on November 10, asking the Dutch for political asylum. This was granted, and he lived out his life there. His abdication was announced in Berlin on November 9 by Prince Max, the chancellor, though the kaiser did not sign his abdication document until November 28, 1918. He died on June 4, 1941, having seen Adolph Hitler's early triumphs, including the conquest of the Netherlands. Details of the kaiser's flight to Holland are in Walter Henry Nelson, *The Soldier Kings: The House of Hohenzollern* (New York: G. P. Putnam's Sons, 1970), pp. 429–440.

129. The crown prince returned to Germany in 1923, on the promise of good behavior. He joined the Nazi party in 1931, as did two of his brothers and two of his sons. This is discussed in ibid., p. 442.

130. The U.S. Army of Occupation was designated the 3d Army and placed under the command of Major General Joseph T. Dickman. On May 2, 1919, Dickman was replaced by Lieutenant General Hunter Liggett. On July 2, 1919, after the signing of the Treaty of Versailles, the 3d Army ceased to exist, and the U.S. contingent in Germany was redesignated the American Forces in Germany — the AFG — until they were withdrawn from the Rhine in January of 1923. The commander of the AFG was Major General Henry Tureman Allen, who had brought the 90th Division to France and led it through the Meuse-Argonne. He later commanded the VIII Corps and, briefly, the VII and IX Corps. He led the AFG with distinction.

131. Townsend's memorandum was dated November 16, 1918; in it, he requested permission to make careful and detailed color studies of the St. Mihiel and Verdun battlefields; to "carry out a number of paintings of incident and battle in the air"; and to do careful oil paintings, asking for adequate time to complete them. He also promised to undertake portrait sketches of commanding field officers of the AEF. His memorandum was approved on November 19, 1918, by Major James, chief of G-2-D, although he seems to have done little regarding the portraits. These documents are in Record Group 120, Entry 224, Case 70, Drawer 3, Folder 2.

132. This British publication, which focused on official British combat art, devoted its issues to special subjects, one being the war art of British combat artist Sir William Orpen. For a fine study of British war art during World War I and later, see Meirion

and Susie Harries, *The War Artists: British Official War Art of the Twentieth Century* (London: Michael Joseph in Association with the Imperial War Museum and the Tate Gallery, 1983).

133. A traveling exhibition of examples of the combat art was organized at the Corcoran Art Gallery in Washington, D.C., by the American Federation of Arts. It proceeded to New York City as part of the Allied War Salon, on view from December 9–31, 1918. The exhibit traveled to Pittsburgh, and apparently to other cities as well. While it was in New York, a viewing by editors of principal magazines was arranged by the Committee on Public Information. Some forty of the drawings were chosen for publication in nationally circulated popular magazines. However, the war art has never been the primary focus of any official publication, though some of the individual artists later published selections from their works.

134. This advancing army was part of the Allied forces following the Germans as they evacuated the territory, as stipulated in the armistice document.

135. Metz was a city of considerable importance. Heavily fortified, its strategic position dictated its inclusion in that part of Lorraine taken over by the Germans following their defeat of France in the Franco-Prussian War of 1870–1871. By the time of World War I, the city had a large German population mingled with the native French. Metz was the objective of the U.S. 2d Army which was poised to begin an attack in mid-November, but was, of course, forestalled by the armistice.

136. Dunn was a car buff with a good knowledge of auto mechanics.

137. Captain James Norman Hall, of the 94th Pursuit Squadron, had formerly been a member of the Lafayette Escadrille. He was shot down and captured on May 7, 1918. Released after the armistice, he later gained fame as coauthor, with Charles Bernard Nordhoff (who had also flown in France), of a well-known trilogy — *The Mutiny on the Bounty, Men Against the Sea,* and *Pitcairn's Island* — and other books.

138. In the summer of 1918, General Charles Mangin was given command of the French 10th Army, which played a notable role in carrying out Foch's offensive operations late in the war. On the eve of the armistice, Mangin's army was poised to attack Lorraine — an attack that was not carried out. However, Mangin, a native Lorrainer, subsequently did enter Metz.

139. Marshal Michel Ney, the Duc d'Eichingen and Prince de la Moskova (1769–1815), was one of Napoleon's marshals and was actually born in Saarlouis in the Saarland, Germany.

140. Another account of this accident is in Mitchell, *Memoirs of World War I,* p. 297.

141. Each squadron of the group known as "the Storks" had a different stork as its emblem. Captain Georges Guynemer, France's second-highest-scoring ace, with fifty-three enemy aircraft destroyed, was a member of this *escadrille.* He was later listed as missing in action.

142. General Billy Mitchell, who was present, stated that Mangin fell "off his horse on his head and nearly killed himself." See his *Memoirs of World War I,* p. 297.

143. Marshal Henri Philippe Pétain, the hero of Verdun, was made generalissimo of French forces in May of 1917; he held that post until the end of the war.

144. Laurence La Tourette Driggs was an author, attorney, and aviation expert. He visited the front on several occasions as a guest of the Allies. In New York City in 1919, he founded and was the first president of the American Flying Club of the

Front for U.S. aviators who had flown over the front in wartime. He became a well-known lecturer and writer on aviation subjects.

145. Lieutenant Charles Nungesser was France's third-ranked ace, with forty-five victories at the war's end.

146. Dr. Wilhelm Solf was the German foreign minister in the cabinet of Prince Max of Baden's government, which took office on October 3, 1918, and which completed the armistice negotiations.

147. Details of the U.S. deployment are in Keith L. Nelson, *Victors Divided: America and the Allies in Germany, 1918–1923* (Berkeley: University of California Press, 1975), pp. 26–30.

148. Captain Aymar Embury 2d was a sculptor in civilian life. He designed the Distinguished Service Cross and other medals for the army.

149. First Lieutenant Grantland Rice, poet and sportswriter, who was previously at the *New York Tribune,* was on the staff of the *Stars and Stripes.* After the war, he returned to the *Tribune* for a number of years and wrote widely in the field of sports.

150. The adventurous correspondents were Lincoln Eyre, of the *New York Herald;* Frederick A. Smith, of the *Chicago Tribune;* C. C. Lyon, of the Newspaper Enterprise Association; Herbert Corey, of Associated Newspapers; and George Seldes, of the Marshall Syndicate. Seldes, the first of the men to return, was sent to GHQ for questioning. The other four were apprehended in Berlin and returned to Trier (Treves), where press headquarters was then located. The five faced a long court-martial interrogation but were eventually reinstated, provided that they would submit the material gathered in Germany to army censors. By then, their news was dated and of little consequence. Details of this incident are in Crozier, *American Reporters on the Western Front,* pp. 268–78. Crozier's dedication to this book reads: "To the Five Runaway Correspondents, Whose Resourcefulness and Courage in a Lost Cause Served the Best Traditions of American Journalism."

151. Jo Davidson was a U.S. sculptor and artist. He sculpted busts of Marshal Foch, President Wilson, General Pershing, and the French premier, Georges Clemenceau, among others, which were displayed at several museums and palaces in Paris.

152. The French president at this time was Raymond Poincaré.

153. These troops were part of the 39th Infantry Regiment, 7th Brigade, of the 4th Division.

154. The literature on the peace conference is voluminous. The course of events can be readily followed in: Ferdinand Czernin, *Versailles 1919* (New York: Capricorn Books, 1965); Harold Nicolson, *Peacemaking 1919* (New York: Grosset and Dunlap, 1965); Arno J. Mayer, *Politics and Diplomacy of Peacemaking* (New York: Vintage Books, 1967); and Ferrell, *Woodrow Wilson and World War I,* pp. 135–177.

155. The classic account of the German involvement in the treaty is Alma Luckau, *The German Delegation at the Paris Peace Conference* (New York: Columbia University Press, 1941).

156. Margaret Wilson, one of the president's daughters, aspired to a professional singing career and spent time in France entertaining the troops.

157. The peace conference began with a series of informal discussions on January 13, 1919, involving the principal delegates. It was formally opened on January 18 at the French Foreign Ministry at the Quai d'Orsay Palace in Paris.

158. There are several days missing in Townsend's diary at this point, but in the first two weeks of January 1919, he established himself in a studio at No. 4, rue Belloni, moving in on January 12. This served as his quarters and studio until he departed France in May of 1919 for the United States. See Report from Captain Townsend to Chief of G-2-D, G.H.Q., AEF, February 28, 1919, in Record Group 120, Entry 224, Case 70, Drawer 3, Folder 2.

159. The Big Five were President Wilson; Lloyd George, the British prime minister; Georges Clemenceau, the French premier; Vittorio Emanuele Orlando, the Italian premier; and Baron Nobuaki Makino, of the Japanese delegation. The head of the Japanese delegation was the Marquis Saionji, who arrived only in April; Makino headed the Japanese group in his absence. Clemenceau was elected president of the peace conference.

160. Robert Lansing was the U.S. Secretary of State, though Wilson kept the conduct of U.S. foreign affairs mainly in his own hands or permitted his unofficial confidant and envoy, Colonel Edward Mandell House, to represent him in diplomatic activity. Lansing did perform some notable service at Paris, however.

161. Though he failed to name the interesting character being described, Townsend was obviously referring to the British prime minister, David Lloyd George.

162. On September 23, 1917, Major General Tasker Howard Bliss became army chief-of-staff in Washington, retiring from that position on December 31 of that year. Later, he served as the U.S. representative on the Allied Supreme War Council and, after the war, as one of five U.S. commissioners to the Versailles peace conference. Smythe remarked upon his wisdom and learning: "Bliss's learning was tremendous. He would have ornamented any university faculty, provided the professors could get used to feeling second-rate in his presence. A scholar in uniform, he knew geology, French, Spanish, Italian, Latin, and Greek, which he read as easily as his native English — a language he wrote with clarity and spoke with force." See Smythe, *Pershing*, p. 7. On October 6, 1917, while chief-of-staff, Bliss was given the temporary rank of lieutenant general.

163. Vittorio Emanuele Orlando became prime minister of Italy on October 30, 1917, and led Italy's delegation at the peace conference. Giorgio Sidney, Baron Sonnino became Italy's foreign minister in November 1914, serving throughout the war and at Paris afterward.

164. Bernard Mannes Baruch, a well-known financier, headed the economic section of the technical advisers to the American Commission to Negotiate Peace. Baruch had been chairman of the U.S. War Industrial Board during the war.

165. Herbert Hoover, who had made his international reputation principally in mining engineering, was named chairman of the American Relief Commission in London in 1914; and in the following year, he headed the Commission for Relief in Belgium. From 1917 to 1919, he was the U.S. food administrator. Having emerged as one of Wilson's trusted advisers, Hoover served as the head of the Supreme Economic Council during the Paris Peace Conference. Formed in February 1919, the council was in charge of food and raw materials for Europe, and responsible for dealing with problems of communication, finance, and maritime transportation.

166. Arthur James Balfour was the British foreign secretary, receiving his appointment on December 7, 1916. In this capacity, he accompanied Lloyd George to the Paris Peace Conference.

167. Frank Brangwyn was a noted British poster artist.

168. Major Augustus John was a Canadian war artist.

169. Alfred Charles William Harmsworth was better known as Viscount Northcliffe. He founded two London newspapers, the *Daily Mail* and the *Daily Mirror*, later acquiring control of the *Times*. In World War I, he was, among other things, director of propaganda in enemy countries.

170. These two sailed from France on board the U.S.S. *North Carolina*, being the first official artists to leave and the only ones to sail home on a warship. See telegram from Captain Harvey Dunn to Chief, G-2-D, January 23, 1919, Record Group 120, Entry 224, Case 70, Drawer 3, Folder 7.

171. The Hotel Crillon was the unofficial headquarters of the U.S. participants in the peace conference, though the official headquarters was at No. 78, rue de l'Université. Other offices of the U.S. delegation were adjacent to the Crillon at No. 4, Place de la Concorde, directly above Maxim's, the famed old restaurant and cabaret.

172. Leon Bourgeois, of France, was permitted to speak as a "Special Delegate for the League of Nations." One observer who was present noted Bourgeois's "over-long speech." This detail and others pertaining to the events of this period at Paris are in Lord Hankey, *The Supreme Control at the Paris Peace Conference, 1919* (London: George Allen and Unwin, Ltd., 1963), pp. 44–45 and *passim*.

173. Lord Hankey indicated that Baron Sonnino spoke at this time for Italy. See ibid., p. 44.

174. The Delsarte system of calisthenics was named for François Delsarte (1811–1871), a French teacher.

175. William Morris Hughes was the Australian prime minister and head of the Australian Peace Delegation. He was described as "an undisguised skeptic" in Hankey, *The Supreme Control*, p. 45.

176. Paul Hymans was the Belgian minister of foreign affairs and an acknowledged spokesman for the minor powers at the peace conference. He later became the president of the first Assembly of the League of Nations.

177. Eleutherois Venizelos was the Greek prime minister and ably represented his nation at the peace talks.

178. Ray Stannard Baker was chief of the press bureau of the American Commission to Negotiate Peace.

179. Lord Robert Cecil was British parliamentary under-secretary for foreign affairs. Like Leon Bourgeois, Lord Cecil was allowed the privilege of a seat as a "Special Delegate for the League of Nations." He played a large role in drafting the League of Nations Covenant and won the Nobel Peace Prize in 1937.

180. George N. Barnes, the Labor member of the British War Cabinet, was chairman of the Commission on International Labor Organization and represented labor interests at the Paris Peace Conference as a British plenipotentiary.

181. Former colonial territories and certain conquered areas were designated as mandates and were granted to various nations to, at least theoretically, supervise rather than to annex outright as conquered territory traditionally was. Mandates were to be prepared for eventual independence.

182. On March 25, after Lloyd George returned from London and Wilson came back from Washington, the peace conference turned its attention primarily to German matters.

183. Bernard Naudin, a contemporary French painter and engraver, was also a war artist of World War I, best known for his graphic scenes of trench life. Mlle. Lissagaray was a friend of the Townsends from their stay in France before the war.

184. Anatole France was the pen name of Jacques Anatole François Thibault, a writer, humanitarian, and author of such novels as *Penguin Island* (1909) and *The Gods Are Athirst* (1913); the latter was about the French Revolution.

185. Henry Cabot Lodge, Republican U.S. Senator from Massachusetts, was chairman of the Senate Foreign Relations Committee and led the fight to defeat the ratification of the Treaty of Versailles by the U.S. Senate.

186. Lucien Jonas was a French combat artist of World War I.

187. Charles Hoffbauer was a contemporary Franco-American painter then on the Paris scene.

188. The British war artists spent some time at the front but then retired to their fully equipped studios at home to complete their canvases. The U.S. combat artists did not have the luxury of going home to complete their work, hence most hoped to return to the United States as soon as possible after the end of hostilities to complete their work in their own studios. The army, however, discharged them soon after their arrival, and they had to forego their plans, for the most part.

189. This is a reference to English diarist Samuel Pepys (1633–1703).

190. Mrs. Mackenzie was the wife of Cameron Mackenzie, correspondent of the *London Chronicle* and, later, of the *New York Herald.*

191. Ignacy Paderewski was the prime minister of the newly created Polish state. He represented Poland at the peace conference.

192. Peixotto, following the end of the war, accepted assignment to the AEF's Art Training Center at the Pavillon de Bellevue, near Paris, taking charge of the school's Department of Painting. The center was operated by the U.S. Army Educational Corps and was established to allow qualified art students in the AEF to spend time, while awaiting transportation home, studying art under prominent artists, both French and U.S. Townsend subsequently served for a brief time at the school.

193. May Sinclair, *The Tree of Heaven* (New York: The Macmillan Company, 1918). Sinclair was a British novelist; this work describes the impact the war had on a British family.

194. There are several documents pertaining to Townsend's activities during these weeks in Record Group 120, Entry 224, Case 70, Drawer 3, Folder 2. These include orders, requests for transportation, and the like.

195. Poland was reconstituted an independent state at the end of the war, with the Polish Republic proclaimed on November 3, 1918. However, the borders were in contention, especially in the east, and the Poles clashed with the Bolsheviks in Russia, as

well as the Czechs. Though the Treaty of Versailles established some of Poland's borders, it was not until the end of the Russian-Polish War of April to October 1920 and the Treaty of Riga, dated March 18, 1921, that peace was reestablished between the Soviet Union and Poland. Other matters had to be resolved between the Poles and Lithuanians as well as with the Germans and the Czechs. Poles from the United States and elsewhere participated in these armed actions.

196. The 2d Army was officially dissolved on April 15, 1919.

197. Captain William E. Moore was the officer-in-charge of the Photo Sub-Section of G-2-D, in Paris. He was responsible for photographing the work of the combat artists before sending the originals to Washington.

198. German hand grenades, because of a long throwing stick attached to them, resembled potato mashers.

199. Shows of this sort were common in the AEF during this era; more often than not, these were revues and musicals featuring doughboys costumed as female singers and dancers.

200. In 1913, the U.S. Congress adopted the 18th Amendment to the U.S. Constitution banning the manufacture, sale, and transportation of intoxicating liquors in the United States. The amendment was ratified on January 29, 1919, to go into effect the following year.

201. On January 8, 1918, President Wilson, in an address to the U.S. Congress, outlined a peace program consisting of Fourteen Points. Both the Germans and the Austrians asked for an armistice on the basis of these points. Wilson had thought that these would be honored at the peace conference, and though many were accepted and implemented, there were compromises made that Wilson deplored but had to accept. Nevertheless, to Wilson, the points remained the ideals to be attained if possible. Among the peoples who rejected some of the points were the Italians, who had entered the war on the basis of a secret treaty that ran counter to Wilson's first point, which emphasized the importance of "open covenants openly arrived at."

202. On April 24, Orlando withdrew from the peace conference because, in his view, Italian claims were not being properly considered (especially regarding Fiume and the Dalmatian Coast) and because Wilson went over the heads of the Italian delegation, appealing directly to the Italian peoples to support his views. Orlando returned on May 5. Then, following a government crisis in Rome, he left Paris for good on June 12 and was not present at the signing of the peace treaty on June 28. Baron Sonnino was there, however, with other Italian representatives.

203. On April 26, 1915, the Italians concluded the secret Treaty of London with England, France, and Russia according to which Italy was to intervene on the side of the Allies. The Italians were promised a rectification of their borders at the expense of Austria. But following the war, Italian leaders believed their country should get additional areas as well. Some of these claims ran counter to one of President Wilson's ideals, which was ostensibly a guide for the deliberations at Paris — that of the self-determination of all peoples. The Italians, adhering to the Treaty of London, ignored these considerations. Having received Wilson with open arms a few weeks earlier when he visited their country, the Italian people now bitterly denounced him as an enemy of their nation.

204. Wilson rejected plans for a compromise regarding Fiume, such as placing it under control of the League of Nations. He stubbornly clung to the principle of nationality. This resulted in a deadlock, and the Italo-Yugoslav boundary was only settled by direct negotiations between these two nations some years later.

205. A "flaming onion" was a type of antiaircraft shell that exploded in the form of fiery tentacles.

206. See copy of this request in a letter dated April 5, 1919, in 70.57.1–214 LIC.

207. G–1 was that section of the General Staff concerned with administration and personnel.

208. Major General James W. McAndrew was Pershing's chief-of-staff at Chaumont from May 6, 1918, to May 27, 1919.

209. The heavy flying suits then in use were popularly called "teddy bears" by airmen in the U.S. Air Service.

210. Townsend was apparently alluding to James Bell Pettigrew, *Design in Nature,* 3 vols. (London: Longman, Green and Company, 1908).

211. Gaston Oliver Desvalliers was a well-known French artist. The others named were of less consequence.

212. Much of the work of the French war artists — François Flameng, Lucien Jonas, Georges Scott, and others — circulated to much critical acclaim in the pages of such popular French magazines as *L'Illustration.*

213. Tours was the headquarters of the SOS, which, among other things, was in charge of transporting officers and men of the AEF home.

214. Townsend had obviously hoped to visit the grave of his fallen brother, Henri, before sailing for home.

SELECTED BIBLIOGRAPHY

BOOKS

American Battle Monuments Commission. *American Armies and Battlefields in Europe: A History, Guide and Reference Book.* Washington, D.C.: U.S. Government Printing Office, 1938.

Chapman, Guy. *A Passionate Prodigality.* New York: Holt, Rinehart and Winston, 1933.

Chase, Joseph Cummings. *Soldiers All: Portraits and Sketches of the Men of the A.E.F.* New York: George H. Doran Company, 1920.

Coffman, Edward M. *The War to End All Wars: The American Military Experience in World War I.* New York: Oxford University Press, 1968.

Creel, George. *How We Advertised America.* New York: Harper and Brothers, 1920.

———. *The Creel Report.* Washington, D.C.: U.S. Government Printing Office, 1920.

Crozier, Emmet. *American Reporters on the Western Front, 1914–1918.* New York: Oxford University Press, 1959.

Czernin, Ferdinand. *Versailles 1919.* New York: Capricorn Books, 1965.

Esposito, Vincent J. *The West Point Atlas of American Wars,* vol. 2. New York: Frederick A. Praeger, 1959.

Ferrell, Robert H. *Woodrow Wilson and World War I, 1917–1921.* New York: Harper and Row, 1985.

Hankey, Lord. *The Supreme Control at the Paris Peace Conference, 1919.* London: George Allen and Unwin, Ltd., 1963.

Harbord, James Guthrie. *The American Army in France, 1917–1919.* Boston: Little, Brown, 1936.

Harries, Meirion, and Susie Harries. *The War Artists: British Official War Art of the Twentieth Century.* London: Michael Joseph in Association with the Imperial War Museum and the Tate Gallery, 1983.

Hartney, Harold E. *Up and At 'Em.* Garden City, New York: Doubleday and Company, 1971.

Janis, Elsie. *So Far, So Good!* New York: E. P. Dutton and Company, 1932.

Kennedy, David M. *Over Here: The First World War and American Society.* New York: Oxford University Press, 1980.

Lee, Arthur Gould. *No Parachute: A Fighter Pilot in World War I.* New York: Harper and Row, 1968.

Luckau, Alma. *The German Delegation at the Paris Peace Conference.* New York: Columbia University Press, 1941.

Marling, Karal Ann. *Wall-to-Wall America: A Cultural History of Post-Office Murals in the Great Depression.* Minneapolis: University of Minnesota Press, 1982.

Mayer, Arno J. *Politics and Diplomacy of Peacemaking.* New York: Vintage Books, 1967.

Mitchell, William. *Memoirs of World War I.* New York: Random House, 1960.

Nelson, Keith L. *Victors Divided: America and the Allies in Germany, 1918–1923.* Berkeley: University of California Press, 1975.

Nelson, Walter Henry. *The Soldier Kings: The House of Hohenzollern.* New York: G. P. Putnam's Sons, 1970.

Nicolson, Harold. *Peacemaking 1919.* New York: Grosset and Dunlap, 1965.

Park, Marlene, and Gerald E. Markowitz. *Democratic Vistas.* Philadelphia: Temple University Press, 1985.

Peixotto, Ernest Clifford. *The American Front.* New York: Charles Scribner's Sons, 1919.

Pershing, John J. *My Experiences in the World War,* 2 vols. New York: Frederick A. Stokes Company, 1931.

Pettigrew, James Bell. *Design in Nature,* 3 vols. London: Longman, Green and Company, 1908.

Rudin, Harry R. *Armistice 1918.* New Haven: Yale University Press, 1944.

Sibley, Frank P. *With the Yankee Division in France.* Boston: Little, Brown, 1919.

Sinclair, May. *The Tree of Heaven.* New York: The Macmillan Company, 1918.

Smith, J. André. *In France With the American Expeditionary Forces.* New York: Arthur H. Hahlo and Company, 1919.

Smythe, Donald. *Pershing: General of the Armies.* Bloomington: Indiana University Press, 1986.

Stallings, Laurence. *The Doughboys: The Story of the AEF, 1917–1918.* New York: Harper and Row, 1963.

Stokesbury, James L. *A Short History of World War I.* New York: William Morrow and Company, 1981.

U.S. Army. *Order of Battle of the United States Land Forces in the World War,* 5 vols. Washington, D.C.: U.S. Government Printing Office, 1931–1949.

Vandiver, Frank E. *Black Jack: The Life and Times of John J. Pershing,* 2 vols. College Station: Texas A & M University Press, 1977.

Vaughn, Stephen. *Holding Fast the Inner Lines: Democracy, Nationalism and the Committee on Public Information.* Chapel Hill: University of North Carolina Press, 1980.

Weigley, Russell F. *The History of the United States Army.* New York: Macmillan, 1967.

Whitehouse, Arch. *The Fledgling: An Autobiography.* New York: Duell, Sloan and Pearce, 1964.

ARTICLES

"Brothers in Art." *The Art Student,* vol. I, no. 8 (Fall 1916): 243–245.

Harding, George, "The American Artist at the Front." *The American Magazine of Art,* vol. 10, no. 12 (October 1919), 451–456.

————. "Drawing the War." *The American Magazine of Art,* vol. 32, no. 10 (October 1939): 568–573.

Keefer, Kimberly. "The Art of Henry Farré." *American History Illustrated,* vol. 17, no. 5 (September 1982): 30–32.

Reed, Walt. "Harry Townsend: On Assignment During World War I." *American Artist,* vol. 36, no. 358 (May 1972): 62–67; 86–87.

NEWSPAPERS

Bridgeport (Connecticut) *Sunday Post,* October 9, 1938.

New Canaan (Connecticut) *Advertiser,* August 23, 1934.

Norwalk (Connecticut) *Hour,* October 4, 1938; July 30, 1941.

INDEX

Abernathy, Lieutenant Thomas J., 77, 82
Academie Julien (Paris), 4
Academie Moderne (Paris), 4
Academy of Fine Arts (Chicago), 14
Adams, Franklin Pierce, 26, 33, 35, 39
Adams, Herbert, 1
Adriatic Sea, 232
Aerial demonstrations, 153
Aire River, 113
Air operations: French, 89, 91; German, 79–80, 100, 102–03, 246; Royal Air Force, 81–82, 89, 98; Royal Flying Corps, 22–23; Townsend and, 237–39, 249–50; United States, 5, 17, 43, 52–56, 71–72, 76–77, 81–82, 101, 105, 112, 115–16, 118, 127
Aisne-Marne: 58, 87
Allen, Major General Henry Tureman, 160
Allied Council, 129
Allied occupation of Germany, 160–61, 167, 174–92, 247, 248
Allied offensive operations, 58, 87–90, 105–110
Allied prisoners-of-war, 151, 178–79
Allies, combat art of, 2, 250
Alsace-Lorraine, 136
America in Europe, 99
American Expeditionary Forces (AEF): 1, 2, 6, 10, 60, 83, 137, 229, 236; General Staff of, 14, 125; influenza in, 58; organization of, 11–13, 14; press relations of, 166; YMCA and, 240
American Fine Arts Federation, 83
American Red Cross, 44, 46, 47, 129, 146, 151, 174, 240
Amel, 226
Ancerville, 27
Andilly, 19, 22, 23
Annamites, 22, 23, 85

Ansauville, 95
Anti-aircraft artillery, 23
Apremont, 92
Arabians, 208, 210, 211
Argonne, 105, 107, 110, 116, 222, 227
Arlon, 169, 226
Armistice: 132, 137–38; celebration of in Paris, 138, 140–41; negotiations of, 136–37; terms of, 139
Artillery operations: German, 32–33, 41, 60, 62, 64, 97, 98, 116; United States, 18–19, 37, 38, 41, 61, 66, 93, 108–09, 116
Art of the American Expeditionary Forces: criticism of, 104, 217–18, 232; exhibits at General Headquarters, AEF, 6, 131; production of, 104; use in war effort, 1–2
Associated Press, 60, 63
Atlantic Monthly, 121
Aubange, 226
Aulnois, 91, 92
Austria: 100, 126–27, 132; military forces of, 113
Austria-Hungary, 136
Austrians, 118
Australia, 211
Australian troops, 87
Avery, Walter L., 71
Aylward, Captain William James: 1, 137, 141, 150, 156, 217, 231; in Coblenz, 178; in Luxembourg, 163; in Paris, 172

Baccarat, 17, 25, 26, 40, 220, 223
Bahnhof Platz, 186
Bailey, Herbert R., 49, 98
Baker, Johnny, 37
Baker, Newton T., 11
Baker, Ray Stannard, 209
Balfour, Arthur James, 200, 202